'**Rocket Ron**' **Haslam** was youngest of ten brothers and of Langley Mill, and started racing in 1972 at the age of just fifteen. He won his first major title, the British TT Formula One Championship, in 1979 and went on to win three world titles and four British championships in his glittering career. His many victories included two in the treacherous Isle of Man Formula One TT and a record six in the gruelling Macau GP. He now devotes much of his time to running the Ron Haslam Motorbike School at Donington Park.

Leon Haslam, the 'Pocket Rocket', was born on 31 May 1983, became National Young Motocross Champion in 1995, Scooter Champion only two years later and winner of the Under 23 British Championship in 1999. Among his many other honours are *MCN* Young Rider of the Year in 1998 and Rookie of the Year in 2004. He finished second in the British Superbike Championship in 2006 and was runner-up again in 2008, winning five of the last nine races. In 2009, he is riding for the Stiggy Honda team in the World Superbike Championship.

Ron Haslam, his wife Ann, son Leon and daughters Emma and Zoe live near Smalley, Derbyshire.

Rick Broadbent is a sports writer for *The Times*, for whom he covers MotoGP among other things, and has previously written books on football, boxing and athletics. He lives in Dorset and is saving up for a bike.

www.rbooks.co.uk

ROCKET MEN

by Ron Haslam
with Rick Broadbent

BANTAM BOOKS

LONDON • TORONTO • SYDNEY • AUCKLAND • JOHANNESBURG

TRANSWORLD PUBLISHERS
61–63 Uxbridge Road, London W5 5SA
A Random House Group Company
www.rbooks.co.uk

ROCKET MEN
A BANTAM BOOK: 9780553819366

First published in Great Britain
in 2008 by Bantam Press
an imprint of Transworld Publishers
Bantam edition published 2009

Addresses for Random House Group Ltd companies outside the UK
can be found at: www.randomhouse.co.uk
The Random House Group Ltd Reg. No. 954009

The Random House Group Limited supports The Forest Stewardship
Council (FSC), the leading international forest certification organisation.
All our titles that are printed on Greenpeace approved FSC certified paper
carry the FSC logo. Our paper procurement policy can be found at
www.rbooks.co.uk/environment

Typeset in 11/15pt MPlantin by Falcon Oast Graphic Art Ltd.
Printed in the UK by CPI Cox & Wyman, Reading, RG1 8EX.

2 4 6 8 10 9 7 5 3 1

For my family

Contents

Acknowledgements

It has taken me many years to put my career down on paper but, with the help of Rick, I have finally managed to do so. I keep thinking about things I may have missed out and people I may have forgotten, but I am glad to have told my story to the best of my ability. I would like to thank everyone who has been a part of my life and career over the years.

Rick Broadbent thanks the Haslam family and his own – Debs, Erin and Sam.

ROCKET MEN

PROLOGUE

I WAS UP TO 170MPH ON THE BACK STRAIGHT AT Snetterton when it happened. I highsided over the handlebars and was spat viciously down the track. The next thing I knew I was engulfed by a huge, black shadow. I was disorientated. Scared. The bike flew over me and crashed down on my body. I don't remember much after that, but I filed two inches off the bone that was sticking out of my leg.

The next thing I recall I was in an ambulance going back to the Queen's Medical Centre once more. The surgeon inserted an iron bar into my leg and left the wound open for two weeks so that no infection could set in. I looked down at the inner workings of my ruptured leg, the bone, the bar and the blood. I remember it all seemed to be moving about; I remember looking at the mangled wreckage of my leg and thinking, This is never going to work.

It was a few weeks before they could do the bone graft. They took some of my pelvis and put it in the hole in my leg. A nail kept the bone together. Then I had some plastic surgery, because they needed extra skin to close over the bone. There was a real fear that I might have to have my leg off.

When you race bikes you never think you're going to crash or hurt yourself even though you know it's going to happen. Something inside you makes you not believe the truth, but this time had been a wake-up call. I thought, Jesus, that was bloody lucky. I was on crutches for a long time afterwards, and I realized that it was going to be a long time before I was race fit. It was a difficult period as I sat down and thought about what I was going to do. More than anything, it made me realize at last that I needed to stop racing.

I was pushing thirty-six, and it had been an incredible trip. From stealing fuel and poaching pheasants I'd risen to the top and taken on the greats, but the road had also been pitted with disaster, tears and torment. Lying in that hospital bed made me reassess it all and where I'd come from. And the most frightening thing was wondering where I'd go next. I could never have guessed that the answer lay with the nine-year-old kid in the corner.

1

TROUBLE AT T'MILL

IT WAS A NIGHT OF SHEER TERROR. IT WAS NOT UNUSUAL for Dad to cause trouble, but for some reason, on this particular night, he didn't limit himself to his fists and, fuelled by drink, he went completely mad. He grabbed a shotgun and chased my brothers through the house in a deranged frenzy. It was bedlam. Shouting and panic erupted as furniture was upended and my brothers ran. It's not an exaggeration to say they were fleeing for their lives, because there was no telling what Dad would do when he was in a state like that. They went all the way through the house, this little man waving a gun at his sons, and in the end they were chased into the pantry, a tiny room off the kitchen. They slammed the door shut and crouched down, praying he'd lose interest and go away. Not this time. The gunshot echoed through the house, and the door splintered. There was a gaping hole left where the bullet had struck. By a miracle nobody was hurt, but it was pot luck that he didn't kill anyone. It might sound horrific to some people, but the truth is that sort of thing was pretty standard in our house. This was the life we had, and for a while things went back to normal. At least, we thought they were normal then.

I never knew my dad, and if the truth be told, I didn't want to. We were a big, sprawling family, but my mother, Florence, was the glue that held us all together. She was an incredibly strong woman and, as it turned out, she had to be.

We were short on bedrooms back in Langley Mill, which is not surprising bearing in mind that, to begin with, there were seven brothers and three sisters living in that little council house. I slept with my brothers, top to tail, in a double bed, until they got a bit older and started wanting more freedom. That's when I went in with Mam. You wouldn't believe it these days, but I slept with my mother from the age of ten until I was fourteen. I was her baby, and so she was very protective towards me.

Things had already gone off in a serious way while I was still a toddler. My dad was a rum sort and he was addicted to drink. He was inside prison more often than he was out, and alcohol was usually the major contributing factor. It was a regular occurrence for him to get into trouble and, while my memories are sketchy because I was so young, I can picture him coming out of prison and giving my mum an awful lot of grief. He rarely worked, doing the odd thing on the side that was barely legal, and would happily take Mam's family allowance and spend it all on booze, giving no thought to the consequences for her or their ten kids.

That was why we were so poor. My grandfather actually had a bookie's shop, a racehorse and five houses. He was one of the richest men in Langley Mill and bought houses for all of his children, all except Mam, because he knew that my dad would sell it and spend the proceeds on ale.

It was hard for my brothers. We were a family and he was our dad, but they were scared of him. It wasn't that he was a big man. In fact, he was small and wiry, with sharp features and narrow eyes, but he had a vicious streak, especially when topped up with alcohol, and he would regularly give my mum a good hiding. It's hard to understand why, but she would keep accepting him back, regardless of what he did or how badly he treated her. I suppose that's what you did in the old days.

It sounds awful, but the Haslam family was built up around my dad's jail time. When he was out, then my parents would have another child, and when he was in there would be a gap until the next one. At the helm was Ken, a hard, stoical figure who wasn't bothered by anything. Dennis, the next-eldest, was different, a bit on the nervous side; and then came Roy and Terry, whom we always called Babe. After him was Molly and then Sheila, Cyril, Phil and Janet, while I put a full stop to Mam's labours on 22 June 1956. She was forty-two and had spent a decade being pregnant. With so many different ages and personalities in one small place it was inevitable that it was a chaotic upbringing.

Dad's crimes were usually related to being drunk and disorderly and to a lack of money. He would break into places but, judging by the number of times he was caught, he obviously wasn't very good at it. It must have been incredibly difficult for my brothers and sisters, who were older and knew what was happening, but I was the youngest and they sheltered me from the worst. They certainly did when things reached breaking point.

We finally got rid of him the day he tried to kill Mam. He went after her with a carving knife, and I have no doubt he would have stabbed her had he caught her. His senses were blurred and the booze vented his rage. Luckily, my mum was always a resourceful woman and she got away by climbing out of a bedroom window and shinning down the drainpipe. She fled to the sanctuary of my sister Molly's house, but my dad hadn't finished. He threatened my brother Babe and got him to take him over there on the back of his motorbike. Luckily, they saw him coming, and Mam crept out of the back door and hid in the next-door neighbour's outside toilet. Dad knocked on the door and Molly, who was heavily pregnant, answered. He shoved a gun in her stomach and asked where Mam was, but Molly kept her calm and said she hadn't seen her, while he ranted and raved.

It was decided it would be safest for Mam to go and stay with my brother Roy who had moved out by then. 'This can't go on, Mam,' Roy said. 'He's crackers and he's dangerous. He'll kill you if you stay.'

It must have been awful for Mam, because she knew Roy was right, but it was still her husband and the father of her kids he was talking about. I suppose she loved him in a strange, twisted way.

My brothers went back to our house with a view to telling him that it was over and that he wasn't to bother us any more. He didn't provide for us, either financially or emotionally, so we knew we'd be better off without him. We were a tight-knit group anyway, and he was the fly in the ointment.

So they went back to the old house and the sight that greeted them proved how Dad had gone completely mad. God knows why – although it must have been largely down to the demon drink once again – but he had emptied all our furniture into the street and set fire to it. Tables, chairs and clothes were burning, and he stood there laughing by the side of this enormous bonfire. What was left he gave to the neighbours. Anyone could benefit but us.

I don't know the details of what happened next, but my brothers finally stood up to him after that blaze.

They threw him out and told him that we never wanted to see him again. He was our dad, but he was just a blight on our lives. He went to live with his brother twenty miles away and stayed there. I only ever saw him twice after that. The last time was in the street, but I had nothing to say and walked on by. I knew what he had done and you cannot forgive those things. He was outside the family circle, and we were happy for him to stay there. The last I heard he ended up living in a shed. Some would say that's what he deserved.

My eldest brother is Ken and, bearing in mind how old I was when all this was going on, he effectively became my dad. He's twenty years older, which means I'm younger than my nephew, but that troubled start brought us all closer together, regardless of the age gaps, and family became all-important, the centre of all we did. If Ken occasionally looked for trouble, Babe was very straight and upstanding. He wouldn't take any crap from anybody but he wouldn't start it either. That was a good quality to have, because there was a lot of crap around in those early days. It was an era of local gangs, when the hard case from Eastwood would challenge the top dog from Langley Mill. It was clan warfare, and pub brawls were common. When you said Haslam, it was like, 'Oh no, not them', but we weren't alone. There were lots of big families, and fighting was part of the culture of the pubs and the streets. There would always be a lot of posturing and pride and someone thinking that he was better than you and vice versa. It became accepted that if you went out to a pub for the night then you would end up in some sort of trouble.

We had safety in numbers for much of the time. As well as my brothers, we had lots of friends and we would go out mob-handed. Sometimes people would feel they could get topside of us and it would go off, but my brothers would always look out for each other. Ken wouldn't back down from anything and, as I mentioned, would actually seek out trouble. There was a point when he enjoyed playing the local hard man. It tended to be fine in the local pubs, where they knew us, but then Ken started going down to Nottingham and came home with more and more bruises every time. Word had spread on the grapevine, and they got to know about the Haslams in Nottingham. That put a stop to those trips.

I tended not to get involved in all of this. I was young and never a fighter. In fact, the worst incident I can remember was when I'd started riding and was at home with a broken collarbone. Ken was no longer a young brawler, but he was still physically strong. There was a knock on the door one evening, and through the window I saw three muscle-bound men with gnarled foreheads and bouncer jawbones outside on the doorstep. Ken had already been to the pub, so he had enough drink inside to make him think he could take on the world, but he never had a chance. I stood and watched as they hauled him into the street and got going. They handed him a terrible, bloody beating, kicking him all over the pavement, and he had no choice but to take it until they were done. When my brothers came home and heard what had happened, they went off on a revenge mission. The bouncers got their payback. It was all tit for tat, egos and aggro, trouble at t'mill.

I don't wish to paint a picture of poverty and violence, because that's not a fair reflection of the whole story. In fact, my childhood was a very happy one. Without much money, we made our own entertainment and had lots of fun. We were resourceful kids in those days, whether it was making ten-foot stilts out of left-over bits of wood or making bows and arrows and taking them into the fields. There were two versions of that particular game. The first involved making an arrow from a nice length of bamboo cane, inserting slits with a knife and putting paper flights into them. Then you cut a groove into the side. Finally, you would wrap a piece of string around it and you had a slingshot. It was amazing how far you could throw those arrows and, being a bunch of competitive boys, we would see who could manage the furthest. The other version was a bit more macho and a lot more stupid. The types of bows and arrows used for this were the ones you bought from shops or, more likely, from mates. They were fairly powerful and spawned a great game in which two brothers would stand at opposite ends of a field. Then one would fire an arrow as high as he could into the air with the aim of landing it as close as he could to the other. If the watcher moved, then he was out and subject to merciless mickey-taking. Most of the time it wasn't as dangerous as it sounds, because you could see the arrow turn over and start its descent, but we did have a couple of close calls.

The worst thing was when the arrow went over your head, because it always looked like it was turning and that made you nervous. I still remember the day Phil floated his arrow and suddenly realized Babe hadn't seen it.

'Babe, the arrow!' he shouted.

'Oh yeah, right,' replied Babe.

Unfortunately, we were always playing jokes and crying wolf, and so he was convinced Phil was just trying to trick him and make him look daft.

'No, I mean it! Look!'

He looked too late to move, but early enough to feel the panic. The arrow crashed down into his shoe. Phil froze. It had wedged into the bit of sole that stuck out of the side. Saved by his beetle-crushers. Babe yanked out the arrow and tore after Phil.

'You bloody idiot!' he yelled. 'You didn't wait for me to look!'

'I told you, Babe,' Phil shouted as he hurtled off to save himself.

The rest of us creased up laughing, but it was a near miss and could have killed him if it had gone another few inches. You didn't think about that, though. We were young and we were indestructible.

Nothing came between us. Brother to brother, sister to sister, we would argue like hell and fire arrows at each other, but if there was ever a problem then, the family merged together. Iron bonds linked us to each other, and having such a hard time with my dad meant that if there was ever an issue the family was always right. Even if one of my brothers was in the wrong, then the family would line up behind him as a united front. We had a sort of dedication and commitment to the family that I think is lacking nowadays. If Mam said 'Go to the grocer's', then you went to the grocer's. There was no argument, no backchat, just an unwritten code of behaviour.

Mainly, though, the focus was on having fun, and there were always lots of injuries resulting from that. We all had old pushbikes and we'd make a track on the road for racing. There was never much traffic in those days. To make it more fun, we disconnected all the brakes and you weren't allowed to put your feet down. That made it hard and your judgement had to be spot-on. If you went into a corner and did two and a half rotations with the pedals, you were fast. If you did two and three-quarters, you would crash, and there were some horrendous pile-ups as people tried to dive down the inside and cut each other up. I would stay out there and have fifty races a night. The best bike I ever had was a decrepit old one that had a basket on the front. It didn't look like much, but it had perfect grip. Maybe it was the extra weight at the front from the basket, but I won a lot on that. I suppose it showed that looks can be deceptive. With hindsight, some cornering skills that would serve me well in the future were probably refined on that old bike.

Some accidents were self-inflicted through rank stupidity. Once, when I was really small, I became fascinated with a seesaw I'd made from a bit of old wood. I put a tin on one end and then jumped on the other. The game then became making the tin go higher and higher. First I did it by dropping a brick on it, which was OK; but I always wanted to take things to extremes, so I dragged a huge lump of concrete around the back of a wall, up a mud bank and to the top. I looked down at the seesaw below and then dropped the concrete. The tin shot up like a rocket, thudded into my head and knocked me backwards. I went home and they washed away the blood and taped up my head. I learned my lesson and didn't do that again.

Lessons of the educational kind were more of an afterthought in this environment. I would say that half of my brothers and sisters were clever in an academic sense and half were at the other end of the scale. Unfortunately, I was in the latter group. I didn't go to school very often, because it wasn't a priority in those days. Now parents and schools would go mad, but there was nobody to push you in the sixties. We were more concerned with putting food on the table and enjoying ourselves, flying down the street on one roller skate because we had only one pair to share between us. School wasn't a priority unless you made it one, and all kids tried to get out of going. Our family was so big, and there was so much going on in the morning, that it was easy to slip away and wander into the fields unnoticed. And that was an education of sorts.

When I did go to junior school I became familiar with the cane and the slipper. It would be for general petty stuff – missing lessons, not listening in class, thinking I was the 'big I Am'. The division of power when it came to punishing errant boys meant the headmaster would use the cane and the teacher would make do with the slipper. One teacher, a Mr Millington, wielded his slipper with great expertise. If you talked in his class, then you were hauled out to the front, bent over and given one of three options.

'So, Haslam, do you want the whitewash, the flying doctor or the standard?'

It wasn't much of a choice. 'Er, the whitewash, sir,' I stuttered.

'Very well.'

The whitewash comprised Millington giving you around thirty whacks of the slipper in little more than three seconds. The flying doctor involved him going to the other end of the classroom and then charging down the aisle at you. The standard was simply the biggest crack you had ever known. I went for the whitewash, but once you'd tried it you would never choose it again. Millington had us taped. Hard and strict, which was no bad thing, and at least he had a bit of imagination when it came to inflicting pain.

I occasionally went to Aldercar Secondary School, where the teachers knew how to deal with the mayhem there too. Lots of the kids smoked, so the teachers would confiscate cigarettes and then give them back at the end of the day. The attitude was 'We know it's going to happen but at least we'll stop it while you're here'. It was a practical solution that I could appreciate. The worst thing about secondary school was also the best – the engineering classes where you'd even get the opportunity to build motor engines. That did get my attention and I wanted to have a go, but my downfall was that the requirement to do engineering was passing your reading and writing tests. I loved the thought of woodwork and steelwork – anything that involved working with my hands – but I couldn't do it because of the problems I made for myself elsewhere.

If my sisters were clever academically, the likes of myself and Babe were clever in other ways, mainly because we were brought up in a practical world in which, if you wanted food, you had to go and find it.

That was far more important than education. Trying to get through the job in hand. Trying to get through the day. Just trying to live. It was as bad as that sometimes.

Mam bore all this with unbelievable strength. I don't know how she did it, because it wasn't that money was tight so much as that it didn't exist. Clothes were always handed down through the family, from brother to brother and sister to sister. Janet, who was closest to me in age, didn't have any new clothes until she was well into her teens. Mam worked really hard and I don't know how she did it with the equipment we had. There was no washing machine, just a steel bathtub, a scrubbing board and ten kids, not to mention the trouble with my dad and his drinking. I remember when we moved to the second house, after my dad went, we had a washing machine with a mangle on the top. We felt like kings.

It did get a bit better in time when some of my brothers were old enough to go to work and they would come home and give their pay straight to Mam. She would then take what she needed to keep us afloat and give back whatever she could. I struggle to imagine that happening today – a working man coming home, physically not opening his pay packet and giving it to his mother. It was a sign of how tight we were and how much we cared for Mam. It may sound like *Oliver Twist*, and it probably was when compared with what we have now, but it was also one of the best times in my life. The build-up to Christmas would be incredible because of the sense of anticipation. There wouldn't be much, but somehow Mam would pull out all the stops and get you something, even if it was only fruit. It's true that you appreciate things more if they are harder to come by, and whatever we got was always enough. We knew there was no money, so we were happy with anything.

The Derbyshire winters were bad because of the biting cold. Like everybody, we had a coal fire in those days, on which you'd boil the kettle, but the problem was that coal was far too expensive for us. The only way around it was to steal some from the truck that came once a week. We took it in turns, although my brother, Dennis, was always a bit nervous about the dark and so he would try to duck his turn and pass it to someone else. It would be one brother one week and another the next. The trick was to go and stand on a bridge and, when the coal truck came under it, jump on to it. Then you'd toss a bit of coal out and leap off before the night-watchman saw you.

That wasn't the only time when we would use the cover of night to bring things home, and it certainly wasn't the only time we took risks. It was what you had to do in those early days to survive. This was an era when it was easy to get hold of guns. Nobody bothered with things like licences and you'd just buy them from your mates or in the pubs. It was rare for someone not to have a gun, even if it was just an air rifle – that was just the way it worked.

Yet, despite all the gangs and the trouble, the guns were never used for anything untoward. We used them solely for shooting rabbits, rats and pheasants. It was how we ensured there was something to eat, either bringing the rabbits home to cook ourselves or by selling them to pubs and shops. If you managed to offload a brace of pheasants, then you'd get a few pence. While it wasn't much, it was something, and money was so short that anything helped. As time went on we also found that we needed money to fund a new habit. It was an addiction that spread through the family. The name of the drug was speed, and the supplier was the bike world.

2

BABE

THE FIRST BIKE I EVER RODE WAS AN OLD BATTERED moped that Babe was using to get to the building site where he had started working. It wasn't much to look at, but it was cheap to run and took hardly any fuel. It was almost a write-off, really, nothing special, a means to get from A to B and nothing more, but to a ten-year-old kid it was a speed machine. So one day when Babe was out I couldn't stop myself and climbed on board. I fired it up and took it down to the canal. I thought I was absolutely flying, when the reality was I was going at no speed at all, but it didn't matter. It was the ride that got me hooked.

Nothing ever ran smoothly in the Haslam household, though, and my initiation turned sour when I hit a pot-hole. The headlight must have been loose, because the force jolted it and it seemed to jump right off the moped before falling into the murky brown depths of the canal. I was really worried, because I knew that Babe would kill me if I had done anything to the bike, and I felt the anxiety rising inside me. The plan had been to go for a quick ride and put it back without him knowing, but now the headlight was missing. Excuses went through my head, but I knew he would see through them all, so there was nothing else for it. I stripped off naked and jumped into the canal.

That wasn't as unusual as you might think. Going starkers was fairly normal when it came to swimming, because you just couldn't get your clothes wet. If I went back with my shirt and trousers sopping then I would get a good hiding from one of my brothers. Clothes were scarce and so you looked after them. Better naked than beaten, I jumped in and began ducking down under the water, running my hand across the bottom, touching all sorts of junk that had found its way down there. It was filthy and I made sure I didn't swallow any of the rancid water, but I kept on searching, thinking, What am I going to do? over and over to myself. Eventually, after what seemed like hours, I found it. I came up like a scuba diver with a bit of lost treasure. I jumped out and fastened it back on to the bike as quickly as I could. Then I got dressed. Luckily, Babe didn't notice. I never ever told him about it.

Babe was the first of us to get into bikes in a big way. There were always bikes of some sort knocking around.

We'd go around dealers and pick up the rubbish that nobody wanted. If the engine was OK, then we took it, never mind the rust and the rest of it. I started riding on scrappy old mopeds, MOT failures, anything we could get our hands on. Babe soon progressed from his moped and after scrimping and saving bought a 750cc Norton Dominator.

He thought he was the king of the road. We all did. I believed that he was truly the fastest thing on two wheels in those early days. The size of the bike and the fact that this was my big brother inspired a deep-seated awe. It was all I knew. Langley Mill was a small, parochial area, a working town in the East Midlands, and I didn't know anything beyond that. He was the quickest guy on the streets of Matlock on his Norton Dominator, and that was the world as far as we were concerned. Nobody could beat him. But within three weeks of having his new bike, Babe had managed to get himself banned for speeding, and that was when he decided to go racing instead. If he hadn't been banned, who knows whether any of us would have gone down the racing route? Maybe we'd have been content being the top dogs on the streets of Matlock.

He started, like everybody did, at a small club meeting. It was 1966, and the first race was at Cadwell Park, which is only in Lincolnshire, just south-west of Louth, but for us it seemed exotic. There was no doubt in Babe's mind that he was going to wipe the floor with everyone, just like he did on the roads at home. 'I'm going to be twice as fast as those blokes,' he boasted.

He finished last. He came in and couldn't understand it. Neither could I. We sat there in mutual shock. My image of my brother was shattered there and then. Babe didn't just think he was going to win, he thought it was going to be easy, and that race at Cadwell opened his eyes. In fact, it opened all of our eyes to the possibility of a life outside what we knew. It was only a club meeting, the lowest rank of racing, but we saw for the first time how it was done properly. Once he got over the shock, Babe dug in even harder. It had been a wake-up call, but he wasn't the sort of person to be discouraged by a setback, and it made him try even harder.

Phil saw what Babe was doing and followed suit. He saved for almost two years to afford a six-speed 250cc Thompson Suzuki. He was obviously talented, but he struggled at first. It was a two-stroke bike and we didn't know much about the mechanics of an engine at that point. In his first year Phil had a mixed time. The bike kept breaking down or blowing up. He did get a second place, though, and people at meetings started to take notice and say nice things. Some even began tipping him for greatness – if he could just finish the races.

We travelled to meetings in an old Ford Thames van that did only 30mph, rising to 40mph down the steepest hills. There was no heater, but it had two seats divided by the engine which had a steel lid on it. Babe would drive, and Phil and myself would rush to get on the tin lid, because that was warm from the engine. It was uncomfortable but it was still the best seat. Babe's girlfriend, Patricia, whom we called Treece, would come along too, so I'd often have to sit on the bike in the back because there was no room on the floor with the toolbox. It meant I had a skewed view on the world. When I myself started racing I didn't know where any of the circuits were because I'd spent those trips sitting in the back of the Thames, looking out of a little square rear window at the grey tarmac. I always said that I could find my way anywhere, just as long as we were going backwards.

When we'd get to meetings I'd take the bikes out, sheet them down and sleep in the van, but whatever the time of year it was always freezing. My favourite place in those early days was Cadwell, because I knew there was an old ambulance in the woods. It had broken down and been left to rack and ruin. The wheels had long gone and the bodywork was rusting, but the best thing about it was there were two single beds in the back. That was a bit of luxury, and I was happy sleeping in the back of a beaten-up ambulance in the woods. We all were, and as soon as we got to the track we would rush for those beds. It got even better when we realized that we could break into the hot-dog stall after it had shut down for the night. We'd force our way in, put the gas on and stay there overnight, making sure we jumped out the next morning before they came to open up. I did that for two or three years but never had the nerve to stay for breakfast.

It was an accident that changed things for us. Babe fell off his new 650cc Triumph Bonneville one day in 1971 and broke his collarbone. Phil took over on the new bike and immediately started winning at places like Cadwell and Snetterton. I think it made Babe realize that not only was he not the fastest thing on two wheels but he wasn't even the fastest thing in the family. Phil had something special, and so Babe decided to help him out. They had a bike each at that point but they were struggling with the costs and so they went halves on a Norton Commando and set about dominating the club scene together. They were hugely successful at that level, winning more than four hundred trophies between them, but there was no doubt that Phil had the greate natural talent. He had that ability to feel the bike and was blisteringly fast.

Mam didn't come to the races. She was too scared; and it was only later, when I had a son of my own and began watching him ride, that I came to understand that. But we became a posse in those early days, Babe, Phil, Treece and me. It felt like we were on the way to something special, and there was no doubt who was taking us there.

Phil was so good that he quickly picked up a sponsor.

By that point he and Babe had pulled the engine out
of the Norton and put it in a Seeley frame. They
entered the unlimited classes, taking it in turns, Babe at
one meeting, then Phil the next, and it went well. So
well that Mal Carter noticed the long-haired skinny kid
on the bike. Mal had been a really good rider, but he
was a big man, and that didn't sit well, quite literally, on
bikes. His attitude was that if he was fourth going into
the last corner then he would either win or crash. He
was that hard a rider, but he had been up against Phil
and he had been both soundly beaten and hugely
impressed. He decided that if you can't beat them you
might as well join them, and that's what he did.

Mal was the boss of the Pharaoh garage in Halifax,
and if he liked you and you were committed, then he
would do anything for you. He was an intimidating
figure. He was burly and had a red, lived-in face. What
hair he had left formed unkempt curls, and he had a
double-barrelled chest. When he spoke you listened.

To start with, Phil was riding the Seeley Norton in
1972, but Mal quickly realized that Phil was special and
he bought him a brand-new 350cc Yamaha. Then there
was a new 250cc. It made life easier for Phil, and he no
longer had to babysit to get the money for his bikes. We
drove around in the Thames and kept the bikes in our
wooden garden shed. That was the workshop, where
all the work would be done on the bikes. Later, we
progressed to a brick garage and that was sheer luxury,

but Mal wanted us to keep the bikes at our place and we were happy with that. It meant it was even more crowded, though, as the council house didn't have enough room for the family, let alone bikes and engines and parts littering the scene, the whiff of oil and petrol in the air. It's not an exaggeration to say we loved those bikes.

'Eh up,' Babe said one night when I'd locked up and we were all in bed, 'someone's nicking your bike, Phil.'

That was enough to rouse him. Phil jumped up and tore down the stairs, still half asleep but scared that his pride and joy was being stolen. Babe looked at me and we went down too. The dogs were making a hell of a racket, and Babe kept on to Phil.

'Someone must be breaking in,' he whispered as we edged along in single file. 'Someone's after your bike.'

Then suddenly I let out an almighty squeal and made the pair of them jump out of their skins.

'Jesus! What's the matter?' Phil cried.

I looked down. 'I've stood on a bleeding hedgehog,' I said. 'That's what the dogs were barking at.'

Phil breathed a sigh of relief but then something clicked. 'Eh up,' he said to Babe, 'how come you knew they were nicking my bike and not yours?'

Babe just laughed. 'A hedgehog, eh? Fancy that.'

Together Babe and Phil were going well. They won a lot and Mal was happy with his new rider. Having been in the same races, he knew just how hard Phil raced and that was what attracted him to my brother. Being sponsored was the biggest break we'd ever had as a family, because we all knew how hard it had been to pay for the bikes. It was the bit of luck that Phil needed. Mal loved it and threw everything at it. It seemed there was no stopping Phil.

I was just the kid brother to the rising star at that stage. I saved up for months and months, and with Babe and Phil's help I bought a great big monster Panther bike and sidecar for £7.50 from the small ads in the paper. I couldn't start it, because it was too big for me, but we ran it with the sidecar for a bit. Then the wheels broke, followed swiftly by everything else, so we converted it into a standard bike. I'd sit on it and it would take two people to shove it to get going.

I had other things on my mind at that point, though. I had started seeing girls, and that was a definite no-no in my family. It was simply not allowed, because they thought that I was too young at fourteen. The Haslam way was to look at girls but not go with them. Well, that might have been the Haslam way but it certainly wasn't mine. I'd been going with one particular girl, called Margaret, and I'd managed to keep it a secret from everybody. I knew all hell would break loose, and so it was a cloak-and-dagger relationship, not helped by the fact that I was still sharing a bed with Mam at that stage, which is a foolproof way of cramping any sex-starved teenager's style.

In many ways Babe was much more than a brother. Now that Ken and Dennis had also moved out to get their own places, what he said went. He was disciplined but mostly fair, and when he said you had to be in by ten o'clock it meant not a minute later. I think he was tougher on me because I was the baby of the family, while Mam would cover for me for the same reason. Their differing attitudes were summed up when I took my life in my hands by staying out late one night with Margaret. I don't know why, but I just decided to forget about the rules, and so it got to half past eleven. We were out with Ken's son Ian, who was about the same age as me, and he was with a girl too. We'd had a good old time and Ian and I were walking home, carefree and happy. Ken's house was further down the road from ours, on the opposite side, and as we turned the corner we saw Ken sitting on the fence outside his house, waiting impatiently for Ian.

'Oh Christ!' Ian said. 'I'm for it now.'

We were out of sight, so I said I'd see Ian later and then watched him make his sheepish way across the road. As he got close, Ken studied him and then pulled out a brush handle and broke it across Ian's back with an almighty whack. Then he physically kicked him all around the yard. I stood in the shadows and watched him take the beating and thought, I've got that to come.

It frightened me to death, so I crept up the road, wondering how I could avoid the same punishment. I hadn't got far when I saw Babe sitting outside our house, shivering in a T-shirt. He hadn't seen Ken give Ian his hiding, but I thought of the broom handle and decided to take evasive action. So I nipped around the back of a house, jumped over a wall and then went through a few back yards, ignoring the dog barks and the flicker of a kitchen light, to get to the rear of our place. I darted in the door and ran straight upstairs, jumping into bed with Mam, pulling up the covers and hoping it would all be forgotten.

'You better not,' she said in the still of the dark. 'He's waiting for you.' I was hoping I might get away with it, but as always Mam knew better. 'He doesn't know you're in yet.'

'Can't you tell him, Mam?'

She sighed and then said: 'I can try.'

So she went downstairs and had to tell Babe that I was already in. He wasn't fooled for a moment. He knew I'd been out, and the fact that I'd tried to trick him now made matters worse. Up the stairs he thundered, and I began to think that I'd be happy with the brush handle. He burst into the bedroom, grabbed me by the neck and dragged me down the stairs. I'd made it twice as bad by trying to fool him, and my legs didn't even touch the floor. Then he started punching and kicking me all over the yard.

'Leave him alone, Terry!' Mam yelled, but it didn't make any difference.

I curled into a ball and took it, screaming out to try to make him think I was more badly hurt than I really was, all the while Mam shouting for him to stop. Eventually, he decided he'd done enough. I was winded and bruised and I stayed on the floor.

The next day, when the dust had settled, Babe collared me again and sat me down. 'Listen,' he said. 'You're fourteen. If you want to go with girls, then go with girls. You're old enough to do what you want now.' I think the beating had been a turning point for him too.

That was when things changed. I moved out at night and started sleeping over at Margaret's mam and dad's house. But it was purely a night-time arrangement and I'd come home first thing in the morning. I had all my meals at home but spent the nights at Margaret's. Mam was very old-fashioned and didn't like it, but Margaret's parents were fine. They gave her the freedom to do what she wanted. That was fine by me.

Nobody bore grudges in our house and the memory of the hiding soon faded. I was a kid when Babe had started racing and I idolized my big brothers and the glamour of bikes. I was given the task of cleaning Babe's bike, although that caused its own problems on one occasion. I had seen Babe use a bottle of something called Gunk to clear oil off his bike, so I thought I'd do the same when he asked me to clean his Norton one night. I noticed that oil was leaking from the chain cover all over the tyre. Blissfully ignorant, I poured Gunk on to the tyre and thought that would do the trick. I thought nothing more of it until I heard Babe come roaring into our house, screaming blue murder. He clipped me around the head and shouted louder than a megaphone: 'What the bloody hell did you do to my bike?'

I was frightened to death and rubbed the side of my head.

'I just used Gunk like you.'

'Gunk!' Babe cried. 'Gunk! That's slippier than oil. You nearly killed me!'

He wasn't lying. Babe had got on the bike and went off down the road with Treece sitting proudly on the back. He probably felt like the cock of the north until he got to the first corner and went straight up a grass bank, narrowly avoiding disaster.

That one was my fault, but there were times which showed he could be equally daft. One of those came when Babe forgot to take the steering lock off his new bike. He managed to go for a good ten miles until he needed to turn off the road and – sure enough – he fell. He was spitting blood that night too, his pride hurt at being thrown from his new bike for such a daft reason.

Nevertheless, after a while all was forgotten, and

Babe even started letting me have a go on his bike. He needed to run it in, so he took it to an airfield and let me get on. The Norton was a big brute of a bike, but I loved it. After the cast-offs and the cobbled-together, I was smitten. Hook, line and sinker.

3

THE POACHER

IF WE WEREN'T TEARING AROUND ON BIKES IN THOSE early days, then we were getting our adrenalin rushes from a totally different source, but one that was almost as thrilling and dangerous. I have to admit that I loved poaching, and by the time I'd become reasonably skilled at it I was doing it just for fun, because there was a bit more money in the house and the need wasn't what it used to be. I did it for the thrill, the buzz, the threat of being caught by the farmers, the gamekeepers or the police. And the hauls could be huge. Sometimes you'd shoot eighty pheasants in a single night, and trying to carry them home was a real test of strength and guile.

Of course we knew that poaching was something you shouldn't do, but we did it anyway. There are few things that give you that taste of pure excitement like going into a pitch-black wood on a mission. It's an adrenalin rush, and the first time was absolutely terrifying. I just followed my brothers. They knew the score and it became a game. With pheasants you knew which woods they were most likely to be in because they were bred specifically for shoots. The downside was that those woods would be heavily guarded by keepers, but that just added to the challenge. It became a battle of cunning and wills. The gamekeepers knew we would be coming because of the numbers of pheasants that were around, and we knew they would be waiting for us.

Our favourite time for a poaching trip was between nine o'clock at night and one in the morning. There would be three of us in a line. Roy would be at the front. He was the seeker, the one who used all his experience to scan the treeline and search out the pheasants. Then there would be Phil with the gun, the shooter, ready actually to bag the pheasants when Roy alerted him. Then at the back there would be me, looking all around for the keepers. Basically, it would be my job to avoid us getting into trouble, but that was no easy task.

You wouldn't believe how black it is when you get into a wood in the wee small hours. It's like being blindfolded. It took me ages to work out how to get around, and the only way to see was by looking along the edge of the woods or the tops of the trees. Nobody would speak, and you would slowly edge deeper and deeper into the darkness, every sound magnified by the stillness, the dank smells of nature in your nostrils.

There were all sorts of traps. The worst was the wire fixed head-high between two trees. That could be really dangerous, because you would never see it in the blackness and you risked being garrotted. You'd fix on the treetops, looking for movement, because that's where the pheasants were, but concentrate too much on the skyline and you could come a cropper. The first man would always carry a stick, which he would hold out in front of him, hoping to catch any traps before they caught us. You'd be walking along and you'd get barbed wire. At other times you'd put your hand out in front of you and feel something cold and damp. Only when your hand was covered with blood would you realize that they'd hung dead goats on a wire to scare you. There would be rotting carcases to put you off and even a couple of mantraps – deep holes dug into the ground and covered over. If you fell into them, then there was no way out until the keepers came and gave you a beating. They were the hardest sort of keeper.

The hardest sort of trap, however, was the tripwire, as we found to our cost one night. Roy was at the front, gently moving forward with his stick held out in front of him, but tripwires were cunning devices. Usually they were about two feet off the ground so that animals could run underneath them, but sometimes they were so low that the first man stepped over it only for the second one to trigger it. The stick would be pointed downwards to try to pick them up, but you could trigger them without even noticing. For the tripwire, a wire would be attached to a tree, where it pulled out a pin that dropped a weight on to the floor. In the dead of a silent night the noise of that sounded like a jet engine and caused total panic. More important, it told the keepers that someone was in the wood who shouldn't be. That's what happened that night. One of us set it off and the weight fell to the ground, unseen but definitely heard. Our cover was blown. The farmers were on to us, and we knew that the first thing they would do was ring the police. The wood would be surrounded in no time.

'Christ!' Roy said. 'Now we're in trouble.'

'What are we going to do?' I asked anxiously.

'Let's go,' Roy said. 'We might be able to get out if we're quick.'

We'd gone a long way into the wood, though, and it wasn't easy getting out. That's when I saw an orange flicker of flame in the distance. Then another. And another.

'It's the police,' Phil said, voicing what we all knew. 'They're already here.'

'They're circling the wood,' Roy said. 'We've got to get out the other end before that circle closes or we've had it.'

We were still walking in single file, holding on to the

edge of each other's coats as it was the only way to stop from getting lost.

'When we get out, stay by the hedgerow or they'll see us cutting across the field,' Roy said.

I could hear my brothers breathing and the thump of my own heart. I could feel the tension, but I always followed my brothers and I did so again. It was to no avail. We saw more torches, each one growing in size, and realized we were trapped.

'What are we going to do now?' I asked.

'We haven't got a choice,' Roy said. 'We're going to have to sit it out.'

So we sat down, hid and waited. It felt like an eternity, crouching there in the dark, catching the glimpse of a light now and again, wondering if we were going to be caught and beaten, but eventually the torches drifted off. Police and keepers wouldn't wait all night to catch you, and so it became a matter of endurance. We sat there and waited until the coast was clear and went home. It was a close shave.

We weren't always that lucky. My brothers were caught a few times and got a few bad beatings from gamekeepers. Two or three of them together could cause some damage. In time, my brothers would click on to the places where that happened, and a few more of them would go, and that meant that if it came to a fight we could get topside of the gamekeepers. It was a good crack.

The first rule of being caught was to deny everything. You throw everything away – guns, pheasants, the lot – and plead innocence. It was very hard for the keepers to prove anything, but that wouldn't stop them giving you a whack if they outnumbered you. In the early days it was pretty obvious we were there because we'd use a huge shotgun that sounded like a volcano going off. Later, we were more savvy and used a .22 with a silencer. I liked shooting and would later build a collection of more than five hundred guns and rifles. We were all decent shots, but the rule was that if you missed twice you passed it on to the next man.

The only time that I actually got caught came in very different circumstances when I was about eighteen. I was coming back from Cadwell Park and driving along a country road in an old Morris Minor. By that time I didn't really need to go poaching and was doing it for fun rather than for meat and money. That day there were lots of pheasants at the side of the road and in the fields, and so we parked up. I was with some friends, Patrick Kelly and the Hollis twins, and we edged on to the grass verge, wound down the window and started shooting. After a while, we'd stop and I'd run out and start scooping them up. I clicked the boot and threw them in. We repeated this a few times and were quite pleased with ourselves. But just as we were getting ready to drive off a police car drew up behind us and an officer got out.

'Er, what are you doing?' he said.

It was a time for fast thinking, so I said: 'We had a puncture but I've fixed it now. We're just on our way again.'

The car was a battered old thing and it didn't take much believing that there would be a problem with it. It was worth about £25. The officer looked at us and walked around the car. He looked at the tyres and then flipped the boot. I grimaced as I saw it open. Why hadn't I locked it?

'What's all this, then?' he asked.

I looked down at the pheasants. More fast thinking needed. 'Ah well, officer, I've got to be honest with you. We didn't really have a puncture.'

He looked at us suspiciously. 'Oh yes?'

'No. What happened was we were driving along and they were coming across the road. We hit them with the car and stopped to pick them up.'

That seemed to satisfy him. 'Yes, they can be silly this time of the year.'

I breathed a sigh of relief and thought we were going to get away with it, but then he spotted Patrick trying to shove the gun under the seat. The copper realized he'd been fed a pack of lies and wasn't happy. Then he dragged us out of the car and shoved us on the ground. He took us to the station, and it was midnight before he finally let us go. The police drove us to a bus stop in a squad car with the sirens blaring and dumped us on the street.

'Get back to Nottingham,' they said.

We all clambered on to the bus, where we got a lot of strange looks from the other passengers. God knows who they thought they were sharing a ride with.

We got a £100 fine to go with the fleas in our ears. Patrick had confessed to everything and we kept quiet. That wasn't because we were being cowardly, but it meant we got only the one fine and so, when it arrived, we split it four ways. Of course it was still Patrick who was worse off, because the police confiscated his car. Now it might not sound like much of a punishment for going around with shotguns in your car, but it was like that then. You didn't get in big trouble for having a gun, because nobody was using them for robberies or anything like that. You had a catapult when you were a kid and then you progressed to an air rifle and then a shotgun. It was natural, and the police knew that. You got in serious trouble only if you were caught with a gun on private land. That was an extra fine.

That experience may have been the only time I was caught for poaching, but it wasn't for want of trying on the part of the authorities. In truth, it was rare that farmers would actually catch you. Their way was to employ gamekeepers or ring the police and let other people mete out the justice, but there were some very near misses and, when four police cars surrounded a field, it meant you had few options. So we waded through swamps and thorns and lakes. It was those nights that taught me how to survive.

There was a time when the police did find us armed with guns but we weren't poaching. Four of us were up at the old railway bank. We were just shooting for fun, at rats and at targets. A girl named Ann was with us. Unbeknown to us, someone heard the commotion and phoned the police. We were so busy with our shooting, and maybe with trying to impress Ann, that we didn't notice the copper walking along the bank behind us. He got to within two strides before any of us realized. One of my cousins, David, sensed someone was there and turned around with his gun in hand. It was just a natural reaction to hearing a noise, but the copper thought that he was pointing the gun at him. He panicked and staggered backwards with his palms spread in front of him. Then he cried 'Ahhh!' and promptly fell backwards down the railway bank. That was our cue. We ran off down the railway track as fast as we could go. I took a gun from Ann so she could run faster, and we fled all the way down the line. We had only been shooting vermin, but we knew we were in trouble because the copper thought we were threatening him.

'I didn't do anything,' David said.

'I know,' I shouted as we ran, 'but he didn't think that. He probably thought you were going to shoot him.'

'Oh God!'

When we got to the end of the line we slid down a bank to hide, but Ann rolled the wrong way and landed on top of a swan's nest. That was scarier than the policeman as the swan spread its wings and began hissing at her. She jumped up and ran to where we were all hiding. Even with us worrying about the police, we couldn't help laughing and we desperately tried to stifle our sniggers.

'It's not funny, you know,' Ann said unconvincingly.

We put the guns out of sight and waited, knowing the policeman would go back to his car and begin circling. Then, after a safe passage of time, we casually walked down to the canal as if nothing had happened, laughing and joking about the swan and the falling policeman.

Animals are always unpredictable, which is part of the thrill of hunting them. Even something as small as a rat can cause problems. My brothers and I would often take pellet guns and go out into the fields after them. One of the places where we knew there were scores of rats was in an old tip by the canal. We studied them and, to our surprise, found out that at night-time they were going up trees and actually sleeping on the boughs. It was easy pickings, so we went out one night very late and made our way down to the tip. If you sat in the bushes beneath the trees you could see the rats' silhouettes on the branches. We got in place and waited. Then Phil clicked on his torch and there, two inches from his face, was the biggest rat you had ever seen. He backed off like greased lightning and pushed us all out of the bushes. That was the end of that trip.

Another time, another brother. Roy was kicking tins around on the tip one day when a rat darted out from the debris. When panicked, a rat will go in any direction, and on this occasion it ran right up his trousers.

'Hey, I've got a bleeding rat up my leg!' Roy screamed.

None of us had seen it, so we didn't believe him. At least, we didn't believe him until we saw his face go white and his hands holding something at the top of his thigh.

'Jesus Christ!' he cried.

We started laughing as he unbuckled his belt, dropped his trousers and let the rat jump out. From that day on we always wore our socks over the bottom of our trousers when we thought there might be rats around.

As well as my brothers and sisters, we had a lodger in our house named Ernie Plowright, whom we called Bunk. He had been a friend of my dad's and originally was his drinking partner, but Bunk was a nice, kind man, the polar opposite of my dad, and we all liked being around him. There was no relationship with my mother, or anything like that, but Bunk quickly became an integral part of the family. He was just a friend who became more than that to all of us. At some point in the past Bunk had come into a lot of money, which is why my dad hooked on to him, because here was a kind, wealthy man who would pay for his drinks. His generosity and the fact that he was never very well organized meant it took about a year before the money had disappeared. That was when he ended up living with us. He was there when all the trouble was going on but, when my dad left, Bunk stayed.

He was the same age as my dad, but that was where the similarities ended. Bunk was a happy-go-lucky soul who could never do enough for you. When the money went, we didn't charge him anything, but he repaid us in other ways. He was a big man, much taller than my dad, and he began to look after me a lot. When I was little, he'd throw me on his shoulders and we'd go looking for birds' nests together, walking the fields for miles and miles. It might sound odd to some people, given that we were poachers, but I've always loved animals, and it was a love that was fostered in those early years traipsing around wet country lanes with Bunk. Langley Mill was a rum neighbourhood in anyone's estimation, so, in the absence of money, animals became one of the easiest ways actually to own something. Bunk taught me what he knew, but I was a quick learner and picked up lots by trial and error. I used to go looking for owls, kestrels, magpies, the lot, and had all as pets at one time or another. It doesn't happen nowadays and would be frowned on, but bird-nesting was common in that era and you became experts on where they were likely to be.

Magpies, I quickly found, were the easiest, because they didn't take much looking after and were incredibly loyal. I would find a nest and keep an eye on it, because other people would steal the eggs. You had to find three nests to make sure you'd get one bird, because there were so many people hunting them. The better-hidden the nest, the better your chances of getting a chick. I'd go back and keep an eye on the nest day after day. When the eggs hatched, I knew it wouldn't be long, and as soon as the magpie had feathers and looked on the verge of leaving the nest I'd take it. At home I'd feed it bread and milk, handle it a while and let it go in the yard. I don't like keeping animals in cages, but the magpies and crows would become tame very quickly and would be happy to land on your shoulder.

Phil also had a magpie that he adored, but it all ended very sourly for that bird. It was a funny old thing that would sit on Mam's shoulder looking for worms as she dug the garden, but it wasn't that friendly with everyone. Our neighbour had a baby at the time, and she left it in a pram outside. The magpie landed on the pram, pecked the baby and drew blood. It was a nasty incident, but time moved on and it was forgotten. Then, one day while Phil was at school, a copper came round to our house. He didn't knock on the door or let us know he was there but went up to the magpie that was in a cage outside. He grabbed it, wrung its neck and threw it in the bin. When Phil came home from school that day and found his pet in the rubbish, it broke his heart.

Later, I had a magpie that caused just as many problems. It would be fine with me and followed me around the yard like a lapdog, but it would dive-bomb everybody else, and the rest of the family would go out armed with a stick. Sadly, that came to an unfortunate end, too, when two of my passions merged to deadly effect – the magpie never stood a chance with the remote-controlled helicopter.

Magpies were easily trained, but I was less keen on owls for the opposite reason. The only way to train an owl is to keep it caged and starve it until it will fly back to you. You could walk with it sitting on a leather strap on your hand, but it wasn't the same as having something that was free to choose to fly to you for no other reason than it chose to.

It was a wild and wonderful world for a kid. When the summers were really hot we used to get a lot of grass snakes too. They were fun, because they were so fast that it was a test to catch them. There were a few adders, but they were poisonous and so presented additional problems. At any one time it meant that we would have snakes, kestrels, magpies, owls, Mam's myna bird, ferrets and, later on, monkeys. That was at a time when it wasn't illegal to keep them, and Mal Carter had got some from an animal park that was closing down. Mam was frightened of them, but I was never one for keeping things captive and so I'd let them run free outside.

There were always dogs, of course. The best was Blackie, a mongrel that got run over three times but was the cleverest dog I ever had. He never went on a lead in his life and was utterly loyal. He was so intelligent that if he thought there was a rabbit in a bush he would bark at it to alert the other dogs. Then, as the dogs stood yapping at the back of the bush, he would go around the other side and wait for the rabbit to come tearing out. The last time he got knocked down by a car he broke his leg, but we thought so much of him that me and my brothers clubbed together to get it plastered rather than putting him down.

The ferrets we kept were there for a purpose, namely rabbiting. That was another art. You'd get a set of nets and place them over four or five rabbit holes before releasing the ferret. It would fly down the hole and you'd wait. You needed a few of you for this, because as soon as the rabbit hit the surface you had to pounce on it or it would get away. They were like quicksilver, especially with a ferret racing up the burrow after them. The farmers actually welcomed us when it came to catching rabbits, because they would get overrun with them, but there were plenty of obstacles to actually getting them. Often the ferrets would get stuck and you'd have to dig them out, which was a laborious task. At other times the ferret would manage to get the wrong side of the rabbit. Then it would be blocked, and you would sit there until the ferret killed the rabbit and physically ate its way to freedom.

With that many animals it was a bit of a menagerie and, like their owners, they needed feeding. So I bred mice to feed to the owls and would catch pigeons for the ferrets. There was an old cinema, the Ritz, that had just closed down not far from our house, and we knew that there were lots of pigeons roosting in the roof there. The building was still in good shape inside, but the doors were locked and chained and there was no way in through the front. We realized that if we climbed up the side of an adjacent building and then leaped across a gap we could get in through a small round window where the glass had been shattered.

When we got in it was pitch-black, but there were loads of pigeons in there, so we'd grab as many as we could and then get out on to the cinema's roof. To get down from there you had to jump into a pile of sand in the builder's yard next door. The roof was as high as a house, and if it hadn't been dark you probably wouldn't have had the bottle to do it, but we did it lots of times, even though you never knew for sure how deep the sand was, and you'd be sweating until you sank up to your thighs while holding a pigeon in each hand.

One day there were a few of us up there. We got into the cinema attic and, as usual, began walking along the wooden beams. They were the only things strong enough to take your weight, and you knew you mustn't set foot on the bits of the floor covered with straw. That would be curtains. Sure enough, on this particular night one of the lads missed his footing and went straight through the ceiling. We peered down, realizing how high we were and how far he must have fallen. Incredibly, he had been saved by the merest of margins. He had fallen through the attic roof and landed on the front row of the balcony. A few more feet and he would have crashed down to the stalls and been killed, but, as it was, he fell only about ten feet.

We snatched the pigeons and made our way out for the descent into the builder's yard, the thin line between success and disaster clear in our heads. It was a line that the Haslams would often cross in the years to come.

4

MY BRILLIANT BROTHER

IT SEEMED LIKE AN AGE, BUT FINALLY BABE LET ME enter a race. I was on his 750cc Norton and I was psyched up. This was going to be brilliant and the adrenalin coursed through my young veins. I was fifteen and had never been so excited.

I had to lie about my age to get into the race, and I was so small and the bike so big that I could hardly get on it. Luckily, the short circuit at Cadwell starts on a downhill, and so I managed to get the bike going. In fact, I got it going far too well in the sense that I let my exuberance get the better of me. I was in the middle of the pack when I realized I was going far too fast into the hairpin. Babe was standing there watching the embarrassing scene unfold right in front of him. I knew I couldn't stop, and out of the corner of my eye I could see the other bikes begin to peel into me. Oh Christ! I thought. I don't know why, but the natural reaction was to stick out my leg. I did it way before the corner and in doing so managed to kick a guy squarely in the ribs and send him somersaulting off his bike. That slowed me and I regained my balance. The incident went out of my head and I went on to finish what I thought was a pretty creditable tenth. However, Babe was distinctly unimpressed.

'What the hell was that?'

'What do you mean?'

'You knocked that rider off his bleeding bike. You kicked him.'

'Oh, that.'

'You go find him and apologize. Jesus!'

It was another Babe bollocking. I didn't fancy the task, but I went and sought out my hapless victim and said I was sorry. He was pretty grumpy and didn't say much. I shrugged. It wouldn't be my last apology.

Babe had seen how I was obviously out of my depth, but I was pleased with myself after my six-lap début. Inside I celebrated. This was fantastic. Soon afterwards, Babe let me have a go on the full circuit at Cadwell. I'd just turned sixteen a few days earlier, and I was nervous and excited but full of self-belief like you are when you're a teenager. The stewards complained, because they thought I was too young to race, but I got on and I achieved the fairly impressive statistic of crashing three times in one lap. First of all I crashed at the bottom of the Mountain. I picked myself up from that one with just a bit of bruised pride and fired the bike up. Unfortunately, I didn't realize the throttle was wide open, and I went haring into Barn and had to throw it on the floor again. The third time I rolled it at the hairpin and had to jump. Babe went mad again. It became a recurring theme in the early days, but there wasn't much damage done to the bike and later we even had a laugh about it.

I was in it for pure fun and less-than-pure girls. I had an old 175cc James two-stroke that I'd take down the old Slack Hill with my mates. We would mess around and try to impress anyone who came past on the old footpath that led to the swimming pool. That proved costly one day when I saw some girls making their way to the pool. I had a friend on the back, and we started tearing over the hill down to the swamp at the bottom. I couldn't have planned it worse if I'd sat down and tried. As we tore down the hill I went for the brake, but the nipple had jumped out so there was no reaction. I tried to stamp down the gears to save us, but the chain came off. There was no stopping us now, and we hit the swamp at full pelt and went hurtling over the handlebars into the black depths. The girls stood on the path laughing at the sight of these two bedraggled idiots in a muddy coating.

'You bloody idiot,' said my mate.

'Hey,' I replied, hooking a thumb back towards the swamp. 'Let's get it.'

He turned around and his face dropped. The bike was now totally submerged but for a handlebar sticking out in defiance.

We ventured into racing old-banger cars on the Slack Hill after that. For a teenager with designs on the opposite sex, having a car of any sort was a godsend, and so we were mightily impressed with ourselves as we careered all over that enormous expanse. Needless to say, there were a few close calls again. One of our friends, Pete Riley, was a bit of a lad who was up for anything, and he climbed on to my roof and hooked his hands into the windows. I started the banger and tried to shake him off. I could hear him laughing on the roof as I slewed from side to side and could see his legs dangling down on either side of the car, but he held firm. I was determined to get him, though, and so I decided to go flat out and then slam the brakes on. I got up to about 40mph, which was as fast as the car would manage before dying on us, and then suddenly, with no warning, hit the brakes. It worked. I waited for an instant and then saw Pete come flying over the bonnet and bounce down the gravel until he came to a stop, bloody and bruised. I honestly thought I'd killed him and can remember a rising sense of terror. He had only jeans and a T-shirt on, and his arms were covered in ugly red marks, but we ran over and saw that he was breathing. We patched him up. You didn't go to hospital in those days.

Babe had helped us get the bangers and we left them out on the Slack Hill. They were rotting, dust-clad things, but we loved them. It was tough love, though, as was highlighted on another occasion. We were racing each other and I was up against my nephew Ian, who had taken the beating from Ken the night I'd got home late with him from Margaret. I had a Ford Anglia and Ian had a Morris Minor. I had him beat, but going into the fastest corner he gave it everything and managed to turn the car at speed. It must have turned over ten times before it finally came to a stop in a plume of dust and smoke. I leaped out and ran over with the others. There were no seat belts or anything like that then, and you had no protection whatsoever. He was out cold on the back seat. We pulled him out and laid him on the ground. We were scared, because we genuinely thought this time we had managed to kill someone. It took fifteen minutes before he came round and we all breathed again.

Perhaps the nearest miss of all was also the funniest. In the middle of the Slack Hill there was a small square of long grass. To vary our antics, we decided that we would race through the grass from all angles, so you effectively had a bunch of teenagers using these rusting relics as lawnmowers. We did that for a good twenty minutes before we'd had enough, whereupon a bemused courting couple stood up in the middle and started readjusting their clothes. The earth, very literally, nearly moved for them.

My initiation into the two-wheeled world had been far less dramatic on Babe's Norton, and it was Phil who took centre stage. When huge crowds of us moved on to bikes and started racing on the Slack Hill, Phil was always the quickest. He was the one we all knew was destined for the top. I helped him out as much as I could by cleaning his bikes and just being in the background. I lurked around so much that it got to the point where one day Mal asked me if I wanted to ride in the open class. I was made up to have a go on Phil's 250 and I did well. At least, I did well to start with, battling my way up to fourth on the last lap, before someone sat up in front of me and I touched him. Down I went. I could see that Phil was disappointed, but neither he nor Mal said much. We put the bike back together again. Phil went out on it but found that the back wheel was buckled and the frame was bent. It meant Phil couldn't race in the national the next day. He'd probably have won, but he didn't say much. He knew his time was coming.

Mal had seen it too and in 1972 decided to take Phil to the Isle of Man, the Mecca for bikers. Phil rode in the Southern 100 and the Manx Grand Prix, but the latter ended badly when he hit the pavement at Waterworks Corner. Undaunted, he was back on the Isle of Man the following year when there were numerous extra awards on offer for the first person to achieve the mythical 100mph lap in the Manx. In all its rich history, nobody had managed to top that landmark speed in a race that is run over the Isle of Man TT course but is considered to be for amateur riders. This time, anyone who achieved the 100mph lap would get £100 and, for some reason, a replica sword.

Going to the Isle of Man was a two-week job. The first week was practice and the second was taken up with the actual races. I went over with Phil and Mal and we stayed in old tin chalets. Phil and I were in one, with Mal next door. It was a poky little room with two single beds and a sink. The first night Phil snored so much that Mal could hear him through the tin wall, so he cleared off to another one further away. Then, in the middle of the following night, I got up and went over to the sink. I looked at Phil and saw he had a girl with him. I was stark naked and totally embarrassed. I flew back across the room and pulled the covers over me.

Because he was to be away for a fortnight, Phil had been forced to take the first week as holiday and the second as sick leave from his job. It was worth it. Practice started at four in the morning, and I rode around with Phil in the mist and realized this was a special and dangerous place. Then Phil went out and broke the lap record on his 350 Yamaha, smashing the 100mph barrier in the process. He clocked 102.17mph. He was a rising star. He was a rake of a man, but good-looking, with long straight hair and a ready smile. There was a star quality about him, and Mal started gushing to the papers. 'At one stage last year he fell off in seven successive meetings, but now I'm sure he has a tremendous future,' he said. 'Whatever it takes to get him to the top, then I'll do it.'

Phil went to the home of a local driving instructor called Herbie Mills, who had offered the £100 for anyone to achieve the 100mph lap. There were no officials from the Manx Motor Cycle Club there, because they felt the incentive might jeopardize rider safety. In fact, Phil actually fell on the fourth lap of the race, but he remounted at Signpost Corner to put in a 99mph lap and win.

Winning was one thing, but getting the 100mph lap really signalled Phil's arrival. It was the break he needed, and he got a lot of newspaper coverage. There was still the odd barb about his riding style, variously described as hairy and firebrand, but he told *Motor Cycle Weekly*: 'I always leave a margin of safety.'

Back in Langley Mill, a big home-made banner was put up in the street welcoming Phil home, and it suddenly hit me how good he was. Until then he had been just my brother but now he was Phil Haslam, a professional racer and a future star. Even before the Manx, Chas Wilkinson, the boss of Cadwell Park, had agreed to pay Phil to race. He was invited to take part in the prestigious Race of the Year at Mallory Park in 1973 and came fifth against GP legends such as Barry

Sheene and Phil Read, eclipsing them all by winning the man-of-the-meeting trophy.

Mal was now giving Phil as much experience as he could cope with. He rode 250cc, 350cc, 500cc and 1,000cc machines. Anything and everything, anywhere and everywhere. The following March he went to Daytona for the famous American race and held his own. Phil got married to Angie, and they had a baby son, Carl. The world was his oyster when he took the ferry to Northern Ireland for the North West 200, but he crashed on the 350, going straight through a hedge and breaking his ankle. It was a bad, fast crash. He was travelling at 140mph when he aquaplaned on the wet. He caught his leg against a bough, while the bike was totalled after ripping down the hedge like a bionic trimmer. Road racing is a dangerous game and you need to respect that or you can end up in serious trouble very quickly. That accident was a reminder of how you can never take anything for granted in motorcycling, but we knew Phil would be back on the bike soon. In fact, it was sooner than we expected, and the crash kept him out for only six weeks. He cut off the plaster himself, so that he could return, and came a good third at Croft to show nothing had changed. He had the momentum.

I didn't see the comeback, because I'd had a major argument with Babe in the meantime. I say it was a major argument, but the way we often argued in the

Haslam household was without a lot of shouting; it was more what was left unsaid that festered. Actions often spoke louder than words, as I'd found out that night in the back yard with Babe's fury and his boots. This time the problem arose when Babe asked me to clean his bike. At that point Babe was mainly racing at club level with the odd national, whereas Phil was definitely establishing himself on the national scene. As for me, to put it bluntly, I'd found out what women were and I was seeking more time on my own.

If I cleaned the bikes, then I was allowed to go to the meetings, which is what I loved, but my priorities were shifting. I usually did what Babe said, but that day he came home from the building site and found his bike hadn't been touched.

'Ron, why haven't you cleaned the bike?'

I didn't have anything to say, really. I'd been delaying for a while because my mind was elsewhere. 'I'll do it,' I muttered.

'No,' he said sternly. 'You do it when you're meant to, not later.'

He was angry and I knew he was right. 'You don't clean the bike, you don't go racing. You know the rules.'

He stormed out and that was it. I accepted it quickly, because I wanted to be out on the streets. I was barred from going racing but had more free time. And that was why I wasn't there when the first disaster struck.

★ ★ ★

I don't remember where I'd been. It wasn't important. It was an ordinary day. Nothing was happening. It would soon be forgotten. But then I walked into the front room and everybody was crying. There was just a stifling air of misery in each corner.

'What's wrong?' I asked, knowing that the answer would be bad.

Roy took me aside. 'There's been an accident, Ron.' I could feel my heart sink to the pit of my stomach. 'It's Phil.' Deeper still. 'He crashed today at Scarborough. He's dead.'

I remember crying instantly, but it wasn't long before the tears dried up. I was in total shock, like the rest of my brothers and sisters. It was the first death in the family, and it hit us like a steam hammer. None of us knew how we were supposed to react.

I've tried, but I can't remember where I'd been that day. Why would I? It was just a run-of-the-mill day, but then I walked back into a cold house and my world changed for ever. Mal had called the house a few hours earlier. 'There's been a bit of a problem . . .' We were all shell-shocked. Your mind is a mix of emotions at a time like that. Sadness, anger, confusion.

'What happened?' I said, and the story slowly came tumbling out.

Phil had got himself out of plaster from the crash in the North West 200 and carried on as usual. After the comeback at Croft he had gone to the Oliver's Mount circuit in Scarborough on 7 July 1974, riding Mal's Pharaoh Yamaha 350cc, and was leading by a mile when something went. The bike spluttered and coughed and then cut out as he tried to accelerate out of a hairpin. Phil raised his left arm to let the other riders know that he was stopping, and he was about three feet from the edge of the track when his handlebar was clipped by another rider, called Derek Chatterton. That sent Phil into a steel bridge support and back across the track, directly into the path of the next rider. That happened to be Steve Machin, a close friend of Phil's, who couldn't avoid him. He careered straight into him. Phil suffered serious neck injuries and loss of blood and died by the side of the track.

Afterwards, people wondered whether the sun was in his eyes or whether the track surface was a problem. Maybe there'd been too many bikes in the race. But it didn't make any difference. He'd been three feet from safety but he wasn't coming back. It was the most vivid reminder anyone could have about how terrible this life could be. Two weeks later, Steve Machin was killed in an accident at Cadwell. We never blamed him. This was the risk they all took.

I looked around the four corners of the room and kept waiting for the phone to ring again, expecting someone to say it had been a mistake and that Phil was OK. But the call never came. Later, when Phil's body had come back from Scarborough, I went to see him in the coffin, but I wasn't really looking. It wasn't true. That ghostly face wasn't my brother. It took me ages to really accept that I wouldn't be seeing him any more and that he wasn't going to walk through the door and start joking with me, that there'd be no more poaching, pranks, and bows and arrows.

It hit my mother unbelievably hard, but she put all her energies into being strong for her girls, who just couldn't stop crying. She was comforting them and they were trying to be around her as much as possible. I just went deep inside myself. Normally, I was all over the place, doing stuff with my brothers and mates in the streets, but nothing happened after that. I would leave the house and walk the fields for hours and hours, trying to get away but never managing it. I was just passing time, ticking off the days and hoping it would get better. I didn't see what had actually happened for months.

I thought about the argument I'd had with Babe and how I wasn't there when Phil died. I thought about how I'd been intending to clean Babe's bike the following day, and what that argument had meant. I was still riding on the Slack Hill but I wasn't there at Scarborough and that made it even worse. Yet, strangely enough, it was seeing how it affected others that really brought it home to me. Alan Pacey was Phil's best mate and they had started racing at about the same time. They were at school together and then entered racing. The week after Phil died, Alan rode Phil's bike at Darley Moor as a tribute, but he got the reality of the situation much quicker than I did and was completely broken down by it. Seeing Alan like that made it finally sink in.

At that time, riding bikes was a treat for me. Phil was the one who was going to go all the way. Barry Sheene was two years away from being the world champion, but Phil was pushing him on lesser bikes on the tight circuits. Sheene was great on the publicity side of things and had what we would call works bikes compared with the ones we just bought and rode, but there was little in it. People will think I'm biased, but I can guarantee that my brother would have gone to the very top. Everything was there for him, and there was no stopping him. He was ahead of his time. He was twenty-four.

5

WILD AT HEART

AND THAT MIGHT HAVE BEEN THE END OF THE STORY. There were no bikes after Phil's accident. We all stopped. Babe, me and Alan Pacey. Nobody in the house wanted anything to do with them ever again. Beforehand it had been a family affair, a thrill with Bunk and Treece tagging along for the crack. We'd already had some great laughs and highs, but all that was undone by this crushing low. It was hard to fathom. Finally, it had seemed as if we were getting somewhere. Fortune was smiling on us. And then blackness. That was it. Mam didn't say anything, but we were finished. It was time to move on to something else.

It was strange. There was a void without Phil and a void without the bikes that had become a consuming passion for the three of us. Things struggled on like that for months, and then Babe said: 'You know, if it was the other way around and I'd got killed, then I wouldn't want Phil to stop racing.'

'No,' I said.

'He was the one of us who was making a name for himself. He was going to do something. It would have been wrong.'

'I know.'

'I've been thinking.'

I knew what was coming.

'I'm going to start again.'

He wasn't asking me or anyone else for our approval. Babe had made up his mind, so he started racing again. Mam didn't want him to, but she never tried to talk him out of it or stop him. And when Babe started again, that opened the door for me to follow, because he was now the eldest brother left in the house. Mam wanted us to be safe but she also wanted us to be happy, and so she suffered in silence. It was an incredibly brave thing for her to do. As for me, I got through the death of my brother by knowing that he died doing the only thing that he ever wanted to. I thought to myself, Why am I here? and I knew it had something to do with bikes. I reasoned that if you get a chance to do something that you love then you have to take it. Life is pointless otherwise. And I loved bikes. For me, riding them was like winning the lottery, even knowing the dangers and the misery they could cause.

I had started working on building sites, so there was

a bit more money coming into the house, but it was still tough to make ends meet. It was so bad that I started to steal fuel to get me to meetings. I would go to the compound where the gas board had a fleet of vans and climb over the wire fence. I'd have a rubber tube and petrol can with me and would siphon the fuel out of the vans. I was careful, though, and only took a little from each van, to make sure that nobody caught on to what was happening.

That winter of 1974, Mal asked Babe and Mam whether I could take Phil's place in his Pharaoh team. 'If he wants to,' Babe told him.

You bet I did. Suddenly to have a sponsor was a hell of a way to start my proper racing career, but it didn't suddenly mean that we had everything easy. Coming back from Cadwell Park after a club meeting the van broke down, which wasn't such a surprise because it was a ropy thing that was permanently on the verge of collapse. You just did whatever you could to keep it going, even if it meant taping it together. That night we hadn't got far away from Cadwell when the fuel pump packed up. I knew there was a scrapyard about half a mile down the road, so we left the van and started walking. It was dark and there was nobody around, so I climbed the fence and jumped into the yard. I went looking for a Mini, because I knew it had an electric fuel pump that would do the job for us. Finally, after rooting through a sea of mangled wrecks, I found one crumpled beneath three other cars. We managed to pull it free enough for us to get the pump out and we escaped back to the van. The way we got home that night was having someone sit on the bonnet with a pipe connected to a jerrycan and the pump. It got us a little bit further each time. A sponsor, you might say, was an advantage, but it would get you only so far.

I started out on a 350cc and a 250cc. Mal had redesigned the van so that it bore the slogan A TRIBUTE TO PHIL HASLAM on the side next to the Pharaoh's head. He was also sponsoring a rider called Roger Marshall on a 750 at the time. I did well when I stayed on the bike, winning most of the club races I entered but crashing a few times – accidents that I'd term as standard slide-off jobs with no broken bones. Halfway through the season, Mal asked if I fancied going on a 750. I said yes straight away, because I'd always been more comfortable on the bigger bikes. I'd started on Babe's 750cc Norton, so to get back on one was like coming home. I had a few practices on it and then Mal said we were going to the post-TT event at Mallory Park.

This was a big deal. It was 1975, and the race attracted the top guys like Barry Sheene and Phil Read, so it was a chance for me to really stake a claim. I wasn't nervous. Riders always think they will win. They are invincible, and if that sounds like arrogance it's a must for getting on a bike and riding at ridiculous speeds. In fact, when I crashed after five laps it wasn't because the bike was too big and I was scared of its raw power; it was down to me feeling so confident on it that I felt I couldn't make a mistake.

I was never in the anti-Sheene brigade. He had to cope with people saying he had been born with a silver spoon in his mouth and had had it all given to him, but I never had any problems with him. He was mouthy and flash and was always surrounded by women, but I respected him and there's no doubt he had the wow factor. That's not to say I thought he was better than me. I would look at him in those early days and think, I'll be as good as that. Always, in my head, I would think that he was faster purely because he had better tackle. Better tyres here, a faster engine there; it's the racer's way always to find a reason why someone else might beat him. It's never down to sheer ability. He came to find me at that meeting at Mallory and said: 'Listen, son, let me give you a piece of advice. If you want to go faster, slow down.' I smiled. To me I was a kid on the way up, and here was a legend-in-the-making, Barry Sheene, the man of the moment, a year away from being the world 500cc champion, running scared. It made me feel good, although later I came to realize that Barry was a straight-talking, honest guy and never had a truer word been spoken. I did need to rein it in, because I was pushing too hard and I did have lots of crashes. I had a reputation for being a bit hairy and wild, and Sheene would later brand me a nutter. But there was no hidden agenda or mixed message – he was just telling it as it was.

He won that day at Mallory. He cracked his knee on a kerb going through the Esses, but he still finished first, which was a hell of an effort given that it had been only that March when he'd had his famous crash at Daytona, almost killing himself at 180mph, splitting a kidney and breaking six ribs, an arm, his back and his collarbone.

I could sympathize, because I broke my collarbone when I fell coming out of the hairpin at Mallory. I had no throttle control. When I thought I was out of a corner, the throttle was either on or off. I'd open it as fast as I could and was oblivious to any middle ground. I was up to fifth on the Yamaha TZ750 and I thought I was going to win, but then it was over. After that, people started pointing fingers at me and saying the power of the bike was too much for me, but it was really down to my impetuosity and fearlessness. And that started a run of broken collarbones.

I was back at Cadwell within three weeks. The crash had caused £800 worth of damage, but Mal had the bike repaired and that meant I had to race. I was second to Derek Chatterton in three races, and the injury was all but forgotten until I came off again just days later. It was only a light fall, but I knew my collarbone had gone again. Maybe I had returned too quickly, but I got back even faster from that one. Two weeks passed, and I was in the saddle and breaking my collarbone again. Mal didn't say much during this period. He could see that I was trying my hardest, but even he must have wondered what he had signed when I broke it for a fourth time in the space of two months.

I should point out that a broken collarbone is a serious injury – at least in terms of pain. It hurts so much that it's untrue, but I kept coming back quicker and quicker and learned to brace myself on the tank. Mal wanted me back, so I took a couple of aspirins to numb the pain and off I went. The strange thing was that all the breaks were happening in exactly the same spot. I had it strapped up, because it had started to knit, but the breaks were almost identical. That baffled the doctors, who said that shouldn't be the case. It was the fourth break that solved the puzzle. This time the break was on the other side but in exactly the same spot. This was even odder, because it had barely been a crash and yet it had snapped my collarbone cleanly. Finally, we realized that each time I got a bash on the head the chinstrap of the helmet rammed into my collarbone and broke it. It was a shame, because I was proud of that helmet; it was a full-face Bell model, the sort that everybody wanted at the time, never mind the fact that movement was so limited that I could barely move my head or that it sat so low on my head that it was causing more trouble than it was worth.

You didn't think too much about things like having the wrong-sized helmet. It was a lot more amateurish than now, and the protection was limited. I was just pleased, because I had what was supposed to be the best helmet and it was a bonus if it fitted. I used to take my leathers to a local cobbler, who got to know me very well. Initially, the Pharaoh colours were red, white and blue, but before long mine resembled a patchwork quilt with bits of brown and black and yellow, too. I also used the cobbler to sort out my foot problem. I had a habit of not putting my foot back on the foot peg so I used to wear the end of my toes away. The scrutineers wouldn't pass the boots for racing, so I had a set of boots made for scrutineers and another for racing. As soon as they gave me the nod and they had wandered out of sight, I whipped off the new boots and put on my old ones, which had duct tape wrapped around the ends to form a thick pad that would take the brunt of the friction. It gave me more clearance between my foot and the track, and I preferred it. If it got hot, I knew that meant my skin was rubbing on the track.

It worked well enough until one race at Cadwell. I got on the rostrum that day, but there was a trail of blood behind me. Everybody could see it, and when the television cameras picked up on it, so did the scrutineers. 'That shouldn't happen from a new set of boots,' one said. I had to show him my foot. Blood was streaming out of the boot, and when I removed it I'd lost half my little toe. They checked me more often after that to see which set of boots I was wearing. I liked my old set, but I had to admit that they were well and truly shot.

My cobbler pal was an old-school tradesman with a small shop and set of irons. He stuck lumps of rubber on my boots, and I would put Polyfilla in my helmet. Mal did buy me a new set of leathers when the old ones got too unsightly, which didn't take long because I had a nasty habit of falling off a lot in those early days. I wasn't discouraged, though. When I'd been on the 350 and the 250 I'd been falling off halfway down the field. Now at least I was falling off near the front. That made all the difference to me.

Everybody got to know Mal around the paddock. He was this bear-like Halifax garage dealer who had a well-earned reputation as a hard case. He was as tough as iron with a heart of gold, but he wouldn't take any crap from anybody, and on occasions I saw him grab officials by the neck and headbutt them. This was the way he dealt with irritations. One day we were driving out of a circuit when a bike cut in front of us. It was an every-day occurrence at bike meetings when the car park is crammed, but Mal took exception to it. He reached out of the van, pulled the rider off his bike, lifted the visor and punched him through the helmet. There was never any smoke with Mal, just fire. You didn't need to wind him up. Bang – that was it. Short, sharp and simple.

That was good for me, because I did have a habit of winding others up with my riding style, and Mal was my protector. That was the case at Cadwell later that year. I was on my Yamaha 750 on a part of the track where the straight leads into a fifth-gear left-hander. The normal tendency would be to brake hard in the middle of the track, but I was going flat out and managed to miss my braking point every time. I got away with it for a bit but made such a mess of it on one lap that I turned the hairpin into a chicane and ended up going the wrong way down a track. There had been three bikes turning into the hairpin in front of me, and I'd managed to race up the inside, hit every one of their front wheels and knock them all off. If it had been bowling, I'd have been a hero, but understandably they were not best pleased, and one of them came looking for me afterwards. His mood was further soured by the fact that he had a brand-new 250cc bike and it had been his first time on it. Somehow I'd not fallen off. I'd turned around and proceeded on my way, managing to put the mayhem in my wake from my mind. This guy was furious, though, and scented blood. He came storming down the pit lane looking for me. I saw him coming, but suddenly there was a huge wall of flesh and muscle between us.

'Have you got a problem?' Mal asked, fuse already lit.

'I'm going to bloody kill him. Where is he? Haslam!'

Mal palmed him away, and that shocked him. 'You're not killing anyone today.'

That was the last word and the rider knew it. He trundled off, pride hurt and bike battered. 'Tosser,' Mal added as an afterthought.

In retrospect, you couldn't blame that poor rider. I upset lots of people, and they would tell me to calm down and back off. 'You're wild,' they'd say. 'You need to slow down.' I didn't take a blind bit of notice. I was a young spirit and all I wanted to do was to go fast. If it didn't work, then, well, I had Mal behind me.

I had a sponsor and bodyguard, helmets and leathers, but it was still not a living at this stage. The trouble with that scenario was that I couldn't keep a job, either. Mal was demanding and if he wanted me to go testing every Wednesday and Thursday, then that's what I would have to do. For two years I had managed to hold down a job on a building site, working five days a week, but, as bikes became a priority, keeping in work became more precarious. I'd progressed from being a labourer to driving a JCB when I got the sack. Then I drove a tractor for a local firm. That lasted about six months. I had a construction job at Wimpey's, and there were three or four more building jobs, but I was getting the sack more often than I was working. Something had to give.

I proved a lot better at keeping girls than at keeping jobs. All the girls wanted a good time. They didn't want anything serious, just a guy with long hair all down his back and big sideburns. That was me. I was seeing

Margaret, sleeping over at her house every night, but that wasn't enough. I'd already met Ann, the girl who had once fallen on the swan's nest, at meetings. She used to come along with her boyfriend, and she and I got on instantly. She was slim, sparkly and had jet-black hair. There was a definite attraction, and it was inevitable that we were going to start seeing each other. One day I went into the shop where she was working and we got talking.

'I'm taking my brother's pigeons for a flight,' I said. 'Do you fancy coming?'

It might not have been the best chat-up line but it worked.

'Yes,' she said without any hesitation.

The plan was to take the pigeons down the motorway and then let them find their own way home. So we got in the old van and set off, the pigeons cooing in their basket. Ann was shy and quiet. She was just leaving school and was only fifteen. We carried on down the road with barely a word spoken between us. Eventually, after what seemed like an eternity, we got to the right spot, and I pulled in.

'You need to get them out one at a time,' I said. 'Do you want to do it?'

'I don't know,' she replied. 'I've never held a pigeon before.'

'Don't worry. Here, let me help you.'

So I put an arm around her and we both held the

pigeon together. That's when I got my first kiss from my future wife.

So there was Margaret and Ann and another girl called Wendy, who was older and lived in Melton Mowbray. I was never one for one-night stands, but I did have three steady girlfriends at the same time. Needless to say, that caused lots of problems. Margaret would want to see me all the time, and so would Ann, but keeping them separate was a logistical nightmare. It was hard. Mam was bothered by it all, as she didn't think it was right. I'd have a girl at the house and Mam would be on tenterhooks, because she was worried that Margaret might come over and find us.

'Ron, you should stop all this and stick with Margaret,' she said to me one day. 'It's not fair the way you're carrying on.'

'Mam, I'm a teenager. I don't want to settle down.'

It was too much fun and racing was my way of separating my secrets. Margaret didn't come to the races. Ann did, but she was still with her boyfriend, so we had to keep it from him. Ann knew about Margaret, but Margaret didn't know about Wendy, and Wendy didn't know about anyone else. Confused? So was I, but in the back of my mind I wasn't bothered if the truth emerged. If one of them had kicked up a fuss, then I would have told them to do what they liked. I had my bikes and they were fast becoming my true love.

I'd been in the same class at school as Margaret and

we just stuck together after that, but as racing came along with the opportunities it brought I started exploring. Bluntly, I was looking for sex. I enjoyed it so much that it was a case of any time, anywhere, whether in the van or in the park. Ann and I had a regular spot on a big bank. We'd park up, jump over the hedge and not care if we were disturbed by people walking their dogs, which happened a few times. Of course, on those occasions we'd stop and get dressed as quickly as we could, blushing with embarrassment, but it was a wild time. I never was the sort of rider who would go into the paddock to pick up a girl and go home with her, but if I saw someone I liked I would try and get a relationship going. It was just that I tended to have a few of those at any given time. I had a reputation for it, but, while it bothered Mam, nobody said much to me. The night Babe had beaten me around the back yard had been the cut-off point. Things had moved on.

They were changing on the track, too, and the turning point was an international meeting at Cadwell. Mal's way was to put me in as many meetings as possible, just as he had with Phil before me. It meant that within a season I'd probably clocked up five years' worth of experience. The internationals were a step up from nationals, which in turn were a step up from club level. I did them all, but it was that race at Cadwell in September 1975 that would cause a few murmurs in the motorcycling ranks.

You'd never have guessed it from what happened the day before. I'd got to grips with the Yamaha 750 and felt on top of the world. I was at one of those points when I felt I simply couldn't be beaten. It was a national race at Croft and I was leading by miles and decided to push for the lap record. I had the race in the bag, but then I fell at the hairpin with three laps to go. I got back on and managed to finish, but Roger Marshall passed me and I had to make do with second. It was one of the few times that Mal went ballistic at me.

'Why the fucking hell were you pushing so hard?' he screamed.

'I wanted the lap record.'

'Fuck the lap record. You need the win.'

It didn't happen often, but when Mal gave me a bollocking it was a severe one, and this was the worst. I took it on the chin, realizing there was no point in trying to defend myself because he wasn't listening and, anyway, he was right. I just decided that I would have to make it up to him, and, as luck would have it, the chance came the very next day.

Phil Read was there – Rebel Read, the two-times 500cc world champion whose will to win led to him being branded a 'traitor' by his Yamaha team-mate, Bill Ivy, because he disobeyed team orders and battled him to take the 250cc title in 1968. So was Mick Grant – the man who had just smashed Mike Hailwood's long-standing lap record at the TT race on the Isle of Man. Sheene was absent, because he'd broken his leg messing around on a monkey bike in the paddock, but it was a stellar line-up. These were the big guns. Sheene was at the top, but Read was on the works MV, and Grant had the works Kawasaki. Big guns ready to be spiked, as far as I was concerned.

Practice went well, Mal was speaking to me again, and I was third away. By the end of the first straight I caught them both and just pulled away. It was one of those indescribable days when everything comes together. I won the first race and was delighted, not only because it was the first international I'd ever won but also because it repaired the damage with Mal. The second race was a carbon copy, with one significant difference. It started in exactly the same way, with Read and Grant battling each other at the front. And once again I caught them by the end of the first straight, only this time I caught them going way too fast. At first they were too preoccupied with their own battle to notice, and as they braked they clashed. Now, the way to ride Cadwell was strange. It wasn't a matter of how hard you braked at the end of the straight; what you had to do was shut off as soon as you saw the end of the straight, then you had to get out of a wobble before you braked. On that day, I was trying so hard to catch them that I left it too late over the rise. You have to remember that in those days the bikes' handling was a bit suspect. The net result was that I could see that I was going to wipe them both out. You don't think much in situations like that, because it's over in a matter of seconds and you're focused through adrenalin and fear, but I knew that taking out Rebel Read and Mick Grant might even be too much of a task for Mal the protector. But then the miracle happened. As they clashed they made a tiny hole. Somehow I got through it and passed them both while completely out of control. I had no time to be grateful and hit the brakes as hard as I could. The corner was coming up too quickly, though, and so I laid it in, thinking that I was going to crash and accepting the inevitable. Only, for whatever reason, the inevitable never happened. I went around the corner and cleared off. I couldn't believe it. I turned around and saw Read and Grant shaking their heads. I knew then that they weren't going to come after me.

They were pickled off, but I didn't care. All young lads get to a point where they think they can beat anybody, and I was there. My confidence was so high. I got the Folbigg Trophy for the fastest lap of the meeting and had ruffled some illustrious feathers. It was the start of something. I never drank alcohol, but Mal did enough for both of us that night. I had arrived.

6

FIRE AND BRIMSTONE

I KNEW I WAS DOING WELL WHEN I WALKED INTO THE dole office and they had all the newspaper clippings in a brown file on the desk. They found it hard to believe that someone who was winning races and getting headlines could be struggling for money, but I explained that Mal took all the winnings. It made no difference. I'd been caught, and they wanted to send me for jobs. I had to stop claiming the dole after that.

The prize money was paltry in the early days. If you got £100 for a win, then you thought you were a king, but I was oblivious to the financial side of things. I always have been. For me, I wanted to race, and that was the beginning, middle and end of the story. Any money I had I gave to Mam. She would take my dole but provided me with all my food and accommodation. Mal took care of all the other bills, and we had a system that suited me just fine. Eventually, Mal let me start to keep my prize money. It would get spread very thinly, but in time it grew, and where you were once getting £100 you might get three times that. That was when Mal, always the shrewd negotiator, put me on a deal where he took two-thirds and I got the rest. I didn't complain, because he was doing everything for me.

The results kept coming. I was the runner-up in the British 750cc Championship in 1975, but I was more concerned with the international races and I sampled my first TransAtlantic meeting at Brands Hatch that year. Those were big occasions, Anglo-American bun-fights with top names, dense crowds, and a riot of noise and colour. Meanwhile, my style was still causing a few people to watch in horror. One of those was old Percy Tait, later a champion sheep-breeder but then a big name and doyen of motorcycling. Our meeting came at the Stars of Darley race, which is an annual event that sees local lads take on a smattering of stars. Percy Tait was the oldest rider out there, but he was still doing well and was on a four-cylinder Yamaha.

I found myself battling with him for the lead. It was a clash of contrasts, the old stager against a nineteen-year-old kid trying as hard as he could, on Darley's track. We got to the last lap with me just leading, but I knew he was there. I could hear him, and he was pushing me to the limit. I was coming up the last section, which is made up of a left, a very tight hairpin, a massive back straight and then a corner to the finish. I was pushing too hard and cocked it up on the way into the hairpin. I was probably going a crazy speed like 60mph and, because there was no run-off at Darley, I just laid the bike over to the point where I simply had to crash. The last thing I heard was Percy Tait's Yamaha growling before the kill and then I hit the floor. I pulled my hand off the throttle and put it on top of the tank. I was going miles too fast and my leg was dragging behind me. Then the footrest clipped the dirt bank that separates the track from the spectators and thrust the bike back vertical. The bike flipped up and I was thrown forward, headbutting the tank. The next thing I knew, almost magically, my hand landed back on the throttle. I certainly didn't reach for it, but I didn't need an invitation and tore off down the straight and won the race. It was an incredible incident, one of those moments that make you wonder if there's someone looking after you. Afterwards, Percy Tait came to find me and said: 'Son, in all my career I've never seen anything quite like that.'

'Thanks,' I replied.

'I could have beaten you easily,' he continued, 'but I was too fascinated by watching you and wondering how on earth you were still on the bike.'

I grinned. 'It wasn't skill,' I told him. 'Just luck.'

I felt I was going places, but I was still terrified when Mal decided those places should include America in

1976. 'How do you fancy Daytona?' he said one day.

'Daytona? You're joking.'

'Be good for you. See the world, another type of racing.'

'I don't know.'

'Well, get used to it because I've bought the tickets. It's all arranged.'

I was a naive nineteen-year-old. When I started going to the domestic circuits they seemed like far-flung and exotic destinations to me. I was just a kid and not like my son Leon was at that age; I was still in the comfort of my family and had Mam running around doing everything for me. I had never cooked a meal or even made a cup of tea by that point. And now here was Mal saying that I was going to America and that I might as well enjoy myself.

The Daytona 200 is a legendary sixty-eight-lap race run at the Daytona International Speedway. It attracted all the top Americans at that time, and Mal's reasoning was that it would be good for me to see another way of doing things. The plan then was to give me as much experience of as many types of racing as was feasibly possible. I was to learn basic preparation of a bike from a guy called John O'Neil, a works mechanic for Yamaha, in Philadelphia, and then the two of us would travel down to Daytona for the race. Mal would come out later.

I was scared to death. I'd never been away and had

Right ♣ Butter wouldn't melt... Me during my (occasional) schooldays.

Right ♣ In the back yard. Posing for the camera in my best clothes.

Above ♣ 'Oh no, not the Haslams!' The clan out in force at Dennis's wedding. From left: me, Phil, Cyril, Ken, Babe, Mam, Dennis, Val.

Left ♣ My rock. Me and Mam.

Left 🏍 Dreaming. Playing on Babe's bike while he wasn't looking.

Below 🏍 Bikes in the blood. With Phil's son, Carl, and Babe in my workshop.

Right 🏍 The beginning of the road. Rookie Ron on his first bike.

Left and below 🏍 My brilliant brother. Phil and the Pharaoh made a big impression on the Isle of Man. These shots are from 1973, a year before he died at Scarborough.

Left 🏍 The dad I never had. Babe pictured with John Gainey, his sidecar partner.

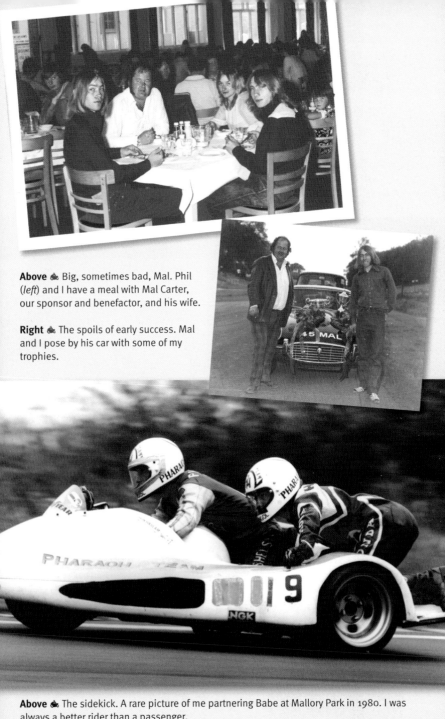

Above ♣ Big, sometimes bad, Mal. Phil (*left*) and I have a meal with Mal Carter, our sponsor and benefactor, and his wife.

Right ♣ The spoils of early success. Mal and I pose by his car with some of my trophies.

Above ♣ The sidekick. A rare picture of me partnering Babe at Mallory Park in 1980. I was always a better rider than a passenger.

Above ♣ Team Haslam. Ann and I had already been through lots of ups and downs by the time I stood on the podium at Hockenheim in 1985.

Right ♣ My right-hand woman. Ann has always played a pivotal role in my career.

Below ♣ A winning team. After all the controversies, we finally get our hands on the TT trophy.

Right 🏍 Farmer Haslam. Our foray into deer farming proved just as hazardous as life on the track.

Below 🏍 Slings and arrows. This was a far more sophisticated bow than the one that nearly killed Babe when we were kids.

Above 🐎 More horsepower. My love of animals and speed meant I really enjoyed horse riding. I even impressed Harvey Smith – briefly.

Above 🐎 The poacher. I have been fascinated by guns since our days hunting pheasants, and have a collection of around five hundred.

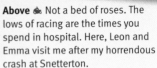

Above 🏍 Not a bed of roses. The lows of racing are the times you spend in hospital. Here, Leon and Emma visit me after my horrendous crash at Snetterton.

Left 🏍 A proud mother. Little did Ann know what Leon had in store for her.

Below 🏍 Happy family – with daughters Zoe and Emma.

Above 🏍 Boy racer. Leon helps his dad down the pit lane in his customized Norton leathers.

everyone to do everything for me at home. I just tagged along to the races and sat on the bike. I remember Mal got me a load of money and gave me a wallet. I had a passport, too. I packed a few clothes and contemplated spending two whole months away from the family nest. It was terrifying.

'It'll be fine,' Mal said. 'John will take care of you. But it's a big country, and the first thing you'll need to do when you get there is get a hire car.'

'You what?'

'Get a hire car. Hertz or summat. Don't worry, you've got plenty of cash.'

'Er, it's not that,' I said.

Mal arched an eyebrow. 'Well, what exactly is it, then?'

'I don't have a driving licence.'

'You what! You're going in three bloody weeks!'

His surprise was understandable. After all, I'd been driving the van for ages. The idea of a licence had just got lost somehow. I had tried but failed the test a couple of times and then I'd forgotten all about it. This was another time that Mal went ballistic. Time was against us, but he had a way of pulling strings, and before I knew it I was in town for a specially arranged driving test. Now it sounds bad, I know, but I knew that there were three instructors at the centre and Mal had told me that two of them would be fine. He had bought them off, and so a pass was assured. The problem was the third one, so I turned up for my test concerned about the odds. They called my name out and I walked out to the car. The instructor looked at me blankly.

'Now, Mr Haslam, get yourself comfortable and then can you please drive out of the car park and take your first right.'

Bugger! It was obvious the odds had worked against me and the one-in-three shot had come up.

'Take your next left.'

I carried on and the nerves grew. What if I failed? I'd have to miss Daytona.

'Take your next right.'

We had gone for about four miles and I could feel my body tensing. Then the instructor said: 'Right, Mr Haslam, putting it bluntly, you can do what the fucking hell you like.'

I took a double take before realizing this was one of the men in Mal's pay. They were some of the best words I'd ever heard. We drove around a bit and talked until it was time to go back, whereupon the instructor went straight back into perfect testing mode.

'Thank you, Mr Haslam. I'm pleased to inform you that you have passed your test.'

When I got to Philadelphia International Airport, John the mechanic picked me up and drove me straight to the motel. It had a kitchenette, but I spent most of my time at McDonald's until one night when I thought,

Stuff it, I'll make something. I'd seen Mam cook sausages, but I'd obviously not been concentrating. She had cooked sausages in brine, but I got some proper ones and threw them in the pot and tried to boil them. When I ate them they were still raw, so I ended up back at McDonald's again.

I was a little boy lost and I looked like it, too. I had no muscles and looked like the runt of the litter, but I suddenly found myself with loads of time on my hands. The plan had been for me to go to the workshop about a mile from the motel and watch John build my bike. The trouble was that the bike didn't arrive for five weeks, so I was left to click my heels in an alien place where I didn't know a soul. I wandered around and marvelled at the big American cars, but I soon got bored by the concrete strip of fast-food joints and bargain stores. I decided I might as well use the time to train, so all I did for those weeks was pound the streets and then kill myself doing sit-ups back in the room. I had a set of chest expanders and used them constantly. When I'd finish I'd collapse, but there was no television and no phone, just a bare room with a bed and a cooker, so it wouldn't be long before I was back working out. I'd do press-ups with my legs on the floor and then, for variety, press-ups with my legs on the bed. I actually came to enjoy it and so I kept working. It was all that kept me going, because I wouldn't actually speak to anybody for days on end. It was a case of anything to relieve the boredom, but that period changed my physique. I went there a skinny boy and came home a man.

In all my time there I had only one night out. I went to a party with some Americans, and it was like one of those things you see in a film – the air was thick with marijuana and people were throwing up. Others were lying on the stairs, totally out of it. It was like a cross between a hippie commune and a frat-pack party. I gave it ten minutes and then cleared off. I wasn't into that. It was tough being away, and I felt truly lonely for the first time in my life. Nowadays, of course, you could just ring someone up and that would make things so much easier, but that was a generation away. The one thing that I did have was an old-fashioned tape recorder. I had a plan to tape myself speaking into it and then send the tape back home. At that point I'd never done interviews or anything like that, and I managed the considerable achievement of feeling embarrassed even though I was the only one in my room. I clicked the button but after a few seconds clicked it off again. I tried a few times. Eventually, I did manage to get a few words out. I still have the tape today, but it is not a classic piece of family history.

'*Click* . . . Hi, Mam . . . *click* . . . Hi, Babe . . . *click*.'

I was chronically homesick, so I was thrilled when a package from home was waiting for me at the front desk. I quickly unwrapped it and shoved the cassette into the old tape recorder and waited for the messages.

'*Click* . . . Hi, Ron . . . *click* . . . Is this on? . . . *click* . . . Hi, Ron, it's Mam . . . *click* . . . Hi, Ron, it's Babe.'

It was somehow reassuring to know they had experienced the same awkwardness.

The only way to beat the blues was to get busy, but that was hard because I had no mechanic skills at that point. I could do bits and bobs, but that was it. I'd been looking forward to having John show me how to build a bike, but it came so late that he didn't have the time to do that. Instead, he just had to work flat out, around the clock, to get the job done. I did get to try my hand at making spoke wheels for the Yamaha assembly line, which is a hellish task, but it wasn't the learning experience I'd been hoping for.

Finally, when the bike was built we loaded it up into the back of a fancy van and set off. It was around 900 miles. There were three of us, and two beds in the back. While someone took the wheel the other two would get some sleep. We drove for two days without stopping apart from to fill up with petrol. 'Just stay on this road for four hours,' John would say before bedding down. I was just glad I had a licence.

You knew about things by reputation in those days. There was no internet or twenty-four-hour news channel to take you abroad, so there was an air of mystique about going down to Daytona. I had no idea about racing on a banked oval, and after I went out for my first two laps of practice I came in with blisters on my hands. Nobody had told me it was perfectly normal for the bike to shake on the banks. As a novice, I'd been fighting it and trying to stop the wobble by gripping as hard as I possibly could. I'd barely started before I came in dripping with sweat and absolutely drained. I thought that after my training regime I was super-fit, but I felt like giving up. Then, after a few more laps, I was so tired that I physically couldn't fight the bike any more, so I just let it wobble. To my surprise, it didn't get any worse, and I relaxed a bit, finally realizing that the banked sections at Daytona completely flatten the bike's suspension.

One of my enduring memories of Daytona was the strictness of everybody out there. Compared with the meetings in the UK, it was like having the Gestapo run things. I took my shirt off in the paddock and suddenly heard this thunderous voice behind me.

'What are you doing taking your shirt off?' he yelled. 'Do you think we all want to look at your horrible body!'

It was the same with sandals. They were banned from the paddock. It was a shock to me, because I was interested only in racing. How you looked was irrelevant. But this was the American way, and when they said they shut the doors at nine o'clock they damn well meant it. Before a minute past, they threw everybody out, whether your bike was ready or not.

I was always a bit nervous of Mal because of the way he was, the hair-trigger temper, and because he was from this strange place called Halifax, which was alien to Langley Mill folk like us who saw Nottingham as an adventure. But I was happy to see him when he turned up a few days before the race, and for him America was a paradise where you could shoot anything you wanted with the sun on your back. He was in his element.

The race was a big deal. There hadn't been too many people there in the build-up, but the crowd was huge when we lined up on the grid. It occurred to me that here I was, finally doing something on my own, without my family covering for me. That was more frightening than racing itself. The race started well, but Mal was doing the refuelling and he failed to fasten the cap on. So I got to the end of the pits, turned and went down. The clip had come undone and leaked fuel all over my tyre. That was the end of that fleeting shot at glory.

The journey was far from over, though, and Mal saw to it that my education became more cosmopolitan by the day. After America, the next stop on our 1976 world tour was Europe. There would be me, Mal and his mate, Ivan, working our way through different countries. Mal would kip in the caravan and I'd drive. In fact, I did all the driving because Ivan still couldn't. I took us down to Imola and then to Paul Ricard, coming eighteenth and ninth respectively. Ivan had never been out of the country, and the first lesson he learned was you can't drink the water over there. Two days later he came out of the toilet.

Mal loved it as much as I did and he threw money at it. The one thing he wouldn't do, though, was pay for a mechanic. I think he wanted me to learn my trade because he thought it would be good for me. But he also had a very simplistic approach to these things – the bikes would be delivered straight out of the crate and we would run them. He'd say: 'One's got slicks, one's got intermediates and one's got wets. Take your pick.' By now bikes were my life. Girls took second place. I didn't have a social life, because there was no time for it, and no sooner had I got back from one meeting than I got on with sorting out the van for the next. Mal was fantastic and gave me so many opportunities, but in truth it was almost too much. We travelled the globe under the Pharaoh banner, but there was never any respite. If there wasn't a big meeting that week, then he would shove me in a club meeting instead. You might think that sounds like he was in it for the money, but it was simply the case that Mal loved racing so much. He needed his fix. We'd go to somewhere like Croft, and he'd make me start at the back of the grid because it was obvious I was going to win. It was a step down, and so he never let me finish a race, because that would be taking a trophy away from up-and-coming lads who were trying to make a name for themselves.

I didn't care where I was racing as long as I was. Club

meetings or internationals were all the same to me. I even tried speedway. I didn't really stop to consider how far I'd come, and I never really thought that it wouldn't work out. Every time I went out there I thought I was going to win. Mal did everything to bolster that belief, but he sponsored lots of young lads at the same time and had a soft spot for someone who was trying his heart out but had no money. Mal, meanwhile, had money from all over the place – he had his garages in Halifax, dabbled in CB radios when they became the trend and also had a farm complete with buffalo.

He also had a disastrous personal life, which he hid from me. In 1970 his wife, Christine, had been involved in a car crash that left her paralysed from the neck down and killed their son Malcolm. BOY DIES AFTER THREE-CAR CRASH shouted the headline from the *Halifax Courier* that Christine saw when she woke up, heavily sedated, in hospital. It was horrific, yet that was by no means the last tragedy to befall the family. Mal and his wife had split up by the time she committed suicide by overdosing on sleeping tablets some nine years after her accident; and then, in 1986, Kenny, their son and a speedway star, shot his own wife before turning the gun on himself, thus orphaning their two children. It was a life that Mal managed to hide, and I only learned the full, traumatic facts later. How he managed to live with those things I do not know, but perhaps racing was a release.

I've still got an article from a 1977 *Motorcycle Racing* magazine which has a feature on Mal, and he pulls no punches as he talks of his time inside and nutting the odd person. 'I've broken every law in the book, been done for assaulting the police, and I've been in every cell in Halifax and Bradford for fighting,' he told the reporter, who probably couldn't believe his luck. 'I was scrapping because I had a rough upbringing. I supped out of jam-jars as a kid, and we never had carpets. I didn't see electric lights or a wet toilet until I was fourteen. We weren't brought up; we were dragged up. We lived on bread and jam, bread and dripping, bread and sauce, and we used to fry chips on a Tilley lamp. It was that bloody pathetic.'

He talked openly of almost killing people, breaking their jaws and not knowing when to stop, but he said he had changed when he went into business. And he absolutely loved bikes and would do anything for me. He was angry when I lost the 1975 British title when I was disqualified for swapping my bike and again when Steve Parrish got the Grovewood Award at the end of that year instead of me. In that same article he said it took him six months to recover after Phil's accident. He continued:

The poor lad died in my arms. It was a terrible tragedy and it knackered up my life. I was never the same man. I had already lost a son and then it was like losing another. I was like a father and I did everything for him, but I always knew he'd get killed and I always felt he was too good to live. At night, when he'd be in one bed and I'd be in the other, I'd stop awake many a time looking at him and saying to myself, 'You poor sod. What the hell are you doing it for?' Now, watching Ron ride, I'm so frightened for him and scared of losing another member of the family. The day Phil died I walked down that 140 yards to the paddock and all I wanted was for Ron to ride for me. I wanted him to be Phil.

I could never be that, but I was doing my best. Looking back on it now, that magazine article explained a lot about Mal and the way he was with me. There was no need for him to feel guilty, but I suppose he felt he was the one who had encouraged Phil and given him the opportunities.

In the meantime, Babe had decided to stop racing bikes. Babe was good and fast, but he knew he wasn't the king of the road as he had been back on the streets of Matlock. His short black hair was now flecked with grey, and he accepted the taunt of time. So he turned his attention to sidecars and teamed up with a friend from Langley Mill called Bonner Freeman, Phil's brother-in-law, and got sponsored by the landlord of the Miners' Arms pub in Eastwood. Mal wasn't as interested in sidecars, so I began to take over and put a bit of money Babe's way whenever I could afford it.

For me, things were definitely on the up, highlighted when, in August 1976, the factory Suzuki team asked if I'd trial one of their 500cc bikes. It was an honour and a thrill to see what the top guys got to ride. This was Barry Sheene's bike, and it would give me the opportunity to see whether I was right in believing that he had it easy because of his equipment. The date was set, and the venue was Oulton Park in Cheshire. They wanted Sheene to ride, too, but he flatly refused and said he wouldn't be there if I was. It wasn't personal, but Sheene knew that I was a promising rider, so he had nothing to gain and everything to lose. That just made me feel even better. I felt that Sheene was intimidated. It was big news, and Ann came along to watch with her boyfriend. Unfortunately, by the time she got there I was already in hospital with a broken wrist and two broken fingers. It couldn't have worked out better for Sheene. I did three laps and then went for the brake at Cascades. I quickly found out that the brake had come undone, so I headed across the grass into a ditch. It wasn't much of a test. My first time on a proper factory 500cc bike ended in embarrassment with me sitting on my backside, but I'd already tasted enough to know that the works machines were in a different league.

All I needed was another chance, and it came the following year at the British Grand Prix. Mal had got hold of a Suzuki and secured me a wild-card ride in the race, but more important in the long run was the fact that Gerald Davison, the top man at Honda UK, had noticed me and paid Mal £250 for a one-race deal. They gave me the bike that Phil Read had won the TT on that year and put me in the Formula One support race. The temptation to ride for Honda on a four-stroke, when all I'd really ridden before were two-strokes, was too much. It was the first time I'd sat on a bike with what I'd call true works backing, and it went like clockwork. I just cocked my leg over the Honda and rode. I won the race by a massive eleven seconds and, significantly, my lap times weren't far off the best times set in the Grand Prix itself. Honda wanted me and gave me a contract for the following season that would be considered bizarre today. It meant that I could ride the Pharaoh 750cc Yamaha for Mal as well as riding the Formula One for Honda. Mal wasn't ready to let me go. He would tell everyone that I was the greatest, and for my part I was happy because I owed him so much. Not least the fact he had got hold of a Suzuki and secured me a ride in the actual British Grand Prix later that same day in 1977. It had been big news in the Haslam household, and word spread through Langley Mill and beyond. It seemed hard to believe that this kid, who had messed around on pushbikes in the roads and gone on midnight poaching shoots with his brothers, should now be on his way to Silverstone. What's more, I was on a Suzuki, which was the same make ridden by Sheene, who had already wrapped up the world title and was heading to Silverstone for a championship party.

The family were excited by the news and all made the trip. I tried to keep calm by going out into the campsite and flying my remote-controlled aeroplane. One of the Japanese Honda engineers came over. He was called Takeo Fukui and asked if he could have a go. In our broken discussion I tried to explain to him how to use the controls, and off he went. I got it really high for him and then handed him the control box. He smiled a broad grin and then did the only thing that he shouldn't have done. He put the plane in a sheer dive. I knew that it would still be OK as long as he didn't try to pull it up, but of course he did just that. The net result was the wings snapped off and the engine and body started hurtling down towards the campsite like a bullet. That was when Fukui handed me back the controls. There was nothing I could do. People were milling about, riding bikes and drinking beer. I winced. We were incredibly fortunate that that metal bullet hadn't hit anyone. Fukui was very apologetic and then wandered away. He's now the president of the entire Honda corporation, and Leon is riding for them. The wheel has come full circle.

I might have bonded with one of Honda's top men, but there was a problem when it came to the Grand Prix. I had gone well on the Honda in the support race, but the Suzuki was a different beast altogether. I'd already had my accident the previous year, and my ability to get on with the mechanical quirks of the Suzuki had not improved. It had a completely alien disc valve and no end of things unsuited to my aggressive style. The bike was brand new and I never knew what it was going to do. With no testing, I lined up for the British Grand Prix in front of thousands of adoring Sheene fans and wondered what the bike had in store for me.

It didn't take long to get an answer. I lost it after the back straight, and the bike chucked me up into the air. It was a dramatic highside. Then the bloody thing caught fire, because it had magnesium carbs on the side that ignited as soon as they hit the ground. It was a spectacular sight, but it meant I didn't enjoy my first taste of GP racing. I was unharmed and learned a lot, but it was a bittersweet experience. I don't know what went through Mal's mind when he watched that bike burning on the back straight. Money never entered my head, but that accident was going to result in a huge bill, because the Suzuki was the top bike at the time and, as the smoke spiralled into the sky, it was clear there wasn't going to be much left of it. To his credit, Mal realized the Suzuki was only going to cause us problems; he got shot of it soon after that and we went back to my beloved Yamahas.

I wasn't the only Brit struggling that day, even if my

crash was worthy of only footnote status in the bigger scheme. Sheene was the man the crowd wanted to see, but he had been suffering with head gasket problems, so he borrowed the bike of his friend, Steve Parrish, to qualify on pole. In the race itself his Suzuki blew its gasket again, and in a fit of rage he drove his bike into the garage wall, bending the forks badly enough to wreck the bike. Parrish, meanwhile, was having a great race and looked set to win it. He was still leading on the last lap when Sheene went to the pit wall and held up a board on which he had chalked the message GAS IT, WANKER. Sure enough, Parrish did just that and crashed. Pat Hennen, an American, went on to win the race, took third place from Parrish in the championship and bagged a factory ride with Suzuki as a result.

It was a harsh lesson for me, too. I tried the 500cc Yamaha in a few races after Silverstone but it wasn't competitive. The factory Yamahas were good, but the ones you bought over the counter were simply not up to the job. In contrast, the Suzukis you could buy over the counter were strong, but I soon went back to my 750cc Yamaha and tried to eradicate Silverstone from my mind. Everything in racing revolves around winning. That's what drives the circus and fuels the dreams. Jumping in with the big boys had been a shock to me. I had always thought that if you had stuck me on equal machinery with some mileage on the clock, then I was the best. All racers think like that. But then reality hits and tells you that you're not as good as you thought. That's when lots of guys quit, but I was ravenous for more. I'd take the fall, heed the lesson and move on. I was still young, Sheene was getting older, and I knew I'd be back.

7

THE KNOCK

WHEN I THINK OF THE ISLE OF MAN I THINK OF PHIL. HE was a record-breaker and the future king of the roads. He was the one who was going to drag the Haslam family from Langley Mill to the back pages. He was the 100mph man who tamed the treacherous turns and early morning mist. But that was all a distant memory, and now I was the one flying the flag as I caught the ferry in 1978.

I went to the Isle of Man because I wanted to be a Grand Prix racer. To some, like Barry Sheene who was a long-term leader of the anti-TT brigade, the two were poles apart. Sheene went to the island once in 1971 and crashed at Quarter Bridge. His view was that it was too dangerous and that if you made a mistake, then you might well end up dead. The list of casualties over the years proves that he had a point, but his stance didn't go down well with those who thought it was the spiritual home of motorcycle racing, and he got a lot of flak when, eventually, it was stripped of its world championship status.

I can see both sides, but what I do know is that Barry Sheene was never afraid of anything. He rode on other road circuits, including Oliver's Mount, which had claimed the life of Phil, and you can't pretend Sheene was not a brave rider. All I can say is that I fell in love with the place very early on in my career, and if that curried favour with the fans, then so much the better. I was there to get noticed and get into GPs because that was the elite, the endgame.

The Isle of Man is a one-off. It's about bikes going at breakneck speeds along country lanes, the roar of finely tuned engines yards from terraced houses, the scent of petrol hovering over an entire island. I'd been there before with Phil, sleeping in the old tin chalets, but this time it was different. Mal hired a car for me so I could run around the course and learn it. I remember thinking that it would be impossible; there were so many twists and turns, and it was so long, that it seemed it would take twenty years to get to grips with it. But Mal's way was always to push me and make me do the laps wherever I was racing. In fact, in the 1978 season alone I raced in 250cc, 500cc, 1,000cc, Formula One and Formula Two races. It was the bike version of cramming for exams.

Even Mal knew that the Isle of Man was different, though. He always encouraged me to push myself and go harder than maybe I should have. He didn't want there to be anything in reserve and would force me to go faster, but he knew that you couldn't do that with a rookie and the Isle of Man. Instead, he told me to back off and just take my time. 'Learn the course,' he said. 'That's what you need to do first.' He was right, too, but there was still a buzz when I went out for practice at the crack of dawn when there was so much mist on the Mountain that I could barely see in front of myself. I did what Mal said and, although I came fourth in the Formula Two race, I was never going to trouble the front runners that year. Nevertheless, I had the taste and knew that I would return.

I was well aware of how treacherous riding on the roads could be. I'd had a terrible experience the previous year when I was battling with Geoff Barry in the Killinchy 150 race in Ulster. Geoff lived down the road from me and was my main rival in the race. There was a very fast section between hedgerows where I was losing time to him because I didn't know the circuit. I got it all wrong and didn't realize there was a kink. I was going far too fast and I was going to take him out. I was panicking when, suddenly, as if by magic or some sixth sense, he eased up. I went flying through and somehow managed to miss him. I breathed a sigh of relief, knowing how close we had been to disaster.

Half a mile down the road I put my hand up to acknowledge my mistake and wave him past. I dropped in behind and tried to follow him round. On the next lap he fell off in front of me at a slower chicane and went flying head first into a dirt bank. His bike somersaulted back and clipped me on the shoulder. It ripped my leathers, but somehow I managed to stay on. I knew it was bad, because I watched Geoff hit the bank and he didn't move, but you never know for sure until someone tells you. When I heard that he'd been killed, I felt sick. I also wondered what would have happened if I hadn't waved him through. Would he have pushed so hard if he hadn't been in the lead?

You can never, ever get complacent in bike racing. Do you think about the danger? The simple answer is no. You know deep down that sooner or later you're going to crash, but you manage to hide those thoughts away in another part of your brain. The dangers were never dormant for long, though, as I found out when Mal sent me to an American backwater called Loudon to race against the great Kenny Roberts, the man who would supplant Sheene as the world's greatest rider in 1978. When I raced him, Kenny was still to become the world champion, but he already had an aura about him. I was confident in my own ability, though, and felt I could take him on in his own back yard.

It took me most of practice to realize just how fast you could go around the huge banked corners. They were all fourth gear and, once I realized that, I began to get faster and faster. What I didn't learn quite as quickly was that, when the bank drops away, you had to level the bike up. I kept it laid over, and so, as I came out of a corner at 130mph in fifth gear, I had the biggest highside that you've ever seen. The bike instantly caught fire, and I was bashed against the banking and somersaulted down the track. Despite all the broken collarbones and the wrists and fingers, it was the first time I'd had a major high-speed crash – and I knew about it. The skin had been shredded in lots of different places, and there wasn't a part of my body that didn't ache. To this day I've never been so battered and bruised by a crash. Even so, there was never any question of me not racing the following day. We worked all night to rebuild the bike, but I was hurting everywhere.

I managed fifth place, but the truth was I was scared to put too much effort in, and that can be absolutely disastrous for a racer. The sport is based on self-belief. If that goes, then you're on the fast track to the scrap heap. Most riders get The Knock at some point in their career, and for a period it will completely destroy them. When you're in the throes of that downer it's the hardest thing in the world to claw yourself back. Belief ebbs away, and that depression can last for a week or a year. For others it never ends, and they join the ranks of ex-racers, undone by a sudden onset of reality and the dangers faced.

I had The Knock after the TT in 1978. It started during one of the TransAtlantic meetings between the best of the British riders and the Americans. There was a huge crowd, and Donington was awash with leather and excitement. I was trailing one of the Americans into the Esses at Donington Park when he shut off quicker than I'd anticipated and I ran into the back of him. At that point I wanted to stop what was happening and rewind. I knew that he should have been accelerating when he was braking. Things became cloudy, and I thought this wasn't right. It all happened in a nanosecond, because the last thing I remember was hitting the back of his exhaust. Then I was flung into the bales and knocked unconscious.

It took me the rest of the season to get over The Knock. The first thing I did was try to be safe, but that was the worst thing I could have done. Being safe caused more problems. I tried to keep a little back in reserve and increase the margins for error, but that meant I had to push harder in other places. I held back in the areas where I was more nervous and tried to make up for that elsewhere. It was a balancing act that never worked. So I finished up with a slower lap time. And then I started crashing. I thought, Christ, I'm crashing like I was before, but now I'm slower, too. It was a downward spiral and, regardless of the willpower I mustered to combat it, the stark fact was it kept happening.

It hadn't even been that bad a crash. Certainly, it didn't compare with the one where I lost a lot of my skin in Loudon. But I kept thinking about what had happened and how the other rider had done something I hadn't expected. It was the realization that my fate wasn't in my own hands that troubled me. I'd see others riders come off and slide into banks, brush themselves down and get back on, but they knew the cause. It might be oil on the track. Solution? Don't hit the oil again. You might have locked the front brake. Solution? Don't lock the front brake. Simple. But I'd been knocked cold by someone else's mistake. You could have argued that I anticipated wrongly, but motorsport is all about anticipation.

I suffered and started riding a long way off people to make sure the same thing would not happen again. I started giving myself a gap, and the first thing that happened when I did that was people started tearing past me.

'What's wrong, Ron?' Mal said.

'I don't know. I'll be OK.'

'You're pushing too hard.'

'Don't worry. I'll be OK.'

I said the words but I wasn't convinced. Mal was always one for driving me as much as he possibly could. He was a hard taskmaster, but he could see this was something serious and so he started telling me to back off. But there was something inside me that wouldn't let me give in. Call it bravery or stupidity, but I started pushing ridiculously hard in the wrong places. And as the bruises worsened, so did the blues.

Mal was an unusual sponsor. Lots of them would warn their riders about crashing and immediately sow a seed of doubt that affects your riding. Mal wasn't bothered about the money or the machinery. He just wanted me right, but that was a struggle. It was a terrible period in my life and it lasted for months. 'What's wrong? What's wrong?' I couldn't answer. The truth was I knew I was frightened; I was a nervous wreck on certain bits of the track. I didn't want to hurt myself, but I was actually hurting myself more. I wanted the excitement and I wanted the adrenalin rush, but I didn't want the pain.

Nobody said much at home. Everybody knew that I had a problem, but there was nothing anyone could do. So after another crash I might get a 'hard luck' or a 'you'll do better next time', but it didn't help. There were the barbed comments too. Nobody would say it to my face, but I knew certain people were saying that I was finished. Even in the family someone would say: 'What's up – couldn't you catch them?' They were throwaway remarks, really, and they didn't know they were cutting such deep, slashing wounds. It is down to your will in the end. How much do you really want it? Do you want it badly enough to get over this massive hurdle? Is the nervousness bigger than the craving? If it is, then it's over. Lots of them don't get over it.

Make no mistake. The Knock can even dethrone the greats. Take Fast Freddie Spencer, who would become part of my life soon enough. He was the fresh-faced genius from the Bible Belt who was to light up the motorcycling world by becoming the 250cc and 500cc world champion in the same year. You'd talk to him and he would have no idea how he was doing it, because he simply had so much confidence and skill. But then his wheel broke one day in South Africa in 1984 and Freddie fell. He didn't win the title that year but managed to bounce back brilliantly the following season. He was different after that crash, though. Beforehand he wore the thinnest leathers, but after that he was heavily padded at every race. While Freddie could still do it, the effort of will he needed to achieve it was enormous. Within a few years the shining star just faded out.

It makes no difference whether you are a club racer or a double world champion. The Knock bridges all classes. You might go your whole career and not get it until the very end, but it hits everybody at some point. Ninety per cent of riders will start blaming other stuff, because they don't want to believe that it's them, so they will say the brakes are terrible or the tyres are off. Sometimes the excuses are genuine, but much of the time it's down to a rider not being able to take it beyond a certain point. They ignore the little beacons of doubt telling them that they're not up to the job.

I went through this period and I simply didn't know what the hell I was doing. Later, people would suggest that I didn't have the self-belief that others had, but I disagree with that. The only time I doubted myself was during that one period. I backed off from everything else. There were no girls for a while and I went into hiding, because I knew something was deeply wrong. This was my career on the line and also my love. I went into a quiet place and would try not to think about it, but that only made it worse. It went on meeting after meeting and I got to the point where I actually dreaded going racing. If a meeting was cancelled I'd think, Thank God for that. I was in a super-hard job that I no longer wanted to do, and that scared the crap out of me.

Luckily, The Knock can go as quickly as it comes. For me, it began to change when I sat down and thought, What else can I do? I'm sitting here and I'm still young. If I stop racing, what is left for me? I couldn't come up with anything. Nothing was ever going to give me the same thrill and pleasure. Once I realized that, it made me push through. Be practical, I told myself. There's no option.

Somehow I got myself together and, believe me, it was one of the most difficult things I have ever had to do. I thought that if I killed myself, then it would be while doing the thing I loved. That was the worst-case scenario and I could live with that. I honestly didn't care if I did die racing. That's what happens sometimes. I accepted that. I also thought about Phil. Why had I carried on when he died? It was because I wanted to continue where he had left off. He'd done so well and there was a part of me that didn't want his name to die. I wanted to carry on the tradition, and doing it for someone else eased the burden. Those two things came together and pulled me through. Nothing else mattered.

I don't really know for sure why it lifted, but I got through it and the following season I was back to my old self. I started well, and no longer was my priority merely to survive. I wasn't scared of dying any more, and that felt great.

I was now able to progress. I'd been the runner-up in the British 750cc Championship in 1975 and was second in the 1978 British Formula One series. I was actually a world champion in 1979, winning the TT Formula One title, albeit that it was only run over two rounds at the TT and the Ulster Grand Prix. I was also second in the *MCN* Superbike Championship. That year I got the offer to join the official Suzuki team as a works rider, but I decided to stay with Honda. I hadn't raced in a GP abroad and didn't feel I was ready. It was nice to be wanted, but I thought I'd be better off staying with Honda, who said I could ride a few GPs in 1980.

My ties with Mal were weakening. He was my sponsor, manager, everything, but now I was a Honda rider, too. I was preparing Mal's bikes and was flat out trying to fix them and get them ready for races. That wasn't slave labour, because I was happy to do it. I had become quite skilled at it since I was that novice in America and preferred looking after my own bikes. That showed on the one occasion when Mal decided to invest in a mechanic for me. The man he actually employed was Howard Gregory, who went on to work for Kenny Roberts, but my riding went to pot. It wasn't that Howard was not setting up the bikes well, but I just felt something was missing. It wasn't trust exactly, but when I sat there watching Howard work on the bike some of the fire seemed to drain away. It took me half a season to adjust to going from running around trying to do everything to sitting back in a caravan with my feet up.

The trouble with working so hard on Mal's bikes was that it meant I was running late for Honda. Bearing in mind that this was a huge corporation with a rich history in GP racing, they were less than impressed when I turned up a couple of times and found the crew waiting for me in the pit lane. I signed a new deal with Honda but kept Mal as my manager. It seemed like a compromise that might keep everyone happy, but it was never going to be enough for Mal. He wanted control, and he didn't like following me around when he'd been calling all the shots and deciding where we would be racing. As for Honda, it's fair to say that Mal, what with the drinking and fighting, wasn't really their sort of person.

I cannot thank Mal enough for what he did for me and my family. We wouldn't be where we are today without his unstinting support, and I owe him a debt of gratitude. He was hard but fair with me, and I gave him plenty of excuses to erupt. One of those came when he bought a Formula Atlantic racing car. It was basically a scaled-down two-litre machine that looked like a Formula One car. Mal was always one for his toys, and he bought the very car that had just won the championship. He asked if I fancied débuting it at Donington, which hadn't been open very long at the time. I jumped in and set off. At that time Donington had a surface that was very pronounced and grippy. Even though the car had slicks and it started to rain, I thought I'd be fine. In fact, I found I was quicker than everyone in the wet and was loving it. Right up until the point where it spun. My motorbike rider's instinct took over and I shut off, which was the worst thing to do, and the car ploughed straight into the pit wall. It was beyond repair. I hadn't realized the difference in tyre temperatures on big cars like that, and it was a disaster. Mal's new pride and joy was a mangled wreck, and he never got the chance to even sit in it. They were good days with Mal, though, and, despite all the crashes and the spills, the trauma of

Phil's accident and the destroyed Formula Atlantic, I look back on them with great affection. But the writing was on the wall, and Mal knew it.

I'd been everywhere with him – Daytona, Imola, Paul Ricard and the Isle of Man. I'd started on the Island on a 250cc Cotton that we nicknamed the Billy Cotton after the band leader. But times were changing. Mal didn't care for Honda muscling in on his act. In turn, they'd ask him not to do the pit boards because he was giving out different information to me. I'd be racing 250cc, 500cc and 750cc bikes with Mal, and then climbing on the Formula One with Honda. I was doing that in nearly every meeting. I had people literally wheeling a bike to me when I finished one race to get on another. I loved it, but it was knackering, and when I started having to miss warm-ups Honda thought enough was enough.

Gerald Davison was the top man at Honda and Barry Symmons later became the team coordinator. They took me under their wing. They'd phone up and tell me where we were racing and that was it. Simple. And one of those places was the Isle of Man. The place had been stripped of its world title status, but it still had an aura about it, even if the controversies began to rage all the more passionately during the next few years.

I'd slowly been learning. In my very first race on the Island in 1978 I'd come thirty-eighth, but the following year I was third in the Formula One class behind Alex

George and Charlie Williams. That was the year when I enjoyed a great battle with Mike Hailwood, who had drawn record crowds to the Island by coming out of retirement the previous summer. Hailwood was a cavalier genius, with craggy good looks and a multi-millionaire father who had invited scorn by driving him around in a Bentley. However, Hailwood was the real deal and had a charisma you rarely find. He certainly gave me a wonderful riding lesson on the Island. I had a problem on my bike which meant it would go great for a couple of miles before misfiring for the next few hundred yards. Hailwood had just come back on the Ducati, which was not that quick, but he knew the place like the back of his hand. I must have passed him twenty times only for the bike to misfire and Mike to come past me again. I'd tag on behind him and watch him ride. It was a masterclass. My style at that point involved hanging off the bike, but Mike was the opposite. He was just sitting bolt upright, totally unflappable and seemingly not trying, but he was inch-perfect everywhere. I couldn't believe it and felt it was an honour just to follow him. I liked Mike, and he found me afterwards and commented that I didn't seem to run out of track anywhere. He didn't mind passing on a compliment, which you can't say for everyone in the bike world, and I appreciated it.

In 1980 I was third in both the Classic and the Formula Three races. That was the year that bad blood began to be spilled by Honda and Suzuki. In the six-lap Classic it was Joey Dunlop who broke the course record on the scruffy looking Rea Racing Yamaha that matched his appearance. My team-mate that year was Mick Grant, and he was second and I was third.

The trouble had started earlier in the week when Grant won a controversial Formula One race on the works Honda. Suzuki complained about the size of the tank on Grant's Honda, which had been filled with tennis balls to limit its capacity, but the result stood and the resentment simmered – all the way to the next year, when I would be the victim.

I'd served my apprenticeship and knew that I could win when I made the trip in 1981. It had been a steep learning curve. When I first went there I thought there was no way I would ever work it out. On the short circuits, each lap takes about one and a half minutes and you feel in control very quickly, but here it took twenty minutes to do a lap, and after two weeks I was none the wiser. It meant I couldn't go flat out because I was never sure what was coming up next. It took me three years before I felt I knew every bump and every ripple on the surface. Learning it that way was a huge benefit, because it made the Isle of Man a gentle break for me. The pressure was off, and there was no one there telling me to go harder, faster, better – and, anyway, this was motorcycling's biggest festival, and so nobody was expecting the lad from Langley Mill to win.

I'd had a couple of crashes and been lucky. One of them came at Ballaugh Bridge, which looks pretty innocuous and is just a small hump that you take at around 30mph. I loved jumping and so started to play a little game with myself to see how high I could leap over the bridge. Immediately after it there was a kink right and then a kink left. I got to the point where I realized I could jump straight over the right into the left by clearing three white lines on the road. Where everybody else was arriving in second gear with low revs, I hit it in third knowing I was bypassing the need to turn right. I jumped so high that I could see inside the commentary box that was stationed there. The bloke inside was going mad, and he wasn't alone. Everyone was saying I was too wild and dangerous, but I was just enjoying myself and loving every minute.

Inevitably, I came a cropper. I hit the bridge in third but the steering damper broke and so, when I landed, the bike locked and threw me up the side of a gable roof. It looked horrendous but I escaped with nothing more serious than a sprained ankle. The attitude of everybody was that they had told me so, and I had no option but to take it on the chin. There is a photograph of me from that crash, upside down, limbs splayed like a star, and seeing that now is a reminder of the dangers. But you can never make the Isle of Man safe. If the roads are improved, then that just makes the bikes go faster, and it is impossible to put in run-offs. Even after

Ballaugh Bridge the potential for disaster didn't really affect me. In retrospect I think it was good that it lost its world championship status, because it meant that everybody who went to the TT really wanted to be there.

Road racing is obviously very dangerous, although that is part of the appeal, and I saw my fair share of crashes. I had a first-gear crash down the middle of the road going into the Mountain section, while Phil had one in Ireland when he hit the kerb and was thrown down the middle of the track. He had a space helmet at the time, with a wrap-around visor, but it split and cut his face to ribbons.

And, of course, there have been hundreds of people who have died at the Isle of Man. That's perhaps not surprising, because the most difficult thing in motor-cycling is a road circuit at five in the morning with so much mist that you can barely see your hand in front of your face. It's hard to explain just how frightening riding blind can be. You get by from memory, because it's physically impossible to see through mist on the Mountain when you're travelling at 100mph.

I developed a system where I'd commit the course to memory and get into a rhythm, so I would know that it would be a right followed by a left and a straight. It became natural, so that I just flowed into it. The terrifying part came when you realized your rhythm was out and you'd get to a corner that you thought was another hundred yards up the road. Suddenly, everything is out of time and you're in a panic. Physically, you're lost within yourself and the only solution is to get in the middle of the road, slow down and wait until you get to a marker that rings a bell. You wait until everything connects again.

Once I used a slightly different technique to win a club meeting on an old airfield circuit. I think the technique might best be termed stupidity. On that day the hail was pelting down so strongly that it was sticking to my visor and blurring my vision. If it had been a Grand Prix, they would have stopped it, but anything goes at club level and so we all soldiered on, even though none of us could see where we were going. You couldn't lift your visor for long, because the hailstones were so big that it was like being punched in the face, so the only solution was to keep flicking it up.

My method was to flick the visor while travelling slowly at the beginning of the straight, look down at the edge of the track and then nail it. I counted to five in my head, because I'd worked out that that would take me to the braking point. Everybody else was huddled in the middle of the track, because they thought it was safer, but I'd be screaming along the inside, looking down at the edge of the track. The flaw in this plan was that I had given no thought to what I would do if I caught someone. That was possible, because I was taking so much time out of them that I could easily have lapped the field. I got away with it, but afterwards I thought, Christ, that was stupid. I could easily have had a terrible crash from piling into the back of someone, but I was so pleased that I'd found a way of going fast in the hail that I didn't stop to think. These days they'd say I was out of my mind.

I'd learned my lessons from the Mountain mist and airfield hail and was a more mature rider when I arrived on the Island in 1981. This time I knew I had a chance and was confident when I lined up for the start of the Formula One race. Graeme Crosby had a chain problem and so wasn't allowed to set off at his allocated time. Instead, he was made to start from down the field. That meant it was down to me and Joey Dunlop, but Joey had to change a tyre at a pit stop and I was flying. Only the bike could beat me now, so I backed off a little. Finally, I passed the flag and doubled back on myself to celebrate. Ann was there and hugged me. The mechanics were all slapping my back. I couldn't have felt any higher. And in the midst of all the jubilations, sparing a thought for Phil, nobody noticed that Suzuki were spitting blood a little further down the road and talking feverishly to Crosby, who had ridden a good race to make third place from the back of the field.

My joy was short-lived. Word came through that Suzuki had protested, but initially I thought, So what? The rules were clear, and I'd already stood on the rostrum. They couldn't do anything now, could they?

The rest is a blur until I remember Barry driving past a few hours later and winding down his car window. 'Ron, I'm sorry,' he said. 'We've got a problem.'

I still refused to believe it would be serious and was actually in the hotel at the function that night expecting to receive my award. I was on the stage when they read out the names and they said Crosby had won.

'No, no,' I said. 'You've made a mistake. I won.'

'They changed the result,' the announcer told me.

I was numb, but the team were furious. I found out that Gerald had already done his best for me. He had stormed into the meeting room and asked the organizers: 'What on earth is going on?'

'We've decided to remove the four-minute penalty,' he was told.

'You can't. Ron would have pushed harder if we'd known Crosby was in the race.'

Gerald was right. We were constantly worried about running out of fuel, so I was told to ease off. Now they were giving my title away and Gerald was seething. He said: 'It's a scar on the history of the TT. We've got professional teams and an event run by rank amateurs.' Gerald said that Geoff Duke, the famous racer and one of the committee members, couldn't even look him in the eye.

The rules were there in black and white. If you go to the back of the grid, you lose time for each place. But now they'd decided that they were waiving that particular rule. The blokes on the team couldn't believe it. They'd known that Crosby was effectively out of contention that afternoon. After my first lap I had nearly a minute's lead. There were boards all over the circuit, and I could see that Crosby's name was nowhere. I was so far in front that I thought I'd slow, because I was concerned that I might be jinxed and the brakes would fail or the engine would break. The course was 226 miles, and there were plenty of opportunities for something to go wrong, so with the benefit of a big lead I cantered to victory. At least I'd thought it was victory.

Honda tried to get the result reversed, but the decision was now set in stone. Crosby was the winner and I was second. Honda were outraged, so much so that they painted their bikes black and had all us riders dress in black leathers for the Classic race at the end of the week. Joey did his best, raising the lap record to 115.4mph before running out of fuel, but Crosby went on to secure a double. We were slaughtered in the press for the protest, but Gerald replied that it had been a dignified protest against a rank injustice. The truth was that he had actually wanted to withdraw the team before realizing that the only ones who would suffer from that were the fans. So we wore black, and the festival ended sourly. It was the black of mourning.

I went back the following year and finally got an undisputed win in the Formula One race. Grant had been the early leader, but his engine went and I beat Joey to first place. It was a popular win, because of what had happened before, but under all the relief and joy something had changed for me. As soon as I had that first win, I didn't enjoy riding as much. It took the fun away, because suddenly I was expected to win. If someone was quicker than me, then I would have to push myself beyond eighty per cent to beat them. When it got beyond that level, it was no fun. I wouldn't accept losing, so I started to feel the extra pressure. I had wanted the TT win for so long, but once I had it nothing was the same again.

8

SCRAMBLED BRAINS

THERE WAS SOMETHING MOVING ON THE TRACK AHEAD. It was like a line of oil, but it was shimmering, and as I got closer I realized that it was a huge snake. I lifted up my bike and somehow managed to miss it, but I knew that Joey was right behind me. I slammed on the brakes and turned around. I got off and walked towards the streak of grey. It was motionless, and I noticed it had a wide, flat bit just below the head. I reasoned that Joey must have run over it. And that's when it reared up. I realized the flat bits were folds of skin and I came face to face with a spitting king cobra.

It's fair to say that Joey Dunlop and I were not the most worldly of people. I was a lad from Langley Mill and he was a working-class hero from Ballymoney. We were shy, didn't say much and liked the company of close friends. It was inevitable that when we started travelling the world with Honda we were going to be in for a serious culture shock.

I went to Suzuka for the eight-hour endurance race with Alex George in 1979, and we were second. After that I was a regular visitor to both Suzuka and Macau, where I won the Grand Prix a record six times, and my eyes were opened to the wider world. It was a place of snakes, cavernous fish tanks, and deranged shopkeepers asking whether you wanted your monkey dead or alive.

At the end of the 1980 season I continued my education by going to Australia to take part in the Swann Series. That was great. It was just me and a couple of mechanics travelling around for four weeks, and the atmosphere was like a club meeting. The distances between the tracks were huge, so we'd get halfway and then kip down. I enjoyed the whole experience, because racing had become serious and it was like entering a time warp and emerging back in the good old days. There was no pressure to win, and if you lost it didn't matter because there would be another race the next day.

The facilities weren't up to much, and everything was pretty basic, but I liked it because racing was becoming work as well as pleasure. You built up to win a championship, and the pressure filtered through to you. That wasn't fun. On the bike I still enjoyed it as much as ever, but the day before I'd be slowly winding up. In

Australia there was none of that. You raced, and that was it.

It was down under, at places like Sandown Raceway and Adelaide, that I first came across Wayne Gardner. I had a big target on my back, because I was the only Brit, and I was on a substantial bike, and Wayne was happy to take potshots. God, he was quick! He was wild and hot-headed but he was fast. You never knew if he was going to finish the race, but you knew that he could ride the bike. It was pretty obvious that he was going to go all the way. A couple of years later, Wayne was signed by Honda Britain and was a team-mate. He was on his way.

I did OK in Australia despite one strange crash when the wind just lifted me and I took off like an aeroplane. I was only about four feet in the air, but it felt like high altitude. Then the wind placed me down sideways and I slid along the track. The bike was badly damaged, but when I got to the pits the mechanics were laughing and singing 'You picked a fine time to leave me, front wheel' to the tune of 'Lucille'. That brought me back into the fun side of riding, knowing that these guys could see the humorous side of any situation. It was what I needed.

Joey had the same approach as me. We wanted to win, sure, but we were racing because we loved it. There was no thought about money or fame or anything else. We were bikers. Simple as that.

One incident in South Africa, after that meeting with the king cobra, showed how we were on the same wavelength. Honda had just brought out the 1100R and we went to Kyalami to test it. All the Japanese top brass were there to witness their baby in action, but because it was so new there was only one bike. I'd been there before, but Joey hadn't, so after I'd done a few laps I came in and said: 'Tell you what, Joey, why don't you jump on the back?' There were a few anxious looks from the development team, but Joey was up for it.

'Sure,' he said and cocked his leg over. The Japanese were looking at me as if I was mad. This was their new state-of-the-art model, and I was giving pillion rides. We set off and did eight laps before I thought I might as well let Joey have a go. But instead of pulling in I just stepped aside on to one footrest and let Joey shuffle forward. We were going around 100mph at the time and the Japanese went absolutely mad. Barry Symmons was there and had his head in his hands, but we didn't even think about it. We hadn't planned it or anything, but that was me and Joey – we just thought the same way.

We'd got to know each other from the road circuits. His wife, Linda, and Ann got on really well, and you never felt out of place with them. There were no airs or graces with Joey, no pretence. You could walk into his house without him knowing you were coming and he wouldn't bat an eyelid. Even now it's like that at our place. Recently, someone arrived unannounced in our kitchen, and we were all talking to him. I assumed he was someone Leon knew, and vice versa. It was only after he'd gone that we realized none of us had the faintest idea who it was and that it must have been a fan!

Another man who was the salt of the earth was Willy Gibson. When we went to Ireland, Mal would disappear and stay up drinking until three in the morning. I didn't drink and so I tagged along with Willy and his family, who were incredibly hospitable. They just took us in, no questions asked. Just like Joey.

We thought the same and even looked the same to an extent. Neither of us bothered much with barbers. Joey had a mischievous expression and a crooked smile that often had a cigarette hanging from it. He had a thick Irish brogue and marks on his bike to represent the dogs he had killed while racing. They were like the crosses a fighter pilot might have chalked on the side of his cockpit during the war. I was staggered by the number. Joey must have killed fifteen dogs and yet he had never fallen off once. That might not have impressed the RSPCA but it impressed me, because I knew from experience how frightening it was when you hit an animal. It happened to me when I was riding on the Mountain section on the Isle of Man with Ann clinging on the back at around 160mph. It was early morning and so I let rip, flat stick. It was sheer luck that the hare didn't hit the front wheel and bring us crashing down, but it couldn't avoid the fairing.

'Oh my God!' cried Ann. 'Go back, Ron. We've got to see if it's OK.'

I turned around and came to a stop by the side of it. I can assure you the sound of a dying hare is one of the most awful things you will ever hear, like the crying of a distressed baby. Ann was devastated, but it was too far gone. I had to put it out of its misery and be thankful that we, at least, were OK.

The risks were everywhere on the roads. Babe and I had gone to the Ulster Grand Prix one year, and I had settled in behind Joey in the race. There was a section by a windmill where I wasn't as fast as him. There was a slow rider in front of us, and Joey was going past before the upcoming bend. I didn't want to lose Joey, because I wanted to get a tow off him, but just as I hit the throttle he eased off. I snatched the front brake, clipped Joey's back wheel and was thrown up a cart track. Joey was scared to death. He stamped on his brake, chucked his bike on the floor and came running back to me. It wasn't his fault, but he knew that he had changed his mind and that that had caused the spill. Ann was back in the pits with Barry, and they heard over the Tannoy that I'd crashed. Then, when Joey didn't come round either, they must have been fearing the worst. Eventually, I limped back and saw Babe waiting on his sidecar. He should have been on the road but had refused to go out until he knew I was all right. I put up my hand and off he went.

That bond I had with Joey meant it was good to have him when we travelled east, but it didn't mean there wasn't a competitive edge. The Suzuka eight-hour race is a huge deal for the Honda factory on their home track, and the first thing you want to do is to be the fastest man in your team. The circuit is like Alton Towers on drugs, with a fairground by the side of the track, a yellow roller coaster, and huge tanks where the fish get caught and thrown back a thousand times a day.

The race itself can be equally baffling. When I first went there in 1979 I thought you'd be at ninety per cent, but you're actually at a hundred per cent all the time. You have anything up to fifty-five minutes on the bike before you get off and let your team-mate have a go. You dismount and watch the others. The second time you get off and have a bit of a rest. The third time it feels like you've had no break at all. You've just collapsed on the table at the back of the garage and someone's telling you to get your helmet on. Your hands are curled up. The physio stretches them and you swear blind that they're going to snap. It hurts so much, but once he straightens them it's beautiful.

The trouble with endurance racing is that you all compromise so that the bike doesn't really suit anyone. I always ran the gear shifter on the right-hand side, but nobody else did that. It made it hard work, but our chances ended prematurely when Joey touched one of the white lines and crashed early on. I'd been the quickest, so I think he was pushing a bit too hard. I knew what that was like, as I'd done the same thing in an endurance race at Brands Hatch when I was partnering Alex George. Alex was older than me, but his lap times were better and that grated. We were a lap clear of everyone and the race was in the bag, but I wanted to be fastest, so I pushed on and fell at the left-hander running down to Clearways. That was the first time I'd seen the team disappointed in me.

'What happened?' Barry said.

'I touched the inside of the kerb.'

'Why didn't you ease back?'

A pause. 'I just touched the kerb.'

Nothing else was said, but I knew Barry knew the reason.

If Suzuka was different, Macau was like the Wild West. Mike Trimby, a racer who became a friend, invited me to take part. It was similar to the Isle of Man but shorter – around nine miles – and Mike organized a holiday in Thailand for each rider afterwards. The first time I went there in 1981 he lent me a bike to take around the course to get my bearings. It was like stepping back in time on to narrow streets with people pulling carts. One night I was going around when a load of lads came screaming by in an old banger with the

Above 🏍 'Rocket Ron'. Leaving Barry Sheene for dead at the start of the Donington Road Race in 1977.

Right 🏍 Have you got any Polyfilla? I look back now on the helmets we used to wear and cringe.

Below 🏍 The thrill of speed. On board the new 1100R.

Right ✍ Any bike will do. Mal's son, Kenny, was a speedway champion and I was happy to try my hand too.

Left ✍ Weathered leathers. Riding at the Cadwell Park international in 1975 with threadbare gear.

Above ✍ Yam Yam. I loved the big Yamahas but rode anything. Here I'm on a 350 at Mallory Park in 1975.

Left ⚜ Hair apparent. I felt I'd made it when I got my first GP contract in 1983, and my sideburns were in their pomp, too.

Right ⚜ Refusing to toe the line. I smile after an early win at Brands – despite the shredded toe that had the scrutineers fussing.

Above ⚜ Happy days. I get my knee down on the Rothmans Honda in 1985.

Above ⟡ Chain reaction. I don't know it yet, but I'm an accident waiting to happen after my chain breaks at Ballaugh Bridge on the Isle of Man.

Above ⟡ Fall guy. Crashing is part of the game, but you never believe it's going to happen.

Above 🏍 It's just my pride… The aftermath of my showboating crash at the TT.

Above 🏍 Elf hazard. We had our ups and downs with the Elf in more ways than one.

Left 🏍 Looks can be deceptive. The Elf was a striking machine, but we were often knocking our heads against a brick wall, or the tarmac.

Above 🏍 The development rider. I gained a reputation for testing new bikes, and I loved it.

Above 🏍 No fizz. The Pepsi Suzuki year started with high hopes but went flat very quickly.

Above 🏍 The finale. I bowed out of GPs on the Cagiva with fewer fingers than I had started with.

The man in black. I came home to ride for the much-loved Norton and was staggered by the welcome.

number plate painted on by hand. I went around the next corner and they were sideways in the road. I had nowhere to go, because they were completely blocking all escape routes. I hit the brake and aimed for the barrier and the bonnet. The bike wedged in the gap, and I was thrown head first over the barrier. Meanwhile, the lads just shunted their car back into the road and set off. They were complete hooligans, shouting and pointing and not in the slightest bit bothered about the bloke who had just disappeared into the bushes.

I dusted myself down and carried on. I saw people sleeping in tin shacks by the side of the road and kids with deformed legs working as beggars. We later found out that their parents would strap their legs up their backs because it made them more twisted and induced more sympathy. I went into town and saw someone living in a garage with a settee and a chair. He was one of the rich.

Mike drilled the dangers into me. This was a place where you simply could not go wrong.

'It doesn't matter if you're last,' he said. It was a place that was beyond making mistakes, but the bare fact was I pushed harder than on the Isle of Man because it was shorter and I could learn it quicker. I listened to Mike and decided to enjoy it, but it turned out that was good enough to win it in 1981. I came to love the place and won every time I went. The second time was on the four-stroke Honda, and I was up against the top Japanese guy on a two-stroke. I beat him in the first leg but could hear him all over the back of me in the second. He was close enough for me to hear his fairing scraping and his engine screaming. I felt the contact. I covered the white line and he went down. I was pleased he'd fallen because I'd felt he was going to beat me, but I was relieved he wasn't hurt.

The only other time I came close to losing was when Didier de Radigues, a Belgian rider, came over. He pushed me harder than I really wanted to go on those tight roads, but because I'd already had a hat-trick of wins I felt I was defending something. I think my experience helped me. I knew that at the top end of the circuit it was all about rhythm. You started slow and built it up. The rhythm was more important than the raw speed, and you didn't crash by spinning the bike from under you, but by getting out of time. That happened to me a few times, and I rubbed the leather off my arms on the barriers, but I was able to back off before coming to grief.

I started to get a reputation out there. I liked to wander around and see the local life, and people would stop and point at me. It was a bit like how Joey must have felt on the Isle of Man. He was the King of the Roads and I was the King of Macau. The pair of us were traipsing around one day and came to what I thought was a pet shop. There were lizards, eels, snakes and monkeys all slithering and jumping about. Now, I liked monkeys, as I've mentioned before. I even had one at home. I won a race at Donington in 1980 and was on the podium for the presentations. They started lugging this huge, angular trophy across the track for me. 'I don't want that,' I said. The man on the mike was confused, because it wasn't like me to be awkward. 'I had the same one last year,' I explained to him, 'and my monkey impaled its arse on it. The vet's bill was horrendous!' In Macau I was intrigued by this monkey and was watching it when the owner came out from behind a wooden table brandishing a big knife. He wanted to know whether we wanted him to kill it for us, which is when I realized this wasn't a pet shop but a convenience store. I was strictly a pie-and-chips man, so I told him to leave it. Meanwhile, next to us, a local pointed at a chicken fluttering around in a basket and the storekeeper picked it up and pulled its head clean off before handing the flapping body to the satisfied customer.

It was therefore with a deep feeling of anxiety that we went to Macau's famed floating restaurant. Joey and I weren't the most adventurous of people when it came to cuisine, but Barry was up for anything. Once he had tricked me into eating frogs' legs by getting the kitchen staff to purée them and use it as a filling for vol-au-vents. In the floating restaurant he surveyed the nine courses and smiled.

The first thing that came out was what they called a thousand-year-old egg. It was deemed a great honour for us to have these, but they were black where they should have been white, with a green yolk, and a stench that was stomach-churning. It was a delicacy that passed me by, but I pushed it around my plate to make it look like I had tried it. Next up was pigeon, and I was optimistic about being able to tackle this one. What I didn't anticipate was that I would get the whole thing – the head, eyes and beak – and the whole family – baby, brother, father. I had to pass on that too. When the monkey arrived I was relieved to find that they had at least taken the eyes out, but everything else was there. It was the entire animal with the skull cut. Somebody lifted the top of the head off to reveal the white brain. I felt pretty sick by this point and was amazed when Joey tried that. I'd lost all hope when the duck came and, sure enough, it was totally flattened so that all you had was the skin with no meat at all. It's fair to say I went hungry that night.

I look back on my time in Macau with a lot of fondness. The trick was in treating the course with a lot of respect. That was the undoing of Wayne Gardner when he came over. He didn't even make it through practice because he was so aggressive. He was running about two seconds behind me, but I knew Wayne and that he would be pushing too hard. It was pure luck that he didn't injure himself seriously, because when he fell off he almost landed in the sea. Barry stopped him from riding after that, and I think Wayne was secretly a bit relieved. Lots of guys were saying it wasn't a fit place to race and that it was too dangerous.

Like all young riders, Wayne was mad keen to impress when he joined Honda Britain in 1982. We were testing at Cadwell Park one day and I came in and said I wanted to try different forks. We had only one set, but Wayne was watching and copying me. Five minutes later he said he wanted new forks. Barry knew we didn't have any, but made out they'd changed them just to satisfy Wayne. When he came back in, Wayne said it made so much difference, but the truth was his bike was exactly the same as before.

Another time the Japanese sent new carburettors to give us a bit more acceleration. They probably gave us another seven horsepower, which wasn't to be sneezed at, but again we had only one set. As I'd been there the longest, they gave them to me to try at Donington, but while they did give you more power they weren't as smooth and the lap times were actually worse. I told Barry I wasn't bothered about them, which excited Wayne, who said straight away that he would have them. He tried them all the way to last practice before he clicked that they weren't working for him either.

Wayne was a friend as well as a rival, though, and I taught him about Anglo-Australian differences. One of those was the fact that our policemen were a lot sneakier. We found that out one night when we were driving along at three in the morning and I saw a patrol car behind us. It drove past and pulled off at the next roundabout, but before long I noticed some lights behind us again. It was the same car, and as it drew level with us the policeman eyeballed us. Wayne was surprised that they would creep up on you like that, because that simply didn't happen back home.

There's always another side to the story, though, and the police had good reason to have the hump with me. That was because of the night when I got back from overseas and had agreed to hand out the trophies at a local presentation night in Burton. I was absolutely exhausted but couldn't let the people down, so Molly, my sister, and I shot off to the do. I smiled and handed out the prizes, then the lights went down for the disco. I looked at my watch. It was half past ten.

'Come on, Molly,' I said. 'Nobody knows I'm here now. Let's go.'

She got her coat and we crept out and got into my brown Scimitar. Tired and needing my bed, I got my foot down, and we must have reached 100mph when I noticed some car headlights in my rear-view mirror. I stepped on the gas to see if I could lose him, but by the time I got to 120mph he was closing. Then, as he got momentarily held up by another car, I saw a flash of blue.

'Oh Christ!' I said. 'It's the police.'

At times like that bike racers may not be the most rational of people, but I reasoned that I'd been pulling him along at around 120mph for eight miles and so I was facing an automatic ban. That was why I decided to really get my foot down.

It was pitch-black and wet, but I was on my route home and thought that local knowledge would be enough. There was an articulated lorry ahead of me blocking the entrance to a roundabout, so I went the wrong way around it, doubled back and then tried to hook the car the wrong way into a dual carriageway. It was so tight that I spun it around and came to a stop with the police car touching my bumper. It was all or nothing now, and I made the snap decision that if I was going to go down I might as well go down in a big way. I slammed my foot down and got up to 140mph in the wet, swerved over a small island and then lost him on the back roads. I was pleased with myself, although when I glanced over I noticed Molly was as white as a sheet.

I knew he'd be pickled off and would be on the radio, so I parked the car up by the Black Horse pub and phoned Babe. He came to get us and drove back to Mam's. As we got there I saw the squad car turning off its lights and reversing down the side of the house to lie in wait. They knew it was me and so now I really was in trouble. We carried on and went to Molly's and I got into bed, tired and worried, but I'd only been there for twenty minutes when I had another bright idea.

It worked like a dream. We got up and took Molly's VW van back to the do, parking just down the road. As soon as we walked in, the lights went up and the officials came up to me and thanked me for staying so long. We all walked outside and I went into acting mode.

'Oh hell, my car's gone,' I said.

The officials couldn't do enough for me, and the police were duly called. I explained that I'd been late for the awards night and had foolishly left the keys in the ignition – I had to say that because I didn't want the police to smash a window when they found the car. The copper was fine until it came through on the radio that his colleagues had been chasing a brown Scimitar for half the night.

'Are you sure you've been here all night, sir?' he said.

'Yes,' I lied. 'Ask anyone.'

The officials all nodded their heads. I knew the copper didn't believe me, but there wasn't a lot he could do. The only problem was the people from the presentation night were so embarrassed that they wanted to give me a lift home. I insisted we were fine, but had to wait for all of them to leave before Molly and I could sneak off down the road and get into her van.

Two days later the police found the Scimitar, but they didn't tell me for a fortnight, hoping that I'd go back to it. They were so angry that they threw finger-print powder all over it, inside and out. That's a bugger to get off. Finally, I got the car back and went abroad to another meeting, leaving the police to let Molly know their feelings. She was filling her van one day when a squad car sidled up next to her and a copper wound the window down.

'We know it was him, you know.'

Molly played the innocent. 'I don't know what you're talking about.'

'I think you do, love. And there's one bloke down the station who's definitely going to have him, because every time he walks in the rest of us say, "Look, it's Graham bleeding Hill".'

Things weren't going quite so fast as far as my GP career was concerned. Honda's promise to let me ride in a few rounds in 1980 had come to nothing. That was frustrating. I liked riding in Britain and, in the future, I would always try to ensure that Honda let me race at home as much as was possible, but I knew I needed a taste of GPs before having a full-blown season among the elite. That wasn't happening, and it was irritating. I was twenty-four, the age Phil had been when he was on the cusp, no longer a kid.

There were domestic championships to take care of, though, and one of the ones I really wanted was the *MCN* Superbike title. Honda managed to annoy me there, too, when we pitched up at Brands Hatch. HRC always made a 1,000cc Formula One bike and they sent that over. I rode it in the Formula One race and won, so I asked Barry if I could use it in the Superbike race. He refused, saying it was only for the Formula One. I was frustrated by that, because it was much quicker than my bike. If I could have done, I would have told him what I thought, because no rider wants things made harder than they need be. I gave him the evil eye as I left the garage, and if looks could have killed then Barry would have been done for there and then.

I won the *MCN* Superbike and Streetbike titles in 1981, but it was the lack of a GP ride that was grating. Honda were still pursuing their NR500 four-stroke at the time. Ever since the FIM changed the GP racing rules in 1968, limiting 500cc engines to four cylinders and thus giving the advantage to two-strokes, Honda had been in self-imposed exile. But they had spent a few years developing the NR500 and I tested it at Donington and in Japan in 1981. But again they reneged on a promise when they called in Freddie Spencer to ride in the British Grand Prix that year, only for him to retire. I felt it was getting to the crunch.

Finally, the following year, I did get my chance, but by then the NR500 project was almost dead in the water as the factory accepted defeat and put its energy into the two-stroke NS500. I didn't care. I needed to sample the GP life and paddock before I felt comfortable. The NR500 was a hard bike to get horsepower out of, and its endurance was non-existent. I had three rides on it that year at Assen, Spa and Silverstone and was way down the field. The only time I thought we might be on to something was at Spa, when I thought I was going to get the bike's first championship point. I believed I was tenth because Kork Ballington had been penalized for going through the chicane. Then they waived the penalty and reinstated him, meaning I was eleventh and out of the points. It doesn't sound much, but it would have been a huge thing for a four-stroke bike to get into the points in a two-stroke world. Spencer then took the NR500 to America, because they thought it might be a rider problem, but he did a couple of national meetings and came nowhere.

All that development went into the car world, so it wasn't wasted, and Honda turned to their three-cylinder bike. Again it didn't have a lot of horsepower, but it was so light and agile that it made up for it. I got the call to partner Freddie for 1983 and, after all the frustration and waiting, I now felt I could do anything. I'd travelled the world and dealt with raw monkey brains and giant king cobras. Now I was going into the lion's den.

9

DEPARTURES AND ARRIVALS

IT IS OFTEN THE CASE THAT THE BEST AND WORST OF times are actually the same. Swings and roundabouts, highs and lows – you succeed in one area and struggle in another. That was the case in 1983 when my professional life was out of kilter with my personal one, and a dream ride in Grand Prix racing was undermined by Ann fleeing to a London shoe shop with our unborn son.

It had started brilliantly when Honda asked me to partner Freddie Spencer on the NS500 V3. The NR project was finally scrapped as Honda gave in to the era of two-stroke engines and set about winning the world title with Spencer, a twenty-one-year-old kid from Louisiana who had already served notice of his incredible potential by winning two GPs the previous year. I'd had a taste of GPs myself that year, but my best position had been that disputed eleventh in Belgium. Freddie, meanwhile, had served notice of a revolution.

Nobody knew Freddie. He had boyish looks and was a clean-cut American hero. Where I'd be covered in oil and had a biker's long hair and leather, Freddie was neatly shaven, well turned out and had the air of a choirboy. He never mingled with people and just did his own thing. He would get on his bike, practise, qualify, race and go straight back to his motorhome. He loved basketball and was always flying home to watch his team, but he spent most of his time at the track locked away from the rest of the paddock. He was a loner, which suited me fine because I was much the same.

People may have thought that both of us were a bit arrogant or aloof, but that wasn't the case. The fact is that we were shy and we liked the company of those we were comfortable with. For me that meant Ann, for Freddie that meant himself. One of the curious things about him was that he only ever spoke to one mechanic. That man was Erv Kanemoto, the Japanese-American tuner. Freddie would tell him what he thought and then go off without saying a single word to anyone else. It was an approach born out of total shyness. He might have been the fastest thing on two wheels and would go on to become a legend, but he was just a normal guy with the same insecurities as the rest of us.

I found that out when I discovered we had a common

bond. One of the ways I'd pass time at tracks was to play with remote-controlled helicopters. I'd build them, fly them and sometimes crash them. Freddie was just as interested in remote-controlled cars, so we had a joint interest. We probably spoke more about that than anything during our time together, and suddenly this man who had won almost every race going without breaking sweat was ordinary.

Having him as a team-mate was both the best thing in the world and the worst. On the upside it meant that you had the absolute elite in your team, but the downside was that whatever you did you weren't going to be as good as him. So I did get ranked as second-best, and that was irritating. Every race was so hard because the first thing any rider tries to do is beat his team-mate. It just so happened that mine was the best rider in the world. I would have beaten him a couple of times, but for some hard-luck stories, but this was a man who took on the world in both the 250cc and 500cc classes and wiped the floor with the lot of us. He wasn't so much a hard act to follow as an impossible one.

The hardest thing for a rider to accept is that there are people who are better than you. Now I have to admit that there were a couple who were faster, but I still think that on my day I could have beaten anyone. I didn't get the same equipment as Freddie, because he was the lead rider and the man the whole of Honda was pinning its hopes on. He would go out and produce a lap time that was so incredible it would leave you scratching your head. I could produce the same lap time, but the difference was that Freddie could do it every day.

I was happy to be guided by Honda. I'd been frustrated that Honda spent so long out of GPs, but when the opening came I seized it. Gerald ran things very efficiently, and I trusted him like I'd trusted Mal, although they were chalk and cheese; Gerald is very well spoken and later went on to forge a second career by becoming an expert on Chinese art. I was never bothered about contracts and never even saw one. Gerald would say this is how much you are getting, and I would accept that, because he was not the sort of man who would rip you off. Honda's way was to give you a low retainer, which would rise the longer you stayed with them. I think I was paid £20,000 in that first season, with a ten per cent rise as it went on, but Gerald was very fair. It was more a gentleman's agreement than a legal document and that suited me. Gerald believed in me and knew I was honest on the bike. We got along well. I was never interested in money, but I did make sure I was well insured. All I wanted was to be covered for whatever it was that my contract was worth, so that if I fell off and was out of action from day one, the money would be taken care of. It meant that my head was clear to concentrate on riding. It cost me a hell of a lot in insurance, but it was worth it for the peace of mind.

I didn't fall off when the 1983 season started at Kyalami in South Africa. I had an advantage, because I'd done some streetbike racing there just beforehand, but I was struggling in qualifying while Freddie was absolutely flying. I couldn't work out how he was going so fast, and then I misjudged my brakes at the end of the straight. I was going way too fast, probably by about 20mph, so I had to square off the corner by slowing right down. The strange thing was that it gave me about half a second, and that's when I realized what Freddie was doing. He was actually squaring off the corners all the time. I did it by accident and shot up the time sheets, but Freddie was doing it on purpose, because he realized you could actually make time by slowing like that. It gave me a hint of Freddie's talent. We were all thinking, How the hell does he do it? and now I knew. I took it on board and finished third behind him and Kenny Roberts, the triple world champion.

I was third again at Le Mans two weeks later and seemed well set for a great season. It was an impressive start by any standards. This was what I'd been dreaming of. I'd wanted to come to the GP world earlier, but there hadn't been anything good available, and I knew there was no point coming in on poor machinery. Now that patience seemed to have paid off. I knew I could ride and here I was, bagging two podiums in my first two races in my first proper season.

Sport never stands still, though, and today's hero can

quickly become just another man in the field. It was interesting to note how my relationship with Barry Sheene changed over the years. To begin with, he was the undisputed number one, the double world champion whose crashes and girlfriends made *News at Ten*, and I was just a long-haired bloke with woolly sideburns causing mayhem on the domestic circuits. In those early days, Sheene was the man to beat. I went to Donington Park, my local track, and thought that I could take him there. They had decided that whoever was leading at the end of ten laps would get a £2,000 bonus. That was a lot of money, and I rode my heart out to take the lead. I was first after seven laps and started counting them down to the prize. Three. Two. I was still in the lead. I could feel the cash. Then, at the end of ten laps, Barry was first. After eleven I was back in front. He was such a bloody good rider and publicity man that he had just been playing to the cameras. He was on a factory Suzuki GP bike so could have pulled away, but he toyed with me and made sure it looked good for the viewers before getting his bonus. He had the machinery and, in truth, he beat me more often than not. I was always thinking, I'll get you next time, but he was good and he had the engine and the tyres to take advantage.

But a few years on, the tide had turned. Here was I getting third place in successive GPs while Barry was struggling down in tenth and seventh after moving back to a Suzuki from Yamaha. As I was getting better, so his fortunes were nosediving. He was still enjoying it and was taking the bikes back to his workshop, but his career was plateauing whereas I was a man on the rise.

He was always a bit nervous of me, because he said I pushed him too hard. He won the Race of the Year at Mallory Park one year, and I was second. His bike broke down just after the finish, so he came and jumped on mine to do his victory lap. What he didn't know is that I ran two steering dampers on either side, turned right up, and he fell off on the hairpin. He came back and went mad at me. 'How the bloody hell can you ride that bike!' he yelled. 'I can't even turn the bleeding thing.'

Sheene had already been through everything. He'd peaked and won two world titles and had been as strong as the best, but we were moving in opposite directions. Barry had moved from Suzuki to Yamaha in 1980, but he wasn't the same and then he had his second disastrous crash at Silverstone. I don't know why he moved to Yamaha – maybe it was for money, because he had a way of pulling in the big sponsors – but it wasn't for the bike and it proved a massive step backward. He came back on a Suzuki in 1983 but it was just a production version, and he would finish the season in a lowly fourteenth. The following year would be his last. By contrast, I was six years younger and just starting.

I always found Sheene dead straight. He wasn't what you'd think from the fast-talking, wide-boy exterior. In reality he was very down to earth. He didn't want to be on a pedestal and just wanted to be one of the normal people. He was the sort of bloke who couldn't care less if he had the wrong sponsor's jacket on the podium. I liked him for that and bought a motorhome off him, but there was no doubt that our respective positions had changed. At the start Barry would be at the top of the paddock in his enormous motorhome, surrounded by a white picket fence, whereas I'd be down among the mud and the rabble at the other end. But I was now the top British rider taking on the Americans like Spencer, Roberts, Eddie Lawson and Randy Mamola. I can't say it didn't feel good.

But life, especially in motorcycling, has a habit of bringing you down to earth with a thudding bang. In the next race at the famous Monza track near Milan, I was on course for a third successive podium place until the bike broke. I slid down the road and could see that I was going to slam straight into a white post that was on the side of the track. I rolled away to miss it, but left my arm behind me and the impact snapped my wrist. I don't know how I managed to get back for the next race from that, but you didn't miss races in those days. You just took the knocks and climbed back up.

I didn't finish any of the next six races, as the mechanical problems began to mount. You can probably put some of the blame for those non-finishes on Freddie too. As a team-mate he was pretty useless because he didn't know how he did things. It was a natural ability that I've never seen in anyone before or since. I had those podiums in South Africa and then in France and thought that was my standing in the world. There was only Freddie I felt worried about, because he always seemed to have so much in hand and didn't seem to know where the boundaries lay.

The thing that you do in those circumstances is ride harder to try to bridge that divide. I needed that bit extra and thought I could get it either by sitting tight and gaining experience or pushing harder and taking it over the top. I was impatient and chose the latter and it cocked me up. You go balls-out and try to compensate for what's missing, but it's an impossible task because you cannot see where you can possibly make up time. The result was I'd always make a mistake, whether running off the track or crashing into a white post. I was fighting Freddie and an internal battle.

I also began to wonder about the equipment, and that wasn't just paranoia. When you think that someone is on better machinery than you, the tendency is to ease back a little, because you know that all he has to do is ride as hard as you and he'll win. I used to be amazed at the strain Freddie would put on his engines. He was destroying them and would have them squealing and in danger of exploding before the end of the straight. I realized there was a lot of time to be gained if I followed suit, but I just couldn't do it. I couldn't get my head around the way he treated his engines. Then, halfway through that season, I found out that he ran the engines once and then they were giving them to me. That explained why they were changing his engines so fast, but he was leading the championship by that point so there was no use in me bleating about unfair treatment.

The frustrating point was Freddie didn't need a leg-up from anyone, but he was getting it anyway. It was the same with tyres. We had contracts with Michelin, but it was basically up to them to give you whatever they wanted. You could argue as much as you wanted, but it would do no good, so I kept my mouth shut. There was no doubt that Michelin wanted an American to win the title, because that's where the market was. Everybody was bitching, but there was nothing anyone could say, really. Freddie was on a three-cylinder engine, and the horsepower was nothing compared with the rest. He was winning fairly and squarely and only Kenny Roberts, who was rumoured to be retiring at the end of the season, seemed capable of stopping him.

Those were not the only problems now facing me as my personal life in 1983 had reached a crossroads and I looked as though I was charging head first down the nearest cul-de-sac. I was twenty when I started seeing Ann, who still had a boyfriend at that time, and we had already been through a lot together. I remember Mal

Carter ringing Ann on her sixteenth birthday and asking her to go over to the Isle of Man with us. She turned up, barely out of school, having caught the train to Crewe, changed at Liverpool and then taken the ferry to the Island. We stayed at the Perry Vale Hotel, and I knew she was special, but I was still seeing other girls, too, including Margaret. Bikes had become my life and the endgame had been to get into GPs and test the dream against the best in the world. Girls were not an afterthought, but they were definitely secondary. And then Ann collared me at Oulton Park one day and said: 'I'm pregnant.'

'That's great,' I replied, and I meant it.

'But you've just got your GP contract, Ron.'

'It'll be OK.'

'But you're going to be all over the world. You're just starting out.'

I began to realize that it might not be as easy as I thought, that there might have to be a lot of compromise and that this might not be the best world to bring kids up in. At that time, women were not encouraged in the paddock and it was very much a man's world. It was macho, outdated and wrong, but Ann realized that far quicker than I did.

We were both open and honest about our relationship, but that didn't stop the hurt. Much later, Ann told me how she had taken a detour and driven past my house one Bonfire Night while working for a delivery firm and had seen me with someone else. She said she was heartbroken at that sight, but she vowed that she wouldn't get mad when she confronted me. She was true to her word and, in fact, she even apologized for driving past my house. She will tell you that I had a hold over her and if I asked her to jump, then she'd ask how high, but I wasn't stringing her along. I just wanted to be a GP racer. It's what we'd dreamed about, Babe, Phil and myself, when we were kids growing up, messing around on bikes without brakes, losing Babe's headlight in the canal and getting banned from the streets.

I never hid the fact that I was seeing Margaret, but Ann had reached a point where she didn't want that any more. It was too hurtful for her to carry on with this half life, even though we weren't married, and so she made a decision. She was two months pregnant and the baby was due in May 1983, slap bang in the middle of my début season. Ann's family weren't posh, but they did things properly. Couples courted, got married and had children. We were doing it all the wrong way around and she felt that deeply.

The first thing she said was that she wanted to keep the baby. There was no way she wanted to get rid of it, because that wasn't right. I felt the same.

'I don't want you thinking I'm trapping you,' she said.

'I don't.'

'I don't want anything off you. I don't want you changing for me. You're in GPs now.'

'I can still be a dad, can't I?'

'I don't know, Ron. I don't know if you can.'

She clearly felt that I couldn't, because not long after that she cleared off down to London. She didn't tell me where she was and I was shocked when I found she'd disappeared. I think I'd still been expecting her to be there when I phoned, but she wasn't. She'd made good on her threat to leave. I had no idea where she was, because she hadn't left a contact number for me. She had just upped and moved down and, although I didn't know it, she was living in a communal flat in Ealing and had begun working in Clarks shoe shop.

It was a turning point for Ann. We were with each other, but it wasn't as though we were partners. We never thought that's how it was going to be. Now I know that Ann was under a lot of pressure. She was an unmarried mother-to-be living at home and her mum didn't like that. So she made the brave decision to go it alone. And for a while life just went on. I had races to go to and the GP circus was a blur. I had no idea how Ann was, and we never officially told each other we had split up, but it wasn't a relationship at that point. She wouldn't tell me where she was living, and I was getting to grips with my first season among the elite and having Fast Freddie Spencer share a garage with me.

Looking back, I know that Ann wanted to show me

that she didn't depend on me. At that point I was still free to go wherever I wanted, with whoever I wanted. There was no firm commitment and I was happy with that. So was Ann. At least, I thought she was, but the pregnancy changed everything and made her reassess. And as the months drifted on without us seeing each other, it made me change too.

Ann was still very young at that point and she knew what bikes meant to me. She had it in her head that if we stayed together, with a child, then she'd be wrecking my GP career. She didn't want to be responsible for that and so she made a sacrifice. The time apart made me realize just how much she meant to me. I wanted her back, but her mother wouldn't give me the phone number. Then I broke my wrist in Monza. Ann had been reading the paper at the bus stop in Ealing one day and read HASLAM CRASHES OUT. She must have still felt something, because she rang the house. She told me she rang because she thought I'd still be travelling home from the GP and, anyway, Treece, Babe's girlfriend, always answered the phone. But I'd got home early and I was the one who heard it go. I picked up the phone and we talked.

'When are you going to come home?' I asked.

'I'm not,' she replied. 'I'm staying here. I've made some new friends.'

'But you're having our baby. Come home. I miss you.'

'It won't work. What's changed?'

'I have. I've split up with Margaret.'

There was a pause. It was true, but Ann had heard it all before. Finally, she told me she would be staying in London.

I saw her once before the birth. She did come home and we talked again, but Ann was strong-willed.

'Why don't you come back and we can go to GPs together?' I asked.

'I've made up my mind,' she said. 'You have to decide what you want.'

'Come back, Ann.'

'Not like this. Look at the size of me. What will people say?'

So she went back to London. She'd put on four stone and had high blood pressure, but she was adamant she was going to go her own way and so she kept working in Clarks. She would say she would ring me at eleven and then purposely not phone, but the time apart had made me realize that I didn't want the other girls and that I wanted only her. The wild days were over and I was ready to settle down.

So I started my rookie season with Honda in GPs with the backdrop of a confused personal life. I had those two third places behind Freddie and then the rot set in. I didn't finish in Monza or Hockenheim and then went to Spain. By this point Ann was almost due and she was still living away. Spain was a write-off and Austria was just as bad. I had just got back when the phone rang. I shouted at Treece to leave it and scooped it up.

'Ron, it's me. We've had a baby boy.'

I couldn't believe it, although I knew it was happening and felt bad that Ann had given birth alone in Ealing Hospital. The guilt was huge. I raced down to London and we met in the Holiday Inn at Heathrow. We both knew that our lives had changed and that we needed to be together. The feeling was still as strong as ever. I'd tried to support her up until then, but she'd backed off and refused. Now we had a child and we knew we wanted the same things.

I went from being a selfish bloke who wanted to do whatever he liked to wanting all that to stop. She said she wanted no commitment from me, but that wasn't enough any more. I went inside myself and realized I wanted her and our child. There were no blazing rows, but I made it clear. So, finally, as I got ready to fly to Yugoslavia, Ann came home with Leon.

We stayed with her mother for about a year and a half. Then we went to Mam's. Leon slept with us and went everywhere with us. It was agreed that if a team wanted me then they would have to accept there was going to be a baby around. In that era it was unusual and lots of people frowned on it, but all my teams were fine with it. If I was going racing, then from now on it would be me, Ann and Leon. Team Haslam. That's even more the case today, with Leon riding, me helping and Ann organizing. It's hard to imagine it working with one of the prongs missing.

I was careful not to give anyone an opportunity to complain, but I refused to have it any other way. It wasn't a case of proving anything to the team, but I wanted Ann to know that it didn't affect me one bit Leon being there. It quickly became obvious that it wasn't a problem and that any fears Ann had of being a distraction or of jeopardizing my position were unfounded. And, to be fair, Ann did all the work. She changed nappies and I got on with my job. If ever Leon played up or was crying, then she would be out of the door like a flash. She made problems disappear and then she would give me all the support I needed. If I was grumpy or mad or had fallen off, then she wouldn't fire back at me. We knew each other so well, but Ann was the cornerstone of my success.

It was good to be a family again. Babe didn't make it to my races, because he would be competing somewhere else himself, and it had been strange without Ann. Other members of the family still came. Mam even came to Assen for her one and only overseas GP. She didn't watch the race but sat in the motorhome. She was nervous and didn't like travelling. She only came to Assen because it was the closest one and you could get there without taking a plane. I took her around the town and we looked at the shops. She had only been as far as Skegness before and was baffled by the Dutch language. That afternoon she got terrible blisters on her feet from walking around, so I carried her home.

The motorhome was not exactly a de luxe thing. It was a twenty-three-footer but, believe me, those extra three feet made a difference. I was considered a bit unusual because I would follow the Honda truck from circuit to circuit in my motorhome as I didn't know any of the places. It was good to have Ann and Leon there with me. The motorhome was always full of people; while I was used to that from home, Ann wasn't. She would walk the streets with Leon to get some peace from the madness of the GP paddock, but our thoughts had turned to settling down.

Back in Langley Mill there was still me, Babe, Treece, Bunk and Mam. When we came home, Ann and I slept on the sofa at Mam's with Leon next to us. We knew we wanted to be together, though, and that's why Ann wasn't there at the British Grand Prix that year. Instead she went with her dad to an auction, where we hoped to buy a rambling, run-down farmhouse in the little village of Smalley.

There were three races left, and Freddie had a five-point lead over Kenny Roberts. I was down in ninth after all my mishaps, but I qualified in sixth and told a journalist that I felt my chances of winning were 'pretty good'. Poor old Barry Sheene was way down in eighteenth on his privately entered Suzuki.

Things were slowly improving on the track. Maybe it was a coincidence that things were sorted out at home, but maybe not. I'd had a couple of failures in Yugoslavia and Holland but finally was back in the points in round nine at Spa. That first year with Freddie was hard, but it became really enjoyable. Compared with the Yamahas of Roberts and Lawson, I thought I got a hundred per cent out of what I had. I was never the jealous type and never envied anyone for anything they owned – the only flash car I ever had was an old E-type Jag that I built myself – but I was envious of tyres and engines. The only downside to that season was Freddie, because everybody would always be over his side of the garage and fawning over him.

At the British Grand Prix I finished seventh, but it was another black day for the sport. Norman Brown of Northern Ireland and Peter Huber of Switzerland died after a collision on the exit from Stowe corner. The race went on for another two laps before we all stopped. Now you look back at the well-worn leathers and smattering of hay bales and shudder.

The season ended dramatically. Freddie and Roberts were vying for the title with two races left when they came together at Anderstorp in Sweden. Kenny blamed Freddie for the accident, which saw them both run off the track before finishing first and second, and later said he had three kids and didn't need some young guy taking him out. He also said he felt like punching

174

Freddie out of the back of the car as they went on their lap of honour. I just thought it was one of those things that happen in racing. That meant it came down to San Marino, with Freddie leading by five points with one race left. Kenny did everything that he could. He was the sort of rider who would work tirelessly at his job. Rugged and with an acid tongue, Roberts never suffered fools. He would try things and wouldn't be up there until it got to qualifying, when suddenly it would come together and he would be on the pace. If I had everything going well, and it was a circuit I liked, then I could match all of them, but if it was a place I didn't like, then I knew that whatever I did I damn well wouldn't be able to get Freddie's lap times. He was the natural of the grid and he stayed on Kenny's rear in San Marino to finish a close second. That was enough. Kenny was still angry about what had happened in Sweden, but you couldn't deny Freddie his moment. Did he celebrate? You never knew with Freddie. He was the world champion, and I was eighth, which I felt was pretty good given that the bike had problems for almost half the season. I knew what it felt like to stand on the GP podium and I knew what it felt like to be a dad. It was a good start.

10

ASSEN

THE WHEEL HAD COME FULL CIRCLE BY THE START OF 1984, and I was now sponsoring Babe, and Molly's son, John Gainey, as they moved through the ranks in the sidecar world. They would travel around in the Pharaoh van with the slogan A TRIBUTE TO PHIL HASLAM on the side. We never forgot where we had come from or what this sport could do to you, but we loved it all the same.

Sponsoring sounds a bit clinical and businesslike, because the truth was that I was just helping out wherever I could. In the old days Babe would go home and support the family by giving his pay packet to Mam. Now I was the one who was doing all right, and I spread the money around. Honda were paying me a flat contract fee and, as I mentioned, their deals worked on a climbing basis. As you improved, your cut would increase. My top contract was probably worth £90,000. Freddie would get treble that, but it didn't bother me. I was never in it for the money and was a bad accountant, something that would come back and bite me in later years, but I appreciated that this was an unbelievable sum of money for us. Then there would be smaller sponsors for leathers, helmets and expenses. I just let others organize that and had no idea that the GP gravy train was heading for the buffers.

Babe and John were doing well. Back when I was still with Mal, he'd had a special bike and sidecar made up for Carl, Phil's boy, and had the slogan SON OF PHIL daubed on the front. Carl was only six months old when Phil died, so everyone tried to do what they could for him. It was still a family affair by 1982 when Babe and I raced on the same day in the John Player Nationals at Donington Park. That proved a bleak day all round. I was meant to début the 990cc works Honda, but we had no time to run it in, so I had to ride a streetbike and came a lowly twentieth. Babe and John suffered a broken chain in qualifying and so didn't even make it to the line. At the time those setbacks felt like the worst thing ever and we sulked and scowled; but those were tiny, meaningless disappointments compared with what was to follow in 1984.

The GP world was a more serious place than the one I'd come from. There were some riotous stories, notably involving Barry Sheene and Steve Parrish, but when you had a factory Honda you had to be more serious. You didn't go and get drunk or things like that. For me, that was no problem because I'd never drunk or smoked. The only time I'd have a drink was if it was freezing cold and then I'd have a tot of whisky to warm myself. That's not to say life on the circuit was boring. Far from it. On many occasions I'd get to my hotel room and jump into bed, only to find the legs had been unscrewed and the whole thing collapsed. People were forever playing pranks on each other. It was like a boys' club.

The first time I went to Spa we went to the restaurant in the hotel. Barry Symmons had got to know the owners very well by that point and we had a nice evening. That night I went upstairs, climbed under the sheets and felt something moving under the covers. That's when Ann screamed. I whipped off the bed-clothes and saw a giant lobster lurching about. They'd taken it out of the fish tank in the restaurant and planted it. They'd even taken the rubber bands off its clippers so it could wreak more mayhem. A few seconds later I stormed out and that lobster was flying across Barry's room. After that I did lots of checks whenever I got to my hotel room. It kept you on your toes.

But even with all the pranks and jokes, you'd get to bed early. I didn't want to turn up on the grid reeking of booze when Honda were backing me. There was a lot of that about, but you owed it to them and yourself to be in good shape. It was a world away from the days with Mal, when I'd even done the ultimate no-no and qualified for someone else. That was for a Finnish rider called Teuvo Länsivuori. He had been a top rider once and even won a GP, in Sweden, back in 1974, but he was nearing the end of his career and struggling. You got start money in those days, so Mal asked me to qualify for him. I put on his leathers, went out and got him on the second row. Those were fun days. That carefree, anything-goes atmosphere was there at the Isle of Man too. I remember being in a hotel room with Joey and a bunch of people at three in the morning the night before a race. I treated the TT as a fun event and so did Joey. Someone said: 'Joey, I bet you can't run naked to the sea and back.'

Joey was never one to shirk a challenge and said: 'Sure I can. No problem.'

'Go on, then.'

With that, Joey stripped stark naked and climbed out of the bedroom window. He lowered himself to the ground and then set off through the gardens towards the beach. Now, at three in the morning on the eve of a race, the Isle of Man is buzzing. There were people everywhere, and there was Joey running through them to the sea. What he didn't bargain for was the fact that we'd locked the hotel door and shut the windows. He was screaming and shouting and eventually climbed up a drainpipe and got in through another window. It's fair to say that Joey had a lot to drink that night, but he still got up and won the next day.

There were still characters in the GP paddock. Randy Mamola, now a MotoGP commentator, was always a live wire. He was rude and funny and always had women in tow. He even had stars painted on the ceiling of his motorhome for their benefit. He was a character on and off the bike, and was unlucky never to go on and win the world title. He was second in the championship four times and always seemed to be just a fraction off the top, but he kept his spirits up and enjoyed it. Eddie Lawson was the polar opposite. He was an unbelievable rider but to him it always seemed a job. I reckon that if he hadn't been getting paid, then he wouldn't have been there.

Honda had come to me before the end of the previous season and said that they wanted me to stay. It helped that Freddie was on course to win the championship, because it meant they had achieved everything they had set out to do and so they didn't look further down the line. That said, I think I'd done enough to impress them, and some people were even tipping me as a future world champion. The trouble was that whenever I had a good result, like a podium, I felt I had to do better. I'd ring home, and they would know the result already and celebrate for me. I was always looking ahead. It was less a celebration and more a case of added pressure.

At the start of 1984 it was obvious that Randy, who had switched to Honda, and Lawson, who was the top dog at Yamaha now that Kenny Roberts had retired to run a 250cc team of his own, would be in the shake-up for the title. I hoped to be there too, although Freddie and I were on different bikes when we got to South Africa for the opener. Freddie was on the new NSR500 V4, while I was on the triple.

I had long had a reputation for my flying starts. That's where the Rocket Ron tag came from. Fred Clarke, who did the commentary at Donington, was the first to use the moniker. I liked it. In those days you started by the side of the bike and had to fire it up and get on. I always made sure it would fire straight away by running a bit harder than the others. The speed helped me pull away. Others tried to start quicker and would flounder on the grid. I was never the first one to fire up the bike, but I was usually the first away. It was down to technique and clutch control. When they changed to clutch starts, that gave me an even bigger advantage. The Rocket Ron tag spread and became commonplace. Only Randy studied me to see how I was doing it, but it wasn't rocket science.

My starting would make a mockery of grid positions by always getting the hole shot. In South Africa I was coming through the rain and catching Lawson and Co. when the bike seized up. It was a bad opening. I'd been flying and confident, but it came to nothing. Freddie had it even worse and didn't even make the race after crashing in practice. I was sixth in Misano in the next race, leading at the start but then fading away, although I was suffering from flu at the time. After that, the season took on a predictable shape. I was fourth in five of the next six rounds, while Freddie and Eddie traded wins and Randy settled into the role of last man on the podium.

They were good results. I don't like making excuses, but I was always chasing Freddie. The hardest thing was I couldn't get the same tyres. Then, all the little bits of development would go to him first. The differences were not enormous, but Freddie was the sort of man who could make a yard from an inch. It was enough to put me on the back foot. The year I did better was when I went on Dunlop tyres and he was on Michelin. Tyres make such a big difference it's untrue.

Freddie, though, was something else, and he did get to the point where he seemed to think he was above everybody else, highlighted by what still ranks as one of the most incredible things I have ever seen in racing. It happened at Assen that season. I'll never forget what took place that day when Freddie didn't bother to turn up for practice. That was unusual, even for Freddie, who was getting a reputation for lateness, and I wasn't alone in being gobsmacked. Assen is one of the hardest circuits you could ever go to, and there had been lots of changes made to it since the previous year. Freddie hadn't seen these and yet he wasn't bothering with practice because he thought he didn't need it. That was the only time that I think anyone from Honda gave Freddie a bollocking. I wasn't in the room when it happened, but news spread on the paddock grapevine, and we waited to see how he would react. What he did was incredible. Freddie was upset and so he went to the van, wheeled out his Honda and went out on to the track, even though there were no settings on his bike. He promptly broke the lap record on his first flying lap.

I talked to him and he told me in his deadpan Deep South drawl that he didn't use braking points. That was staggering because everybody did. You picked a marker and knew that's where you needed to start to brake. Not Freddie. He did it purely on instinct and feel. All he had to work off was his talent and confidence, but luckily for him they were bottomless. He came off the track and the Honda man shut up. He realized then, if he hadn't known it before, that he had a genius in front of him.

I was fifth in Belgium, where Freddie won, and then we came to the British Grand Prix at Silverstone. The team was fracturing at that point. Honda knew that they had to develop the four-cylinder bike because it had the edge on power and running the triple was handicapping us, however nice it was to ride. To add to the bad atmosphere, Freddie had to miss the race because he'd gone and got himself injured in practice for a non-GP race back in the States at Laguna Seca. He'd been griping about the V4, but Randy was happy to take over for that race. Randy proved a point, because he won the race and set the fastest lap time.

I was really pleased with third place in my home GP. Everybody has excuses, but the biggest one that I ever had was my visor kept fogging up so much that I had to keep flipping it open to see. There were lots of press coming up to me and congratulating me, but I was never one for a big party. Barry Sheene might go to a post-race do, but we'd wander around the paddock and have a barbecue with his mum and dad instead.

A rostrum in the British Grand Prix was a major thing for all of us, and the family was well represented. Mam would hardly ever watch the races, but she came along to that one and sat in the motorhome. It was a purple patch. It spurred me on too having Freddie there in the garage, and I was elated when I got my first pole position in the next race in Sweden. I liked the Anderstorp circuit and I noted how it was funny that all the Japanese guys in the garage, who would generally swarm all over Freddie, suddenly came over to me. It just shows what a bit of success can do. They ignored you when it was going wrong, but when you were on pole you were their hero. I couldn't believe how easy it seemed. Before that day in Sweden I was chasing the others – Freddie and Eddie and Randy – but now they were chasing me. The tables were reversed. In practice

I'd watch the others and see how out of shape they were and how they were making mistakes, while I was riding within myself and blitzing them. Someone had swapped everything around, but it's hard to explain how it happened.

Freddie came to me in the garage and said: 'How the hell are you getting so much grip out of the turns?' I couldn't give him an honest answer. I had no idea. Freddie tried following me on the track to see if he could pick it up, but I just breezed away from him. I thought that it might change in the race, but I did a Freddie. I rocketed off and they couldn't catch me. I pulled so far clear that I decided to back off, because I thought I might as well take my time. This was my moment. I was going to win a GP. Concentrate. Ignore the blur of colour in the grandstands. Count it down. Then I noticed the bike wasn't as quick in the straights. When you back off, you take it easier around the corners, because that's where the mistakes happen, but you still go as fast as ever on the straights. But now I was slowing. I glanced down and noticed the water temperature was up to ninety when the dial should have been at fifty. By the next lap it was up to ninety-five and then a hundred. I frowned and swore. The bike slowed and slowed and that was it. In the record books I'm just down as one of the seventeen retirements. Lawson won and Raymond Roche was second. But it had been mine. Nobody was going to beat me that day.

It was weird and horrible. I thought I was going to get the monkey off my back about not having won a GP in the world championship, although I'd won plenty in Macau. I was leading all the way and then the bike broke. I viewed it as a victory even if the points went to Lawson. I knew that I could beat the best and suddenly I felt that I could go all the way and win a world title. But at first you can't move on after something like that. You feel physically sick and wonder whether you'll ever get that advantage again. You think you won't. You go quiet. Introverted. It kills you inside. Only later could I reflect on how well I'd ridden.

My success meant I was becoming a bit of a celebrity. People recognized me and, with Sheene close to retirement, I became his replacement in the affections of the British biking public. With celebrity status came invitations to all sorts of events. From corporate dos to prize-givings, I was in demand. There was also a bit of attention that I could have done without, with letters pouring in from women, some of whom were offering their congratulations and some of whom were happy to offer a whole lot more. The most frightening one was a letter from a woman who said she'd had my baby and was calling it Ron. I don't know why she did that because it wasn't true, but it was disturbing. Then there was the time a woman sidled up to me at Oulton Park pushing a pram.

'This is your child,' she said.

I was taken aback as I'd never seen her before in my life.

'I don't even know you,' I said.

She went off after that. I don't know if she did it for a gag, but that sort of thing was not unusual in the bike world. Much earlier in my career, before I was settled with Ann, I did arrange to meet up with one woman who was claiming she was having my child. To be perfectly blunt, she went with quite a lot of men, and so I asked how she knew it was mine. I didn't hear from her again, so I was obviously not the father, but I did occasionally wonder about that child. I think the fact is that bikes and young men are a potent combination and, when you throw in some money and gritty glamour, it can be irresistible.

After my near miss in Sweden I got an invitation to take part in the television show *Superstars*, in which sportsmen tried their hand at lots of different events. It's probably most famous for Kevin Keegan falling off his bike. I was doing pretty well against the likes of Eddie Kidd, the stunt rider, Colin Jones, the boxer, and Robert Smith, the showjumper. Then I turned my ankle while winning the gym section and had to pull out of the last rounds. I was still fourth, and I kept in touch with Robert as I was developing an interest in another form of horsepower.

Things were going well. I felt I could beat the best, we were a happy family, and finally things seemed to be settling into place. There were always incidents with a toddler around, and I'll never forget the time Ann saw Leon wielding a knife at Paul Ricard in France. She screamed and tried to snatch it off him, but that was the worst thing she could do and he ended up stabbing her by mistake. She ran outside with blood pouring from her hand and then suffered a really traumatic experience by having Raymond Roche drive her to hospital. But life was generally good. I was fifth that season, one place behind Freddie, with Lawson taking the title. Silverstone had been the peak and I could still feel the emotion from that day. You get up so high that you think you're never coming down, but life's not like that. And that's when the second tragedy hit.

I'd finished the season with another podium at Mugello in the San Marino Grand Prix and was looking forward to the winter. I'd been in the top four in seven out of twelve rounds, but I knew I needed sponsors to keep me among the elite. The times were changing and the economic situation was biting. Money was harder to find, and that's why the World of Sport Superbike challenge at Donington was a gilt-edged chance to put my name in the shop window in front of a huge television audience.

It turned into an epic battle between me and Sheene. He was on his 500cc Suzuki and I was on my Honda. I led into Redgate, but Sheene pulled me back at

Coppice and led for the next two laps. We exchanged the lead again, but Barry showed his mettle by trying to outbrake me going into the final chicane. We were side by side, the old and the new, two proud Brits fighting for our futures, and I held him off by half a wheel. I felt a bit sorry for Barry. He was waging a battle you can't win, one I knew well from my own career. It was an all-round downer for him. He was still putting in a hundred per cent but no way could it get any better. That's a terrible feeling for a rider. If you don't think you can win, then the enthusiasm ebbs away. It only has to be a long shot, but the carrot of a chance has to be there for you. Sheene no longer had the confidence to push overboard to do that bit extra. His riding began to slip and he knew it was the end. He'd had a brilliant ride, but he decided enough was enough and retired.

Babe was doing pretty well at sidecars by then, and I managed to have a few goes myself. Funnily enough, given what had gone on in the past, we got to know a traffic policeman and he said he fancied trying his hand on the back of Babe's Kawasaki. 'I can't take you, because I'm not allowed to do club meetings,' Babe said. He'd got to a level that was beyond club races at Cadwell, so I piped up: 'I'll take you.' It didn't matter that I was a GP racer. In those days people raced all over the place. The policeman readily agreed and so we set off. The thing you need to know about a sidecar is that, after it fires, it takes a while for the revs to clear and then you set off. The policeman didn't know that, and he thought something had gone wrong. He started to get off the back when I shot off, dragging him down the track. He let go at the first corner, and it was only when the sidecar lifted up at the bend that I looked back and realized he wasn't there. I went around and picked him up. 'Let's take it easy,' I said before the second race. 'I think if we start at the back and work our way through I can still get you a trophy.' They handed them out for the first three places and, sure enough, I managed to work my way through the field into third. But now I wanted more and I could see the two leaders ahead. The gap wasn't so great and I powered after them. Unfortunately, by this point the policeman was so tired that after four laps he couldn't hang on. We screamed down to the hairpin and he got on to the right-hand side way too early. The sidecar rose and, although I managed to get it back down, we spun sideways and flipped. I was jammed underneath but had it lucky compared with my former passenger, who was bouncing down the track. I remember seeing him fly by, literally, and being amazed at how high he got. My brothers, meanwhile, were all watching at the hairpin and thought I must have badly hurt myself. In fact, I was fine, while the policeman escaped with a broken thumb.

I think that cured him of his desire to race sidecars, but I was developing a taste for it. When John Gainey sprained his ankle, I told Babe that I'd go on board with him. I assumed it would be easy as a passenger and it was just a case of hanging on, but I was very wrong. As I was switching sides, Babe hit the power. It flipped me backwards, so I was being dragged along by one hand, facing backwards down the track. I could see Steve Abbot behind me. Even with a helmet on, I could tell he was creasing himself. Luckily, Babe shut off the power and I clambered back on. He didn't even know that I'd been pulled down the track on my backside.

I found it exciting, because the passenger can actually influence the sidecar as much as the driver. I learned that you only hang out enough to hold the wheel down. Too much and you'll end up in trouble. Too little and you get the same outcome. In qualifying at Mallory we got it wrong and began to spin. I jumped on the wheel arch to counter it. It was no use, and we kept spinning right up until we were inches away from the barrier. Babe stayed down, wondering how on earth we'd got away with that, but I was already pulling the sidecar back, thinking we could still get a qualifying time.

In the end, though, you need to stick with what you're best at. That became clear to me when I had a drive in a sidecar with John as the passenger. I found that I was flying past everyone and gaining positions with ease. Very pleased with myself, I had no notion of the raw panic etched on John's face. Unbeknown to me, I was taking solo motorcycle lines, which meant the passenger was on the grass most of the time. Needless to say, I didn't last too long and spun going into the Esses at Mallory. I drove back to the pits and got off.

'What happened?' I asked, perplexed by the spin.

John was incredulous. 'What happened? What happened? I'll tell you what bloody happened. Do you realize I was on the grass? I'm just bloody amazed we lasted so long.'

That was me done with sidecars but, with my racing finished for the 1984 season, I went to Assen with Babe and John for a European meeting. They were going really well at the time and had already won a couple of big races. Babe was living in a static caravan outside our new farmhouse in Smalley and was doing the place up with a lot of help from my other brothers. They were fantastic. I'd come home from a GP and find that mountains of work had been completed. I didn't ask, but my brother Cyril came round once and plastered the entire house. And Babe could turn his hand to anything, whether it be roofing or putting lintels in. The shell was being filled out and it wouldn't be long before it was liveable in.

I returned the favour in a small way by going with Babe when I could and doing a bit of mechanic work for him. Now the season was over it was time to relax a bit, and I was looking forward to the weekend in Holland. Babe had made the switch from solos to side-cars and made a go of it. Now he was at the point, just as I was in GPs, where he thought he could run with the best of them.

It was the Friday practice session and, through the window of the motorhome, Ann saw Babe put Leon, who was barely eighteen months, on the sidecar. She yelled and ran outside. 'Babe, get him off! It's too dangerous.'

Babe grinned as Ann grabbed his nephew. He drove off. It was nearly time for the practice session. He went out with John as normal, but they were struggling a bit to start off with and came back in confused. 'What's wrong?' I asked.

'Don't know,' Babe said. 'The brakes don't feel right.'

'How do you mean?'

'I don't know. They just don't feel quite right.'

They went back out and had just clawed their way up into the top three when it happened. I was standing there timing them, but the seconds ticked by and they didn't come around. That's when I saw the flags were out on the circuit. I jumped over the fence and ran to where I could see the marshals gathering. I got there at the same time that the ambulance arrived. I could see Babe and rushed up to him but turned away instantly. I knew straight away. Then I went up the track to where John was lying in a cloud of hay. 'My knee,' he cried. 'I've done my knee!' I grimaced. He didn't know about Babe.

This is what happened. The sidecar had a new braking

system which failed coming into the tight hairpin. When Babe had pushed the pedal, the front wheel locked and the sidecar went straight. There was now no steering and he couldn't do a damn thing about it. The bales were stacked up against the barrier. The sidecar went under one bale and the top one came out and pushed Babe back, breaking his neck instantly. I looked back and could see one narrow black line on the tarmac. I felt sick to the pit of my stomach. Not again.

I went to the hospital with Babe but I knew that he was dead. The sidecar was taken away and held so that they could have the inquiry, but I knew what had happened. At the speed they were travelling it would have made no difference if Babe had taken his foot off the brake. It was an accident that just happened. Another one. Fate.

The most pressing thing was getting home. Babe's body had to stay in Holland for the inquest, but John discharged himself from hospital and came home with me, Ann and Leon. I drove the motorhome. A few days earlier we had all travelled out in it, full of hope and excitement. We had such a laugh. But now we were going home minus a brother, a friend and a racer. The emptiness was awful. I'd been back to the hospital to say goodbye and was in a state of disbelief. So was everyone else. Treece, who had been with Babe for years, flew home in a terrible state, while we made the long road trip. It was one of those situations where there was nothing to say. It was horribly quiet on that journey home. Barely two words were spoken. You just heard the sound of the engine and then, every so often, someone would start sniffling again.

It took us a day and a half to get back and I don't remember a single road. I only remember taking the motorhome off the boat. The journey back was a total blank. A friend called Ian Clarke had driven all the way down to Dover to meet us and said he would take over in the driving seat, but I said no. I thanked him, but I needed something to concentrate on. I wanted something to do.

By the time we arrived, Mam was completely broken down. Babe was her son, of course, but what made it even worse was the knowledge that I was still racing. First she had the trauma of Phil, and now Babe. Two sons taken by the very thing that they loved. And there was I, in my second year as a GP racer, most of my career stretching out in front of me. Mam didn't ask me to stop, and she knew that I wouldn't. Babe's accident had changed nothing in that respect. Everything was a shambles, the family was crushed once more, but I didn't seriously think about jacking it in. It sounds cruel, but it must have been Babe's time. There's no other way of explaining it that allows you to move on. The brakes failed and there was no stopping what happened.

The fact that Babe had been living at our place in the

caravan made it harder when I went up there. I can still remember how quiet everything seemed. I wandered about in a daze, not knowing what to do with myself. I didn't want to do anything. It was very depressing. There was just a black hole in my head that I couldn't fill with anything. I would wait and hope that somebody might come up to the house, just so I could talk to them and escape from myself, but everybody left us alone because they felt that's what we wanted. It was a really dark period. All we had was time to think, and that was the last thing we wanted.

Like Phil, Babe was cremated. Because of the days we had spent shooting rats they had decided they didn't want to be buried. 'I'm not going to let the bloody rats get me,' Babe had said. So they were cremated and placed next to each other in the same cemetery.

It sounds bad, but the big one as far as racing was concerned was Phil. That was the accident that could have stopped us all from going down this road. With Babe, things had moved on. It was now a good living, and what else was I going to do? Like Phil, this had been all that Babe had really craved, and it was the thing he had put his heart and soul into. I was the same. I wanted to ride bikes. Simple as that. I also knew Babe would have hated it if I'd stopped. It was that easy to carry on.

The farmhouse was one thing that acted as a distraction to any feelings of self-pity. I'd been able to see the potential, but had known it was going to be a long, hard road and that we needed all the help we could get. Now, without Babe, it was harder still in every way. There were times when I'd drift and think it was impossible to lose another brother, but the work was a kind of therapy. And if that didn't concentrate the mind, then the visit from a man in a grey suit one day certainly did. Quite literally, this figure was the taxman, and he was ready to drop a bombshell on us.

Finally, my total lack of interest in financial matters had caught up with me. It turned out I owed around £200,000 in tax. I know everyone pleads the innocent, but I really had no idea. I'd never bothered with the financial side of things, but this was serious. It was hard because Treece was the one who did all the paperwork and put the forms in, but she was grieving for Babe.

The implications were spelled out by the taxman. If I ceased to trade, meaning I hang up my leathers and stop racing, then I'd get a reduction. That was never an option, but this was clearly serious. Racing was all I did so we had to find another solution, but what?

It's at times like this when you realize who your friends really are. One of them was Robert Fearnell, who ran Donington Park. I went to see him with Ann and told him the story. He knew we hadn't been cheating on our taxes and said that he would do all he could to help. 'The first thing we need to do is get you a good accountant,' he said. He did just that. Price Waterhouse came on board and we set about sorting out a method of repayments. It was a long, tortuous slog, and I'd be paying the money back for years. It meant that, when people were looking at me and thinking I was a wealthy individual, they were wrong. The money was good in GPs, but anything that I would have liked to save went straight back to the taxman.

I was also badly advised regarding ploughing money into Babe's sidecar racing. I would have done that anyway, but I was told that I would get tax relief on it. I only wanted the best for Babe, so I bought him the best engines I could get my hands on. I thought that would be coming off the tax bill, but I ended up having to pay back every penny.

It stemmed right back to the Mal Carter days, when the contracts would be in my name. Mal used to sell lots of clothes, Pharaoh Fashions, on the back of the team, but nothing like enough ever came back in. We tried to go back to Mal, but he had gone to ground. It had been a hell of a year, the year from hell. Broke, broken and bereaved, we struggled on and hoped the dark days were over.

11

THE KINDEST LIE

FOR A WHILE IT LOOKED LIKE WE WOULD NOT BE GOING racing in 1985. The money was drying up, the debts were piling up, and Freddie had a new team-mate in the ever-grinning Randy Mamola. I'd finished fifth in the world championship, but even that wasn't enough to guarantee anything in the changeable world of motorcycle racing. By the end of the year, though, I would have scored the most emotional success of my career.

It was curious that Robert Fearnell should come to play such a big part in my life. I am a shy man and generally I don't mix well with high-flying businessmen with lifestyles from a different planet. I never liked flash cars or the trappings of success, and I didn't tend to associate with people who did. But Robert was a self-made man who wasn't like the others and he became one of my closest friends. Having sorted out my tax problem, he then helped breathe new life into my GP career, too.

He set up the Donington 100 Club to raise funds and used his contacts to pull in some big backers. One of them was Patrick Howitt, who ran a printing group in Nottingham. He agreed to invest in both myself and Martin Brundle, the Formula One driver who was with Tyrrell, and we posed for the papers popping champagne corks. Eventually, we got the sponsorship we needed and I re-signed for Honda Britain, riding under the Rothmans banner, with Wayne Gardner, no longer the hot-headed kid from the Swann Series, as my team-mate and Barry Symmons back in charge.

After all the traumas of the previous year, it was good to get away from it all in South Africa for the first race. It was when I got there that I realized just how seriously Honda were taking it after having Lawson and Yamaha snatch the crown the previous season. The paddock was a sea of blue and white, with the Rothmans hospitality unit taking up a large area. Freddie needed more bikes than anyone, because he'd decided to go for both the 250cc and 500cc crowns. It was a hell of a challenge for him, but if anyone could pull it off then Freddie could.

It always seemed to rain in South Africa, which was odd. There was mud on the track and sections that were under water in the days running up to the GP, but everything was fine by the time we lined up for the race. I was fourth in qualifying, one place ahead of Gardner, which was a nice start, because you always want to beat your team-mate, but I knew that he was going to be competitive. Sure enough, we battled with each other for third spot throughout as Freddie and Lawson tussled for the lead. I was third but with a couple of laps to go made a mistake, and Gardner went past. Christ! I finished fourth, which was a good result, but Gardner was third. It was going to be a long, hard year, and we would bring the best out of each other.

Before the next race, in Spain, I was contacted by the organizers of the Daytona 200. They were anxious that they had attracted a much smaller overseas contingent than usual, so they were sending out an SOS. I was happy to help, but when I got there I found the bike I'd been promised was lethal. I was meant to have a race-ready Sam McDonald/American Honda VF750, but when I started wheeling it down for scrutineering before practice the steering damper fell off. I was lucky I had George Dziedzic with me from Honda Britain. He was a wizard mechanic and heaved a great sigh when he found out what was wrong. The only safe option was to rebuild the thing from top to bottom with borrowed tools and parts. It worked well enough, and after two hundred miles in the stifling heat I came in fourth.

That was my first race on a V4 Honda because I was

still on the triple in GPs. That was my downfall, really. It was the same bike as the year before, so there wasn't much development on it. Initially, the three-cylinder bikes had the edge over the fours, but that lasted only for about a year before the tables were turned for ever. Every circuit I turned up at I'd beat what Freddie had done when he'd won the GP there the year before. The bike was no different, but the times were. I thought to myself, Why didn't you do that a year earlier? But the fact was that the target times had changed, and when the goalposts are moved everyone raises their game. So there I was, riding as fast as Spencer had done the year before, but only managing third in Germany and fourth in Yugoslavia because the four-cylinder bikes had been tweaked that bit further. The standards had risen and so, like it or not, my times weren't good enough for a win.

That began to play on my mind a hell of a lot. I'd been tipped for great things and had lots of accolades, but I hadn't won a GP and that gnawed away in my head. That said, it was still a very good season. While I had treated it as an honour to work with the Japanese factory, it felt like coming home with Honda Britain. I was surrounded by people I knew a bit better and I was on Dunlop tyres, which was a major plus, but then there was Gardner. I was beating him and then he was beating me, so it was even stevens, but the difference was that this was only his second season and his progress, if not his riding, was quicker than mine.

I also suffered the ongoing frustration of being able to make great starts and get away from the pack, only for them to start slower and wind up speed, gradually hauling me in. That gave the impression that I was fading and they were improving. It began to be a bone of contention, because I knew I was riding just as well as ever.

When you ride you have an ability to put things out of your mind. The race focuses you like nothing else and demands your total concentration. But in June of that year I knew I wasn't going to just another race. Tracks merge, airports are the same, and you soon forget the details, but I knew that going back to Assen would be different. It was only eight months since I'd last been there, ran on to the track and found my brother with his neck broken by the side of that circuit. Going back would be one of the hardest things I'd done.

Assen is a riot of a weekend for the fans. You get there and you pass kids lining the streets and waving. Then you see the campsites, which are awash with black leather, flags hoisted from tents, and flaming tyre circles. Fumes drift across the site, merging with the smoky remnants of the home-made barbecues. It has an outsider feel, and anything goes. The track, meanwhile, is rich in history, with its banked curves and big cambers. It was also notably grippy, which meant riders could go faster than elsewhere, but gradually they modified it to cut down on the risks.

I knew about the risks all too well, and it was even harder because the corner where Babe had his accident was one that I'd always liked. I wasn't morbid or miserable about it, but I did think that if there was such a thing as an afterlife, then Babe would be up there and it would be a help, not a hindrance. I thought that he would be looking down as I approached that left-hander with the heavy bank. I always seemed to be quick through there without even trying, and, in racing, if you find something where you have an advantage, then you instantly like it. There's nothing better than that feeling of not trying, of letting it flow naturally, the sort of thing I imagine Freddie felt all the time. The rest of the time you're working like hell to go quicker.

In the build-up to the race I did think about Babe a lot. The memories were still raw and I remember thinking that this was the place. The memory of that horrible journey home without him, barely a word spoken and many a tear shed, was still fresh. The Dutch weather was suitably gloomy for such thoughts. Thunderstorms had turned the grass paddock into a quagmire, and the rain was relentless. Nothing bothered the Assen punters, though, and they were out in force for practice to see me fall twice. Nevertheless, I was actually feeling pretty confident. Despite the tragedy on my previous visit, I liked the track and positively loved it when it was wet.

I knew the grip was pretty good in the middle of the track because of the camber and could use that while others were being tentative and tiptoeing their way around. I always knew I could give anyone a run for their money in perfect conditions, but throw in some wet and drizzle and I was even more confident of getting a victory.

Freddie was on pole, and Randy and Lawson were up there. The rain was tearing down, but it didn't dampen the spirits of the huge Assen crowd. The lights changed and we started running. I fired the bike up quickly and powered past a few riders. Randy was away first, a camera attached to his bike as GP racing went state-of-the-art, with Didier de Radigues second on another Honda. I settled into third and was unaware of the mayhem in my wake as I exited the tightest right-hander on the circuit.

At that stage in the season Freddie was seven points clear of Lawson in the title race. He came from the Deep South and so was used to the wet, but he didn't enjoy that afternoon in the sodden conditions with the track snaking its way through a muddy swamp. His mood soured even further when Christian Sarron ran up the inside of the pack, locked the front wheel and went down, taking a bemused Freddie with him. Freddie hobbled away, led by the marshals, until he shrugged them off and went back to the bike, seeing if he might get it going again. 'Look at the bike,' he kept repeating. It was one of those unfortunate things. Sarron said the spray was so bad that he simply couldn't see where he was going. He went on to the grass and by the time he got back on to the tarmac he had missed his braking point. Freddie eventually accepted that, with a bent clutch level, he was going nowhere and walked back to the paddock, accompanied by an apologizing Sarron.

I was away and felt comfortable in second place. Randy had got off to a flier, but he wasn't increasing his lead and I was holding my own. I always felt this was going to be my best chance for a victory and, with the conditions suiting me, I pushed as hard as I possibly could. That was why I was staggered when I saw Lawson come flying past me. 'Christ!' I muttered to myself. I was on the edge, so I couldn't believe that he was going that fast. We came into a series of bends. He hit the first one and went sideways. He hit the next one and ran wide. Then he just couldn't stop it before the sweeping left. He hit the line, ran on to the grass and slid across the slip road before thudding into the bales and earth bank at around 90mph. I knew I'd been going quickly for the conditions because I was going all out for the win, and that crash told me that Lawson had been balancing on the precipice. He passed me for a few seconds and then fell over it.

The truth for any rider is that they are glad when a rival falls, but that thought is quickly followed by the hope that he is all right. I was happy to see Lawson go down because it improved my chances. He claimed he had been only a couple of inches off line, and he had been griping beforehand about how narrow the Assen track was, but he was going far too fast. There was no way I could stay with him at that speed but, as it turned out, neither could he. It might well have been the crash that cost him the title.

Now there was only Randy between me and the thing I wanted most, but he was good in the wet, and the gap stayed constant. From eighth on the grid to second was a fantastic result, but the disappointment was there too. Yes, it would end up being my best-ever finish in a world championship GP, but it hadn't been the result I'd wanted. I'd been close many times and had all the hard-luck stories you might care to hear, not least being the fastest for that whole meeting in Sweden only for the bloody bike to break down.

I was annoyed again when I saw Randy parked up not far over the finishing line. I thought he was just being typical Randy, a showman playing up the crowd, but it turned out his bike had seized up. It wouldn't have gone another lap. I couldn't believe it. That was the luck of the Haslams. Cursing us again.

That result meant I was fifth in the championship, which was good, but Wayne was third, and the competitiveness between us grew. I'd always liked Wayne even though we were polar opposites in many ways. He was a hot-headed, wild kid who liked nightclubbing and would never tire of telling anyone how he would be the world champion one day, whereas I kept myself to myself and was sometimes criticized for not having the killer edge. One incident that sums up just what Wayne was like was when he was driving his old banger with Roger Marshall, another member of the Honda Britain team and another habitual party-goer. Roger said he thought he could hear a rattle in the car, whereupon Wayne said: 'Let's find out.' He swerved from the slow lane to the hard shoulder, up the top of the grass bank and then down again. 'Yeah, still rattling,' he said.

We got on well. I trusted Wayne, and there were a few riders you could not honestly say that about, either on or off the track, with your bike or with your wife. I know one rider who once deliberately took Randy off and forced him into a bank so hard that it was frightening. That sort of thing happened. You learned fast who would give you the room to stay on.

When it came to safety, Mike Trimby did more than anyone to make life better for the riders. In the early days he didn't have any official capacity, but he was an ex-rider and so was sympathetic to us. The circuits hated him, because he was asking them to spend money on altering bits of track or putting in more barriers and bales. They tried to get rid of him, but all the riders rallied behind him and put in money to make him our representative. It was a major development, because the circuits had too much power over the riders. With Mike doing his bit, we could concentrate on racing. No rider wants to be bothered with safety issues. We just wanted it to be the best it could, and when Mike started growing in influence we knew we had someone on our side.

As that season continued, the rivalry with Wayne intensified. We went to Misano and decided to try out a go-kart track near the circuit. Both of us wanted to win so badly, just for our pride and ego, that we almost wrecked the place. Wayne sent me hurtling over the tyre wall and then I repaid the compliment. That sort of thing was normal. Wayne had a hard, square face and an in-built aggression. He had the mouth but he backed it up and, sure enough, he would go on and win the world title in 1987, but that might not have happened had it not been for a dramatic sea rescue when he was still just a rising star. It happened when we had gone to Malaysia and a sponsor had invited us on to his boat. It was moored just off the coast, and there was a group of us, jumping in, sunbathing and generally having a relaxing time. The sea was a pure green-blue and the boat bobbed gently in the water. Then somebody brought up the idea of trying our hands at windsurfing. I was up for it but couldn't get the sail upright. Wayne, being Wayne, was having none of that. 'I'm Australian. I can do this, no problem,' he chirped. Sure enough, he did manage to get upright and grinned as he sailed by. We then watched as the grin was wiped off his face and the wind took him further and further out to sea. It was when he was a speck on the horizon that someone decided we'd better lift anchor and see if we could catch him. It turned out that, while Wayne could manage to stay upright on the windsurfer, he had absolutely no idea how to change direction. If we'd left him to it I doubt he would have survived.

He did return the favour, though, when we were messing around on jet skis in Thailand. We would hire them off a bunch of kids on the beach and go out on them, having received a strict warning not to jump waves. It didn't take Wayne long to sink his, and he duly received an earful of abuse. The next day, unabashed, we returned for more. 'No jumping,' the kids insisted, and we readily agreed. It was only a few minutes later that I realized I had a leak. They were an odd sort of jet ski with an outboard motor, more like little boats, and I was sinking deeper and deeper. By this point I was a long way from the shore and I was frightened. Wayne buzzed by on his jet ski and asked what was up.

'I've got a bleeding leak!' I cried. 'I'm sinking.'

Wayne had a look around his jet ski and, as luck would have it, pulled out a rope. 'Here,' he said. 'Fasten this.'

By now the thing was nearly completely submerged. I fastened the rope just before the jet ski stopped bobbing and sank. Wayne's jet ski lurched and I thought he was going to be dragged down, but he fired it up and gradually towed me to shore. It took about twenty minutes, because the thing was under water, and the kid went even madder than the one the day before. He moaned that I'd been jumping waves, but I hadn't and I gave him the money to have it repaired.

We may have got on as people but as riders we were rivals. That relationship with your team-mate is all-consuming, and Wayne and I were very close in the points standings. He finished ahead of me in Belgium, but I was quicker in France. The gap was just four points. But then, as I was on my way back from an international meeting, I heard that Mam had collapsed. I rushed to the hospital where she was recovering from a massive heart attack. Suddenly, this rock of a woman seemed frail and looked her age. I held her hand, and for the first time she admitted to me that she would be happier if I wasn't racing. I honestly think it was the strain from Babe being killed the previous year that had put her in that hospital bed. A broken heart, if you like. She had suffered such a hard life with all of us racing, something that I was never able to fully appreciate until the bittersweet experience of having my own son do it. I squeezed her hand and told her that she would get better, but the doctors had already told us that she wasn't going to. It was a matter of time.

To make matters worse, it was just days until the British Grand Prix at Silverstone, the biggest day of the year. On the day of the race the *People* ran a story under the headline MY TORMENT which claimed I was thinking about packing it in after all that had happened to Phil and Babe. Certainly, I was going through the wringer, and it didn't help that Honda flew in two extra V4s and handed them to Wayne and Randy, leaving me on the triple. 'The bike is faster than the three,' Wayne told reporters before explaining that his job was to help Freddie to the title. I was fed up with the whole thing. 'It seems like Honda are really rubbing it in, especially knowing how much the British Grand Prix means to me,' I told the man from the *People*. 'Perhaps they're frightened I'll beat Spencer.'

The race was a disaster. It was the wettest GP on record, and the sidecar race was actually abandoned because of the amount of surface water. Wayne's chance of impressing on a V4 foundered because his visor fogged up and he had to go into the pits to clear it. I lasted longer before the same thing happened to me, and I struggled home in fourteenth. Freddie extended his championship lead with another peerless ride. I couldn't have cared less by the end. I just wanted to get back to the hospital to see Mam.

A few days later they let her come home because they knew. None of us truly accepted the situation. She looked like she was improving, but the doctors assured us that was not the case. I went in to see her and decided that I would tell her the kindest lie of all.

'Mam, I've been thinking and I've decided I'm going to pack in racing.'

I knew it wasn't true, but I knew that it was the only thing that would give her peace of mind. She was still with us, still alert and bright, and I hope that helped. I remembered her saying, after Phil's death and then Babe's: 'This shouldn't be happening. It shouldn't be this way. I should go before my kids.' I think that the thought of me, the youngest of the family, still racing was too much for her, so I told my fib. I hope it made her last moments a little calmer. The truth sometimes hurts too much.

12

THE CRAZY WORLD OF ELF

THE ELF PROJECT WAS MAD, FUTURISTIC, AMBITIOUS and ultimately flawed, but it was a hell of a ride in every sense. The origins might have given me an indication of what was to follow if I'd known about them. The story goes that the top man at Elf, François Guiter, was on his way to the Formula One car race at Monza when he stopped off at the house of Serge Rosset, the legendary French chassis guru, and said: 'I'm in deep shit. Can you build me a motorcycle? You have ten minutes to decide.'

My time with the Rothmans Honda team had fizzled out. Nobody told me that I was surplus to requirements, but no news is bad news when it comes to negotiating time, and then we heard that Honda Britain were pulling out of GPs. I'd finished the season tied with Wayne on seventy-three points in fourth place in the championship. Freddie won the title and was the only other Honda ahead of me, but it was clear that they saw Wayne as the coming force and, in truth, he was a little bit stronger at that point. So when the chance to ride the Elf-Honda came up, it seemed the perfect solution. I could develop a new project, which suited me because I was intrigued by the technological side of bike racing, but I would also have a standard Honda for some races.

I still had a shock when I went to France for a grand presentation Elf were giving. I'd already been surprised by the size of the office, which was a huge glass skyscraper. I had merely thought of Elf as being an oil company, but when they began the talk and ran through the history of how they had developed into the fifth-biggest company in the world I was taken aback. This was clearly a huge undertaking.

If that opened my eyes, then they nearly came out of my head when they showed me the first Elf bike after the presentation. I panicked like mad and turned to Ann. 'Christ, what are we doing here?'

I was well aware that Elf wanted to be different and have a sexy, modern-looking bike, but it seemed to be going a bit far to build a bike without handlebars. Instead, it had levers that you pulled and pushed. I scratched my head and pictured myself racing at 160mph on this. Luckily, that version got scrapped. I could well believe that the whole idea had, as I'd been

told, been born of a competition where they asked
schoolkids to come up with bold new ideas and someone had wanted a half bike, half Formula One car.

It was a year of change. I had signed up for a project
that had invited a lot of scepticism, and Ann and I had
finally decided to get married. The plan had always
been to tie the knot before we moved into the farmhouse in Smalley and, although it would take years
before it was completely finished, it was now almost fit
for people. We were tired of living at Ann's parents' or
sleeping on sofas, and now we had Leon too, so the day
of the wedding was to be the first in the home we had
owned and been renovating for more than two years.
The house was still largely a shell, but we had a kitchen,
a living room and a bedroom that were finished. The
rest was falling to pieces, and we'd only just had
the roof put on, but it was enough. Unfortunately,
on the morning of the wedding in the little parish
church in Smalley in January 1986, the newly installed
plumbing sprang a leak. Several leaks, in fact. I was
there in my wedding suit, getting covered in water, as I
tried to fix the pipes and make sure I got to the church
on time. I checked my watch and knew I should be
making a move, but I had to fix the system or else the
place would be flooded by the time we arrived back.
Somehow it worked out, and I dried out in the car.
Robert Fearnell was the best man, and it all came
together. My dad was not invited.

There was no honeymoon because there was no time. I quickly came to understand that the Elf was unlike anything motorcycle racing had ever seen. They wanted a futuristic bike in looks but also in approach. However, always in the back of my head, reassuring me, was the fact that no matter how radical and odd some of the things were, I always had the chance of riding the conventional bike.

The first time I won on the Elf was in Macau. That was a big deal for the team, who had laboured with the Elf 2 and never been remotely near the front. Now they tasted victory, even if the truth was that the bike was a standard three-cylinder Honda painted in Elf colours. There's nothing like winning to boost morale, though, and that was a good start to what would be an exciting and exasperating time with Elf.

At first I wondered who this guy called Serge was. To me he was just a bloke who used to be a banker. He had the makings of a paunch, grey hair and a determined expression. I had no idea about how he worked, what he wanted or his background in endurance racing. Until the Elf bike was competitive, his plan was to run it through the GP weekend until final practice and then switch to the standard bike. That didn't give me much time to get the bike sorted out, but to my mind it meant I could still be a GP winner.

The season got off to a muddled but successful start in Jarama in Spain. I was left on the line and departed shaking my head and cursing my luck, but made inroads and worked my way up to tenth, way down on Wayne, who won, but delighting the Elf crew. We were lucky, though, because the team had misread the regulations and thought the race was being run over twenty-seven laps instead of thirty-seven. Serge was going to call me in to take on extra fuel, but Ann told him: 'There's no way he's going to stop. If you show him a sign saying "gas" he'll think you're being cheeky.' As it turned out, Wayne lapped me, and so I had to do only thirty-six laps, which was just as well because the tank was bone dry.

Tenth place gave Elf their first championship point. It was a modest start but at least it was one. From there on the project swayed back and forth. At times I thought we were getting somewhere and then I'd think we were nowhere near. What was definite was the fact that we put the hours in. The biggest thing about Serge was that it didn't matter how much time anything took. They weren't in this because they wanted a GP bike tuned to high heaven to win races; they were developing something that was unique. If a job had to be done, then it would get done. That went for the whole team. It was the hardest-working bunch of people I've ever been involved with. We toiled literally day and night to get it right, and I'd often wake at three in the morning and go and knock on Serge's door with an idea. More often than not, he would be in the garage because this was his labour of love. It almost killed Chris Mayhew, the chief mechanic, because he'd spend two days solid working on it without any sleep. He was not alone. If you didn't want to work like that, then you wouldn't work for Serge.

Maybe I pushed too hard to make up for the problems, because there were lots of falls and mechanical failures in that first season in 1986. I was in the points seven times and finished in a decent ninth place in the championship. That was no mean feat for a bike under development and trying to be so different. It was enough for Erv Kanemoto, Freddie's tuner and a top man at Honda, to call me and ask me to ride with Freddie the following season. It would have made life a lot easier, but Elf had got me out of a mess the previous year and I felt loyal to Serge. I stayed with Elf, and Erv got Niall Mackenzie instead.

My riding was still good. I showed that at the TransAtlantic races at Donington in 1986. I loved these meets, and the Anglo-American rivalry gave it something extra. You wanted to get the bragging rights and shut up the grinning Yanks. It captured the imagination of the public, too. Thousands would flock in, the surrounding roads would be rammed, and there'd be a riot of noise. I was due to ride a race-prepped Suzuki, but Honda weren't having that and blocked me. In its place I was given a road bike, the new VFR750, complete with tax disc, horn and mudguards. Sheene was commentating and called it 'a bloody disgrace'. There were real fears about ground clearance and it seemed a joke to be going up against rising American stars like Kevin Schwantz and Fred Merkel on a bike from the high street. The rain came down to dampen my spirits further. It was bloody cold. There was a stench of wet leather. It was the sixth leg and it would be one that people remembered for a long time. I went out on my road bike and, sure enough, the race bikes of the rest pulled out huge distances on me on the straights. There was nothing I could do about that, but I could use my skill in the wet, and I wasn't going to sit around and moan about my misfortune. Instead, I used my braking on the corners to start hauling in the field. I took Steve Parrish and Kenny Irons. I couldn't catch the leaders, but fourth place on that bike was an incredible effort. I felt pleased with myself, and Honda could scarcely contain themselves. It had been a marketing coup for them. Thousands of fans had sat at home and seen me give a perfect demonstration of the VFR750's capabilities. I heard that the phone lines didn't stop ringing after that and the shops sold out of them. As for me, I was getting used to riding at a disadvantage.

The following year we were all amazed when the package came from Japan and we opened the crate to find a brand-new NSR. The chassis on the Elf had to be modified because we'd been expecting a year-old

1986 engine, and it took a long time to sort that out. But I had the standard Honda bike and started well, getting podiums in Spain and West Germany. It proved to me that I could still run at the front with the rest. The third place in Spain was a gruelling one, as I'd been due to receive special lightweight leathers to combat the stifling heat. They never arrived, and I lost a lot of weight in the race just keeping Mackenzie at bay. I was so happy I even allowed Serge to shave off my lamb-chop sideburns in front of the cameras afterwards! But as time went on Elf weren't happy with the fact that their successes were in name only. Later in the season I was told I had to run the Elf in the races, too, and that hit the morale of everyone as we drifted from the front to the middle of the pack and worse. Serge never gave up, but you could tell from the extra lines on his face that it was taking its toll.

In truth, the problems had started from day one. I went testing at the start of the project at Misano and I ran off the track twice. The push-and-pull steering levers had thankfully been consigned to history, but we had a swinging arm at the back and front. That looked strange, and it felt it, too, because whenever you hit a bump the middle sagged. The theory was that it would keep the steering constant, like a car, and that it would provide more grip. I carried on at Misano and got to the point of the track where Wayne Rainey would later have the accident that left him paralysed. I couldn't feel much from the tyres, so I was slow. Then I hit a dip and the bike sagged, which gave the sensation of a front-end slide. Instinctively, I lifted the bike up and ran straight across the grass. I was baffled but got back on the track and kept going. I'd managed another four laps before the same thing happened again.

'What's wrong?' Serge said when I came into the pits.

'I don't know. It's the weirdest thing. I keep thinking the front is sliding. I don't care who's on this bike, that sensation is going to make them straighten up.'

Serge, as he did in these situations, went off to sort it out. There was no way the bike was going to work like that because you felt you were falling half the time. Serge saw it as a challenge, though, knowing that he had to make it more competitive while not compromising on the super-modern design. What he came back with was ingenious, a swinging arm that worked on a scissor effect. It meant that instead of dipping in the middle it forced the front down. So we still had this novel swinging arm, but now when you hit the brake the weight went on to the front. It was a bit slower than normal, but at least it felt vaguely like a conventional bike.

The way it worked out at Elf, though, was you solved one problem and found five more. There would be a lot of shouting. Serge would say his way was right, and I'd say mine was. He had a thick French accent, and I was broad Derbyshire. At times it was chaos. Other people would chip in, too. It didn't really matter who got their way, because at the end of the day we tried absolutely everything. For a while, when I was on the rostrum again, I was loving it. I was racing hard at the front and I was also developing something. It was the best of both worlds, but that didn't last.

We had the GP bike to compare the Elf with. It was the same engine, so the power was the same. But the next major problem was the braking. To fit in with the bike's image, Serge had ditched the normal idea of having two discs in favour of having one big one in the middle. It looked good, and looks were half the battle with the project, but the problem was that this was all so new that we had no baseline. There was nothing to gauge it against, no default setting, and those brakes were a bloody nightmare.

The disc was vented to keep it cool, but we never got it as good as we'd have liked. In fact, it was so bad that every so often you'd lose the brake altogether. I don't just mean that you would pull the brake and it wouldn't slow; I mean you'd pull the brake and the lever would come back to the bar. Unfortunately, this always happened at the end of the long straights, meaning that I had a few very lucky escapes. One of those was in Italy when I pulled the brake at 140mph. Nothing. I pulled it a second time. Nothing. By the third time I was frightened and by the fourth I was running off the track. I stamped on the back brake and fell sideways, trying to get off, while the bike tore into a hay bale, levelled up and ripped along the hay wall before coming to a stop without even toppling over. I breathed a sigh of relief but knew the problem was still there.

You might go testing for half a day before it would happen, but the thought that at any moment your brakes were liable to fail plays on the mind. And my riding went to pot then. It was one thing riding without brakes in testing, but to ride at 160mph in the middle of a crowded race was another. I started to back off and leave myself room. I couldn't ride close because I didn't trust the brakes. I started hooking my finger over the brake and just touching it to see if it was there. It was always a relief when it was, but you can't concentrate when you're doing that. Things began to slide.

When Serge came up with a cure, it was a simple one. The problem was that the big, single disc was knocking the pads so far back that they didn't touch. Serge decided the best way to solve this would be to fasten small springs behind the pads, forcing them closer to the disc. They never failed again.

The things we worked through now seem mind-boggling. First we started with a small thin brake disc, then we had a different diameter, different callipers, the big vented version. And that was just the brake disc. There was always something, and for every positive there would be a negative. So, although the springs meant you no longer had to worry about running off the track at the fastest point, they also created a massive amount of drag. So I regained my confidence but was slower. It was like banging your head against a brick wall.

Serge was a warm, driven figure who used to run rally cars and was happy to make the parts inside his house. Step inside and it was like an Aladdin's cave of motorsport, littered with fibreglass bodywork, fins, camshafts, crankshafts – the lot. It totally consumed him, which was great for me because I wanted the thing to improve as much as he did. Chris, too, couldn't have done any more. He was working so hard that he took to sleeping in the workshop. Serge got him a bed settee and a television, and Chris lived there through the season. You had to respect that sort of commitment, and it meant that everybody gave their best.

The enduring problem with the Elf was that the bike was too heavy. We compared it with the standard GP bike from Honda and knew we had to shed a few pounds or we were always going to be struggling for speed. The next innovation was a single-sided swinging arm made of carbon fibre. This was going to be much lighter than the normal alloy and, even though carbon was new and expensive, Serge was excited by the prospect. It took a few months, but, when it came back, sure enough, it was lighter. They'd done all the tests on it to make sure it was safe, and it was actually three times stronger than alloy. At last it seemed that we were winning.

The only flaw was that nobody realized that it flexed. The back end bent with the new addition, so it was returned to the designers. They stiffened it and sent it back again, but still it flexed. So it was returned once more as the frustration mounted. Finally, after an age, the new, inflexible, carbon-fibre swinging arm arrived. It was unpacked amid great enthusiasm, but there was one small problem. It was now heavier than the original. Back to the drawing board again. Back to alloy.

And alloy meant that the bike was again too heavy, so the next grand idea was to build it out of magnesium. That was a failure for one simple reason that was highlighted during qualifying in Germany. It was the end of the session and everyone was pulling wheelies on the massive pit straight. It's a long hill at Hockenheim and everyone was going through the gears and relaxing. I pulled a wheelie, too, but when I put the bike back down the magnesium front end literally snapped. The magnesium was so stiff that it was like glass. The thing snapped between the handlebars and the swinging arm. I had no control. Nothing. The bike snatched the wheel so hard, and I began to veer off the track and towards the concrete wall at 130mph. I tried turning, but there was no response. It was the most stupid-looking crash ever because it was so gradual, just drifting off line and towards danger. People must have thought I had a death wish. I hit the strip of grass between the track and the wall and then ran over a groove that had been left by a car. I fell and slid all the way down the pit lane. It was embarrassing, but it could have been a hell of a lot worse.

The flags were out anyway because it was the end of the session. Serge came running over. 'What happened?' he said.

I dusted myself down and rubbed my back. 'There's no bleeding steering.'

Serge then looked at the bike and could see where it had sheared. He ran back to the pits and grabbed a blanket and threw that over the bike before he dragged it back. There was a fair bit of commotion in the pits. The journalists gathered around and wanted to know what had happened. Everyone was bemused by why I'd just ridden off the straight. There seemed to be no reason for it. 'I just lost concentration,' I said. The more experienced journalists looked at me suspiciously. They knew something was wrong and that the secret was under that blanket. But this was elite motorcycle racing, and you didn't let teams or the media know what was happening. Not when it was something as serious as the bike snapping in two.

Give nothing away. Keep your mouth shut. Tell white lies if need be. That's what happens in GPs. I'd done that when I tested a new gearbox on the four-cylinder

Honda in Suzuka. Randy was riding for them at the time. Just before I got on to the back straight, the gearbox exploded, locked the back end and threw me over the top. It was a place where you should never fall off, and Randy was having none of it when I tried to pass it off as a mistake. 'I just spun it from under me,' I told the reporters.

'Spun it from under you!' Randy said. 'If you spun it from under you, I want one of those bikes!'

He knew there wasn't enough power for me to have done that in that part of the track. Everyone knew there was a problem, but I couldn't say that. Say nothing or blame yourself. That was the professional way.

The magnesium version actually gave you blisters because it felt so sharp. And we still had the problem of the weight. We had one of the most powerful engines on the grid, but the weight killed the acceleration. It also hated the wet, which was bad news for me because that was one of my strengths. The problem was that the bike didn't transfer its weight from the back to the front like a conventional bike, so you had to skim the brake before you pulled it, otherwise it would lock. That detuned me and added to the frustration.

I also had other things to think about in 1987. Ann was pregnant again and gave birth to a daughter, Emma, in January. I was made up and was so happy to be there after all the trauma surrounding Leon's arrival. Having a boy and a girl completed the set, although I wanted more. I don't know why, but I'd my heart set on four kids.

The first race on the Elf 4 came in round eleven of the 1987 season at Brno in what was then Czechoslovakia. From being a regular top-five finisher, I was now down in a lowly fourteenth, and things got worse. We had the standard NSR waiting in the wings, but I was told I had to race the Elf 4. The single front disc had now been replaced by twin steel units. That single disc had been made from the same material as a Formula One car, but the operating temperature was 400°C. It took an age to get to that temperature on the bike, so the writing was on the wall. And then I crashed after just four laps of official practice. 'It spat me off far higher than the motorhome,' I told a reporter from *Motocourse*. 'My leg came down with a snap and that broke my ankle.' I wasn't the only thing damaged, as the Elf 4 was a mess, too. It meant that they did unwrap the NSR and let me use it while they worked on repairs, but I was in a hell of a lot of pain and just sticking my knee out into the airstream was excruciating.

It wasn't surprising that we struggled. In Brazil we spent an entire session changing the front suspension, and the garage was always a hive of activity. We tried everything, and some of it was truly innovative, but I knew the chances of winning a GP on this bike were nil. Elf wanted to try everything, and that meant that, after exhausting everything mechanically, they looked at the rider. They decided to let Freddie have a go on it. Nobody told me. It was a secret operation, and the implication was they wondered whether the problem wasn't the bike at all, but me. Inevitably, it came out that Freddie had ridden the bike in America. 'How did he get on?' I asked casually.

'Not very good,' I was told.

In fact, Freddie's lap times were way down on mine. That pleased me. I wanted the bike to move forward, but I didn't want them to pin the blame on me. I was disappointed, in a way, that they had used Freddie, but I always got on well with the Elf people. With Honda there was a hierarchy and you'd need to go through four people to get to the top. With Elf it was Mr Guiter who ran the show and wielded the power. Yet, for all his wealth and power, I found him a perfect gentleman. It was why we never had contracts; it was all done on trust. At Assen during the first year he came to see me before the race. 'Are you happy?' he asked.

'Yeah,' I replied. 'Everyone's working so hard.'

'Next year this will be your rise.' He jotted down a figure and showed it to me.

'Great.'

We shook hands and that was it. The second year sorted.

Strangely enough, I was fourth in the championship in 1987, which sounds pretty good, but it had been a struggle on the Elf 4. Even the successes had their problems, as was the case when I went back to Macau and gained a genuine win for Elf on their bike rather than on a disguised Honda. I knew Macau like the back of my hand now, and so was confident every time I went there. Sure enough, I qualified on pole and pulled away from the rest of the field. I opened up a big gap and I remember seeing Serge hanging over the wall with a board telling me to ease off. There were one and a half laps to go, and I was thinking, Great, at long last I've got a victory for Elf. That was when the handlebar snapped. Nightmare. I had a big gap, but when it came to braking I had nothing to hold on to. I ended up trying to improvise by hooking two fingers over the brake and twisting the throttle with my thumb. Not surprisingly, my lead began to get smaller and smaller as I desperately tried to hang on until the line with half a handlebar. As I crossed the line I heard a roar and saw a flash as another bike zoomed past.

It was too close to call and nobody knew for sure who had won. I pulled up to the rostrum and flipped the stand from underneath. It came up that I'd beaten a German rider, Peter Rubatto, by roughly half a wheel. I breathed a sigh of relief as Serge dashed over. He was very happy because we'd won but was veering towards giving me a bollocking, too.

'You slowed too much, you slowed too much,' he repeated.

I raised my eyebrows, but once I had him alone, away

from prying eyes, I told him the truth. 'Serge, look.' I
pointed to the bike and Serge saw that the handlebar
was wedged into the fairing. 'I had a hell of a job even
finishing.'

I don't know whether it was the excitement of
winning, but this time Serge wasn't bothered about
keeping our problems secret. 'Hey, everyone,' he
laughed as he lifted the handlebar. 'Look at this.'

I think I went up in his estimation after that. It's not
easy racing when you can't steer.

I respected Serge immensely, even when he would
pick Leon up and leave him hanging from the metal
bars holding up the awning. That was a running joke.
Leon was four and getting used to life in the paddock.
Toni Mang, a talented racer and member of the
Rothmans Honda team, was married to Colette, who
used to be a teacher. She started giving Leon a couple
of hours' tuition every day. It worked well. Then Serge
would lumber around outside the garage and kick a
football against the door with Leon. It was a family. We
had a close-knit team with everybody working as slaves,
so any success was celebrated. Macau was one, and the
land-speed records that got me into the *Guinness Book
of Records* were another. This being Elf, though, they
were not trouble-free, either.

Elf wanted to set some records, because they wanted
the publicity, so we took the bike to a private banked
circuit in France. It was a play day, really, and because

I was good at starting I was the perfect man for the job. The track was a bowl, similar to Daytona but nowhere near as big. It was surrounded by avenues with poplar trees and the odd pensioner out on his bicycle. It was a quiet, rural scene but for the blokes with the bike and the roar of my engine. The records were pretty easy, in fairness, and I clocked them up for the flying kilometre, the standing-start mile and the standing-start ten kilometres. It was amazing that I managed to get one of those because, unbeknown to me, the steering damper had come loose. I went through the start beam and tore around the circuit. I got to the other end of the circuit and stopped. I waited there for about twenty minutes before some of the guys from the pits made their way to me.

'What are you doing?' someone asked.

'It won't turn,' I said.

'How do you mean?'

'I mean it won't turn right.'

I'd been riding at breakneck speed to get a record without realizing a bolt had come out and jammed the steering. It meant I could turn left, which is what I needed to do on the bowl-shaped circuit, but nothing else. I'd broken the record on a bike that wouldn't turn right. That was the Elf.

It was always intended to be a three-year project, so the 1988 season was the last. The Elf 5 had the previous year's V4 NSR motor, which meant the best I could hope for was to dice with the second string. My best finish that season was seventh, which wasn't something I was used to, and it was hard. In the end it was so difficult to find what was wrong that you wondered what you were doing it all for. I'd dropped on to the Elf because competitive rides were hard to come by, and I thought the carrot of the standard bike, coupled with the chance to develop something completely new, sounded a good deal. But in truth it set my career back. I'd levelled off, too, and other stuff was becoming important. I had Emma now as well, and for the first time in my career I was thinking about other things. The Elf had been a brave and bold attempt at something unique, but I needed a bike that could win to get my hunger back.

13

HORSES FOR COURSES

THERE ARE MANY PERSONALITIES IN MOTORCYCLING, and one of the biggest I encountered was Kevin Schwantz. The world revolved around him, whether he was playing golf with sponsors in Japan or riding the Pepsi Suzuki in the 1989 season. We had a year together but barely spoke. It wasn't the comeback I was after.

Schwantz was a great rider. He dressed like a cowboy and rode with a maverick flair. He was daring, occasionally dangerous, and a product of the dirt tracks. The previous year he had signalled his arrival on the 500cc scene by winning in Japan, and by the time I pitched up in the team he was a serious title contender. I couldn't have been happier. After three years toiling away on the Elf, I was now in a team that had genuine championship aspirations and partnering a talented Texan who thought he could beat anyone.

The reality proved depressingly different. I think I had underestimated just how hard it would be to make the transition to Suzuki after a decade with Honda. The closeness of the teams I'd enjoyed with Serge at Elf and Barry at Honda Britain was no longer there. And there was the added problem that the Suzuki had been built around Schwantz and his way of going fast was completely different from most people's. It took me almost all year to get up to speed, and by then it was too late.

The first race of the year was at Suzuka. We had been supposed to fly out to Japan earlier for a major press conference, but it was cancelled because of the death of Emperor Hirohito. There were rumours that the official period of mourning could even affect the Japanese Grand Prix, but they proved unfounded. More's the pity.

Schwantz won and I was foundering down in twelfth. I found it so hard to adapt after three years on the Elf, which called for long flowing lines. By contrast, on the Suzuki you rushed into a corner, held a tight line and exited sharply. I was used to spinning the rear wheel to turn. It was a difficult adjustment, not helped by the tyres I was getting from Michelin. Meanwhile, the team massaged Schwantz's ego and ignored me.

It got worse in the second round in Australia. Schwantz was going well in qualifying and ended up on pole position. I came into the garage and tried to explain what was wrong with the bike to the English mechanics. I was using hand gestures to explain how I thought we could improve it, while Schwantz was over on the other side of the garage with his mechanics. I walked out of the awning and was halfway up the paddock when I thought of something else that might help. I hurried back and, as I came into the garage, saw my mechanics with their backs to me. They were talking to Schwantz and his team, who were all laughing. I caught enough of it to realize my mechanics were taking the piss out of me, mimicking my accent and copying my hand gestures. Schwantz and the rest could see me, and I think they were embarrassed. Finally, the pair turned around and I just glared at them and walked out. I didn't say a word, but I was disgusted. Here I was trying to do a bloody hard job, explaining what I wanted from them, and they were just taking the mickey and trying to impress Kevin because he was winning. It was pathetic, really, and broke me from them. I could never trust them after that, and if you don't have trust you have very little when you're racing.

I thought about the days with Serge and how we'd work together through the night, and then looked at these guys. In comparison to him they made it feel like it was just a job, and I wondered whether they cared less if they were winning or not. There was no use complaining because, at the end of the day, Schwantz was winning races and I wasn't. It's a rule of motorcycling that if you complain when you're losing, then you're whingeing. Because the results weren't happening as fast as I wanted, or had expected, the mechanics just wanted to side with Schwantz. It made the rest of the season very awkward.

I never had a problem with Schwantz himself. He was a fun lad and I respected him as a rider. He was a bit full of himself, blond and vain, and he could be a drama queen if things didn't go his way, but he was doing what he had to do to get to the top. One of the criticisms that used to get levelled at me was that I was a bit too nice. I rode as hard as anyone, but I think that there was an element of truth in that. Maybe you needed to go around saying you were a future world champion like Wayne did or get mardy with your team like Schwantz. They both ended up as great world champions after all.

It was a frustrating time after that because the relationship with my team was irreparable. I was seventh in Spain, but it would have been a lot better had Frankie Chili not pushed me off the track. It was a bit like that for the rest of the year.

Having the family with me was always a distraction. We would park the motorhome at the grubby end of the paddock, among the privateers, and shun the champagne lifestyle. We didn't go to fancy restaurants or take advantage of the hospitality in the paddock. Instead, Ann would cook for us. Leon's teachers set him homework for when he was away with us, and he began writing a diary of his time on the GP circuit. We also had Emma now, who was two and into everything. I was thirty-three and began to realize that I didn't have too long left. Toni Mang was pushing forty when he won the 250cc title, but that was rare and he managed to keep himself super-fit and avoid having his nerve break. For most of us, the truth is that there's no way you're going to go faster once you reach your early thirties. You can hold your own but you're not going to improve.

I broke both my thumbs in a fall at Spa and so had to miss the French Grand Prix. Nevertheless, I was determined to be back for the British round at Donington. I was optimistic, despite the injuries, because the previous year I cut through the field after being brought down on the first lap, by Schwantz as it happened, and rode well after that. The result didn't look good on paper, but I knew what I could do at Donington. There was a huge crowd, and I gave it everything, even though I still didn't feel at home on the Suzuki. I came home in seventh, added a sixth in Sweden and was fifth in the final round of the season in Brazil. I finally thought that I was getting to grips with the bike by the end of the year and certainly felt capable of challenging Schwantz. But the team had already made their mind up and I wasn't retained.

I never talked to Schwantz about bikes or settings or circuits. In fact I never spoke to him much at all. Even when we went on a golfing trip to Japan, paid for by one of the top sponsors, he always had to be the top dog and the star attraction. If someone high up in the factory was talking to me, then I used to get the sense that he really didn't like it. When we played golf, he would talk to those people he felt were important and that was it. Otherwise conversation was a one-way street. That was just the way he was. We didn't fall out or have any arguments, but we were never close.

I did have a problem with the mechanics, though. I had never forgotten the day they had taken the piss out of me, so, at the end of the season, I took my prize money, walked into the garage and chucked it at them. I hope they enjoyed their two grand, and I hope they felt small when they were doing so.

I agreed to join Cagiva, the solitary European manufacturer in the championship, for the 1990 season. I met the two brothers who ran the team, Claudio and Gianfranco Castiglioni, and liked them instantly. They were enthusiastic, and it was clear that no expense would be spared in their pursuit of a Grand Prix dream. I liked the fact that Cagiva was also a family company and that I would be again developing something new. At the back of my mind, though, I accepted that my own dream of winning a GP was fading. I'd been fourth in the world championship on two occasions and had stood on the podium nine times. It was a pretty impressive record, but the first time I tested for Cagiva the

V4 seized, I was catapulted down the track, and the bike caught fire. It was always going to be a struggle to create a phoenix from those flames.

The biggest problem I had was when I got injured testing a new exhaust at Jerez. It had an even bigger power band as a result and that caught me out. I went down and the bike landed on me. My hand hurt like crazy, because the skin had been shredded off my little finger. I went into the medical centre at the track and was told, in pidgin English, that I needed to have my finger amputated. I can't say I was thrilled by the idea, so I was pleased when Dr Claudio Costa arrived and said: 'No, no, no, I think we can save that.'

Costa is now something of a legend in MotoGP. He set up the mobile clinic that attends all GPs and has helped no end of riders. A part-time poet with a flamboyant air, he certainly improved my mood that day in Jerez. He wasn't bothered about upsetting the medics at the track in Jerez. His only concern was saving my little finger, and he couldn't care less about overruling the locals. There was an argument and a lot of pointing, the upshot of which was the locals told Costa that he wasn't allowed in their medical centre. He shrugged, flicked his long locks and adjusted his scarf. He took me outside, put me on a table and injected me. Then he put a pin down the middle of the bone. I'd lost a lot of flesh, so he wrapped what he could around the pin and folded it over the top so it looked semi-normal. After that he took me to his medical centre to have it X-rayed. He was pleased with it, and so was I. Best to keep all your fingers if you can. The downside was I had to miss a couple of GPs as a result.

I was walking down the paddock, just about ready to come back, when a mechanic came riding along on his pushbike. I could see that he was looking at the grid girls in their miniskirts instead of where he was going, so I put out my hand as I dived out of the way. Like an idiot, I had thrust out my injured hand, and, sure enough, he crashed straight into me. He fell to the ground and at first was laughing, but then he realized I was in huge pain and he couldn't have been more apologetic. I think it was seeing my finger, completely bent backwards, that made him realize I was hurt.

I went back to see Dr Costa. I was wondering how on earth he was going to get the pin out now that it was crooked. In fact, it was simplicity itself. He cut my finger open and took a set of pliers to it, pulling the pin out with a single big tug. Costa told me that he didn't think it would be successful a second time, but I wanted to try and so he put another pin in. That was a mistake and I should have listened. The pain was horrendous and, if I caught it on something, then it was absolute agony. I also knew that I was losing valuable time. Eventually, at the end of the season, I accepted the inevitable and went to the local hospital in Derby to have it off. The finger and the nail looked perfect, but the first joint had completely gone. They gave me the anaesthetic and put a sheet around my hand so that I couldn't see.

'I'm sorry, but do you mind if I watch?' I asked.

They looked at me as if I was mad but removed the sheet. I was intrigued to see how they were going to do it and was surprised at how basic the operation was. The surgeon took a scalpel and cut away at my finger, exposing the bone but leaving as much loose skin as he could. Then he took a pair of wire cutters and cut the bone clean off. I had thought it might be a bit more scientific than that, but it worked. Then he nibbled at the bone and folded the skin over the top before stitching it up. I was out the same night and had the stitches out a week later. I expected the thing to fall to pieces, but it was sound.

That might sum up the year with Cagiva. I missed a big chunk – literally in terms of my finger – and there were other issues, too. When I joined, I'd regained my belief in myself after a good end to the season with Suzuki. I was ready to get back on the podium. I thought the Cagiva was based on the Yamaha, which I'd started out on with Mal Carter, and so there was a symmetry there that I liked. The package sounded good, the budget seemed assured, and it was another opportunity for me among the elite. Then I got on it and the bloody thing wouldn't steer. That was especially hard for me coming from the Suzuki, where the steering had been the strongest point. I made suggestions, but they didn't go down well. There was a lot of suspicion, and people took the suggestions as criticism. There was also the fact that the team was a sprawling operation with too many chiefs. Each section of development had its own boss, and nobody was in control. You could come up with the most fantastic idea ever, but they wouldn't want to do it because they hadn't thought of it. They thought I was interfering and picking faults, but I was just trying to move things along. There was a lack of respect on both sides.

You can't run a team by committee, but the saving grace about Cagiva was my team-mates. Alex Barros became the youngest rider in the top class when Cagiva signed him as a nineteen-year-old that year, while Randy Mamola was also there. I liked Randy, who had been a multiple runner-up in the championship but had been off the pace with Cagiva for the past two seasons after leaving Yamaha. He probably knew it wasn't going to happen for him now, but he was still a brilliant rider and a live wire. Whether it was girls or parties, Randy was out for fun. More than anything, though, I respected the transformation that he had undergone. When Randy first started making it he got seduced by the power that came from success and he started upsetting people. He thought he was better than everybody, and that showed. He was a cocky American loudmouth. Nobody liked it, whether sponsors or fans, but Randy acknowledged it and turned himself around. It took a lot to do that, and I had so much respect for him afterwards. You still wouldn't want to go out in a hire car with him, but he was a great bloke and a teak-tough rival.

I took Alex under my wing. He was trying so hard that he was crashing all over. I knew what that was like, when you're young and eager to impress. He'd knock on the door of my motorhome and ask if I was coming out to play. He did the same with Leon. Alex was living a dream, a little boy lost in the excitement of racing motorcycles. He was lapping up every minute of it and had no edge.

We had some fun times. We were testing in Spain and the rain was slamming down, so there was nothing to do. I said: 'Come on, Alex, let's take a car for a spin.' We jumped in and I set off around the track. 'Here, watch this,' I said. As we went into the chicane, I flipped the handbrake and the thing went sideways. I flipped it off and the car levelled up perfectly, without even a wobble.

'Wow, that was good,' Alex said. 'How do you do it?'

'Easy,' I told him. 'You just pull the handbrake and let it off. That gets you into a slide and you control it from there. Do you want a go?'

A few minutes later I was stood by the side of the track watching as Alex approached the chicane. He squealed into the first corner and then proceeded to spin around like a top. Luckily, he didn't hit anything and arrived back a bit shamefaced.

'What happened?' I asked.

'I pulled the handbrake like you said,' he griped.

'Did you let it off again?'

'Ah,' he said, the light bulb flashing over his head. 'I forget that bit.'

Alex was a young lad who was desperate to make it, and I gave him as much help as I could, whether he was going to beat me or not. I wasn't one of those riders who would just tell you a load of bullshit. Yes, you're competing with each other, but I didn't have the ego for all the crap that often went on between team-mates. My problem had been that every time I had a team-mate he was a bleeding world champion. Alex was young, keen and really good, and I was happy to do all I could for him.

There was the offer of a Ferrari for any of the Cagiva riders who got on the rostrum that year. That didn't provide me with any extra motivation. I didn't like Ferraris and would have sold it if I'd been given one. I tried because it was what I wanted to do and for the team. I remember when we went to Spa I got the thing going so far sideways that the Castiglioni brothers approached me. 'Slow down,' Gianfranco said. 'You don't need to do that. You have a family to consider.' The brothers were fantastic people and knew how hard we were all trying. I will never forget them saying that to me.

I took the Cagiva to eighth at Spa, but Alex really showed his potential by finishing fifth. However, by mid-season there were lots of rumours circulating that Cagiva were going to pull the plug on their 500cc team. I spoke to another Italian factory, Bimota, and had a test ride for Norton at Donington in the build-up to the British Grand Prix. There was the real prospect of us being left high and dry before the season ended, but we soldiered on. My last finish that year was a distant eleventh in Hungary on 2 September 1990. I never retired from GP racing and would return as a wild card, but I knew in my heart that it was over.

I had an end-of-season barbecue at the farmhouse and invited all the team. By the end, the mechanics had learned to trust me and they knew Cagiva were going to carry on. It was a time to relax and share a joke. We did a bit of air rifle shooting and then started messing around on my home-made giant stilts. I showed Alex the gym I'd put in the house, and we had a go on the rope ladders.

The trouble with riders is they are always competitive. I used that to my advantage when my sister Janet walked by, with her daughter, Tina, sitting on her Shetland pony. When Tina was on its back you could do anything with that animal, but we knew that it was very choosy about its riders. Feeling mischievous, I said to Alex: 'Hey, I bet you can't ride that little horse.'

He took one look at the pony. Clearly, his Latino machismo had been affronted. 'What do you mean? Of course I can.'

'Go on, then,' I replied. 'I bet you can't stay on for a minute.'

'I can ride a horse.'

The bet was struck. Janet held the pony, and Alex sauntered up to the little thing, sure of himself and his horsemanship. He cocked his leg over it and crouched down, but as soon as he touched the pony's back it kicked out its back legs, ducked its head, and Alex somersaulted to the ground. The mechanics creased themselves at this, and Alex's pride was seriously hurt. He bounced up and approached the animal again. This time he took a firm grip on it and sat down. What followed was like a scene from a bizarre rodeo as this Shetland pony bounced around the field like a bucking bronco with this GP racer on its back, his feet no more than six inches from the ground. This time he lasted around twenty seconds before he was dumped on his back with a sickening thud.

That pony was marginally trickier than the Cagiva. The team did make it to 1991 and somehow managed to sign Eddie Lawson. Quite what possessed a four-times world champion to move to that team is beyond me. He did two days of the first test and sent the bike back to the factory. He said they needed to chop off the front end. It was exactly what I'd been saying, but because it was Lawson they started to listen. Alex was still with the team, and I spoke to him about it. 'It's a different bike now,' he said. To be fair, Lawson got it going fairly well, while Alex went on to ride in more than two hundred GPs in almost twenty years at the top before retiring at the end of 2007. He knows he is always welcome back at the house if he fancies a ride on one of the horses.

14

THE MAN IN BLACK

WHEN I WENT TO SNETTERTON IN 1992 IT WAS GOING TO be just another meeting in a career that had already lasted two decades. Instead, it would be a day that I'd never forget and that would have repercussions for the rest of my career. There I was, flying in my cool black leathers up to 170mph on the long back straight. There's not much in your mind at that speed. You're in a zone. Focused. Buzzing. Calm. And then the crash. Shit. You're out of control. Falling. Hurting. Panicked. It was an enormous highside, and then the pain as the bike landed on me and jolted me back into harsh, bloody reality. My body broke. The bike disappeared. The blackness that marked the end of the man in black and the Norton homecoming.

It had all started with high hopes. With Cagiva saying they were pulling out of GP racing, I'd fished around for a new ride with Honda, Yamaha and even Bimota, but there seemed no way I was going to get a competitive bike. I knew from the Cagiva year that there was no fun to be had in racing on a bike that couldn't win, so I signed a deal to leave the GP world after eight years and go back to race in the domestic championships with Norton in 1991. Barry Symmons, my old team manager from Honda, was in charge, and I was entered for the British Supercup and Superbike series. It was sad to leave GPs, because you know, deep down inside, that you'll never go back, but I'd stopped enjoying it. Looking back, it wasn't staying with Suzuki, at a time when I'd just got to grips with the bike, that took the will out of me. But I still loved racing, whatever the level, so the next-best thing was to come home with Norton. The bike looked so dramatic, all black and gold with matching leathers. People loved it.

I also thought it might give me more time on the farm, where we'd bought fifty red deer and two stags. With thirty-seven acres, I'd wanted to do something to use the land we had. Up until then I used it only for flying my remote-controlled helicopters and then a threadbare microlight I'd bought. So we took the plunge and decided to become proper farmers – a poacher turned gamekeeper in the literal sense. The deer provided me with a healthy dose of perspective, because if I thought the bike world was hard it was nothing compared with the problems we had with our herd. They started when I went up to check on the two stags and found that one had killed the other. Like riders, they were very competitive. They were very expensive, so that was a bad start.

We never named the deer because it was a business, but it was something we did as a family. Leon and Emma would come out with us and we'd tag the ears. Number eighteen was like a pet and would bounce over to us and let us feed it. I did the butchering myself. Shoot it, hang it, drain it, chop it. I just learned as I went along. Ann could never eat anything if she'd seen it alive and became more emotionally attached to them. The first calf born on the farm was a great moment that would have melted any heart. We were over the moon. It made us feel like real farmers who might be able to make a go of this. The next day we went up to see the calf, which was a dead ringer for Bambi, and found that the mother had killed it. That completely did Ann, because she had stroked it and the mother had smelled her scent.

In the first two years we made some money. Local farmers were crying out for venison, because it's cholesterol-free, and it fetched a good price. We sold to them, and in time we ended up with around two hundred animals. It didn't last. Fencing them in was a nightmare and cost a fortune, but that was a minor irritation compared with what followed. First of all, everyone started to jump on the bandwagon, like they do. Then foot and mouth struck and the government started tightening up on transportation. There was a case thirty miles away, and we were scared it would spread to us and they would shut us down. That was bad news when I had my bikes at the farm. So we tried to offload the deer. We ended up having to get rid of them at such a low price that we thought we'd swap them for wild boar. We packed the deer in the back of a truck one day, but as it started to make its way out two of them jumped over the side and made a bid for freedom. We thought we'd keep those two after that, and they continued to reproduce.

The wild boar arrived, and they were vicious things. We had a few hundred again, but we had a problem when they started opencast mining next door to us. To this day I still blame the mine for flooding us out, because we never had a problem beforehand, but suddenly we had water cascading through the fields. They needed to move the water out of the pit, and it ended up coming in our direction. That meant the entire field was under water, and at one time we had sixty dead piglets floating by in a grim procession. That was awful. Standing knee-high in freezing black water, trying to rescue drowning animals and having to discard the dead, was a nightmare. We tried to fight the company, but the next thing we knew we were being fined for moving a footpath. It was the first we'd heard about it, but it cost us £7,000 to redo it and we realized we were fighting a losing battle. We tried to take on the big companies, but by the time we had finished we ended up out of pocket, paying for footpaths and drowned boar.

Only the bigger animals survived, because the water came up so high. It was horrible, and we realized we didn't need all this, not when I was trying to hold down a racing career at the same time. These days we restrict ourselves to just a dozen deer on our thirty-seven acres and it's fair to say they live like kings.

Back in 1991 the main concern I had was getting to grips with the JPS Norton and its rotary engine. That took some adjustment, because it was so different from anything I'd ridden before. When people say it was super-powerful, they're right, but not in the low range. It didn't have great acceleration until you got to the high gears. In first or second there were other bikes that would beat it. I also had a major issue with the brakes. Throughout my whole GP career, my strong point had been the brakes. Whoever it was – a world champion or a living legend – I could hang on to them on the brakes, but when I got on the Norton I was running past corners and having all sorts of mishaps. I just couldn't get the thing to stop. Finally, I realized that when I closed the throttle the back wheel was still pushing me in even though the engine wasn't accelerating. It meant that I had to start using the back brake for the first time in my career. I developed a system to stamp on the back brake to get the speed off, then do what you might term normal braking and then start slipping the clutch to avoid it locking up. The first clutch we had was off a Hillman Imp and was there purely because they'd bought out the factory. So we had a massive clutch like a tractor's until Barry helped me out by getting hold of a slipper clutch from Kawasaki.

Ron Williams designed the chassis for it. The engine was little and light. It was the size of a 250 but had the power of a 750, and the frame wouldn't take it at first. That meant there was a lot of development again. The engine operated like an electric motor and played havoc with the back suspension, because it always pulled it into the floor. We had to go away from the standard practice on frame and suspension. Ron was working on it all the time, and we finished with something so far from the norm that it was untrue.

I was thinking that racing would be easier in England after years of taking on Spencer, Lawson and Gardner, but was I in for a shock! Everything mechanical dropped a level, so the machinery and the tyres were not as good as I was used to, but the competition was just as cut-throat. I had a great big target on my back, too, because I was coming from GPs and had just got going in the first race when it finished. In GPs you try hard to build up a fast pace towards the end, but by the time I built up pace in England it was the end. The races were shorter but they were full-blown affairs with no quarter given and elbows flexed.

The first win came at Brands Hatch that May in the TransAtlantic races. There was a field of past and future stars on the grid that day, including Freddie Spencer, Scott Russell, Carl Fogarty and John Reynolds. But it was an old rival from the GP circuit, Rob McElnea, who proved my main threat in the wet. It was the hardest bike I'd ever ridden, and we'd set it up so that it was very light at the front end. That meant the front was sliding around more than the back, which generally means there's a crash coming, but I carried on. Every other lap the front would be sliding all over the place, but I kept pace with McElnea and Reynolds. McElnea was leading on every lap, and as we started the last circuit of the track I knew that he would be expecting me to try to go underneath him at the last corner, Clearways. Instead, I got such a run out of the bottom straight that I surprised him by going a corner early. I was so glad to beat him and he was suitably gutted.

There were more successes that year. I set five lap records in as many meetings and got the first 100mph lap at Oulton Park, but the high point was riding in the British Grand Prix at Donington. In truth, the organizers let me ride the Norton because they knew I had no chance of winning. It was hard to calculate the cc of the rotary engine because it hadn't got cylinders, but they let me in as a 500cc two-cylinder. I realized then what competition does to people, because in all my years of racing it was the friendliest paddock that I'd

Left ✥ The genius. The peerless Freddie Spencer, my ex-team-mate, and I share a moment in 1989.

Above ✥ Push off, Ron. Barry Sheene once branded me a nutter, but the truth is we always got along fine.

Left ✥ King of the road. My great friend Joey Dunlop and I stand together on the podium. His death was a terrible shock.

Below ✥ The old and the new. I was next in line to Barry Sheene and as my star rose, his faded.

Right ✦ Wayne's world. I had a lot of time for Wayne Gardner, as shown by the time I rescued him from a watery fate.

Below ✦ The maverick. Kevin Schwantz rode with a lot of flair, but this is about the closest we got as team-mates.

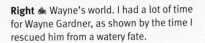

Left ✦ Looking ahead. I knew that having Freddie Spencer as my team-mate was going to be both the best thing and the worst.

Right 🏍 Muck and bullets. Leon the motocrosser would learn how hard the sport can be in painful fashion.

Below 🏍 The 'Pocket Rocket'. The earliest picture of Leon hinting at his future career.

Below 🏍 On the ball. Serge Rosset was an inspirational figure and great friend. Here he tries to keep up with Leon before hanging him from the roof in the garage.

Above ✦ If the cap fits... Leon rolls back the years with a Pharaoh helmet.

Right ✦ Young gun. Leon on his first bike, a 6occ Kawasaki. He's already developed a liking for jumps.

Below ✦ Now listen to me, son. Serge gives Leon the benefit of his wisdom, watched by me.

Below ✦ Following in his father's footsteps. Leon grew up in the paddock, so I suppose it was inevitable that he would be drawn into the bike world.

Above ♣ You know where you're going wrong. I don't give Leon much praise because I want him to improve.

Right ♣ Ice-cool Leon. Note the Kevin Schwantz autograph.

Above ♣ Leon style. I now know that Leon will push it as hard as he needs to. That's terrifying for a parent.

Above ♣ The year of living dangerously. The Italjet season was a nightmare for both Leon and me as I watched and suffered in silence.

Teacher man. Team GB riders Nick Hopkins and James Haydon with Ann and me at Donington.

Left ♣ The eyes have it. Unmistakably a Haslam.

Below ♣ Not just a grumpy old git. I have done all I can for Leon, but nothing can compare to the joy of racing yourself.

ever been in. Riders and mechanics came up to me, slapped me on the back and chatted in a way they'd never done when I was on the GP circuit. I quickly understood that it was because they knew I was no longer a rival. That hurt a bit, but the reception from the crowd was also the best I'd ever had.

There was something about the Norton, being a British bike and looking so good with its black livery, that attracted people to it. Everywhere I went on the Norton I was asked for my autograph far more than when I'd been Freddie Spencer's team-mate standing on the podium. There was something about that black bike that tapped into the romance of biking, and that day at Donington was a bodice-ripper. It wasn't the result, although twelfth was highly respectable given what I was riding, but the noise was absolutely deafening. For the first time in my life I could actually hear the crowd as I went around the track. That was an incredible sensation. It was the same wherever the Norton went. It was a magnet for fans, and people flocked to see me ride it.

It was a good year, all in all. I finished second in the British championship, but I was missing the GP circuit. You start to think about the what ifs and the could have beens. About the second place in Assen and the bike breaking down in Sweden. I was now a farmer and a father of two, but bikes were still such a major part of my life that I couldn't help feel slightly disappointed.

The disappointment turned to real fear before the start of the following season. I was motocrossing with Leon, who was eight at the time, and some of his friends. Unfortunately, I'm not a very good moto-crosser, because I take risks but never get away with them. Sure enough, that's what happened that day. There was a great big ditch that Leon and his mates were merrily jumping. They had the technique to bounce across it on their smaller bikes. I found that impossible on my 250, so had a more basic approach that involved hitting it as fast as I could. Each time I made it across, but then found I was going far too fast to navigate the hairpin on the other side. I was getting a bit annoyed by this, especially as a bunch of kids were managing to do it every time, so I decided to ease off the power just a little. Bad move. The bottom of the bike hit the bank, which meant there was effectively no suspension and I had to take it through my legs. Unfortunately, that didn't work, because I held my legs straight. My leg snapped halfway between my knee and ankle. I knew I was in trouble when I saw my toe flip up and hit my kneecap. I managed to stay on and rode slowly towards the van before gently rolling off.

Everyone was looking at me strangely, because it didn't look as if there had been a problem, but I vividly remember looking down and seeing my foot pointing the wrong way behind me. That made me feel physically sick. I reached down, grabbed it and twisted it a hundred and eighty degrees. I had to look away, because the sound of the bones and fibres crunching was horrendous. Just as I'd done that, Leon sauntered over.

'What's up?' he asked.

'I've broken my leg,' I told him.

Leon looked at my leg and my foot, which was now pointing in the right direction. 'Are you sure?'

I almost managed a smile. 'Believe me, I'm sure.'

Trevor Nation, my team-mate at Norton, chucked me in the side of his van and took me on the well-trodden journey to the Queen's Medical Centre in Nottingham. Halfway there, the pain started to kick in. It was excruciating and I dreaded to think what the damage was. The people at the hospital put me on gas and air to relieve the pain and told me I had a spiral fracture of the leg. I had a plate put in and set about getting back. It was all I needed going into a new season.

As you get older the knocks hurt that little bit more and the recovery takes that bit longer, but I was soon back in the saddle. The Norton remained as popular as ever, but it was hard to get the results in the second season, and then I came to Snetterton. I was going well and had just beaten the lap record when the thing seized on the back straight and threw me down the tarmac. They'd been trying to develop the gearbox, but whatever they'd done it hadn't worked and the bike locked up in sixth gear. The Norton landed on my leg and I was knocked out cold, which was just as well given that my bone shot out of my leg and scraped along the floor at breakneck speed.

It was a horror crash, but you take your luck where you find it, and I was blessed to have one of the most eminent surgeons in the land working on me. Professor Chris Colton was a bike fan and not one of those to look down on people with self-inflicted injuries. He sympathized and got to work on fixing an open fracture of my tibia. For me it was a fascinating process as he inserted an iron bar into my leg.

The first panic was about whether the bone had snapped because of the plate that had been put in earlier. Professor Colton put them right on that one and said the impact of the crash would have snapped anything. I looked at the mangled wreckage of my leg and thought, This is never going to work; this isn't going to happen.

I waited a few weeks in Queen's before they could do the bone graft, and then there was the plastic surgery. It was an amazing piece of skill from the doctor. Ten years previously, four out of ten tibial fractures resulted in amputation, and there was a concern that I might have to have my leg amputated at the knee. Lying in hospital, that was my main fear, but the bone graft worked perfectly and I didn't even have a limp when I walked again. Only a fool ignores a wake-up call, though. I could walk, but running at the front again was a different thing.

I had already resigned myself to the fact that I wasn't going back to GPs. That was undisputed. The dedication you need for GPs is total. There's no other thing in your head. That's all it can be. But I was thinking about my family, the house and the farm, so many other things beyond the race paddock. Now I knew the scary truth. I needed to stop racing.

In GPs everything is a stepping stone. If I do this, then it will allow me to do that. Now I'd reached a point where I couldn't see anything to take me forward. All I could see was a levelling off. It was daunting to think it was over. I did continue to ride after that. I did the Triumph Series for fun. The concept was a one-bike series so that everybody was equal. I helped police the bikes, but it was obvious that the tyres people had differed wildly. It was cheating, really, so the fun went from that, too.

I was casting around for something to do. I was approaching my thirty-sixth birthday when I had the crash and needed something else. I wasn't wealthy, because of the tax bill we had struggled with for years, and I needed to be busy for my own mental health, too. It was my best man who once again put me on a new path. Robert Fearnell had been trying to get young British riders into the 500cc elite for years, and I thought that if I couldn't race in GPs, then the best bet would be to give some kids a leg-up. Robert was doing it purely for love of the sport and for Britain and asked if I'd like to help. I said yes, and Team Great Britain was born.

Robert helped out by getting sponsors and giving us practice time at Donington, but I needed more. It was a shock to my system to suddenly have to go out there and tout for money and backing, when I'd spent most of my career with a nice factory contract. I was naive when I started it, because I thought that my name and the backing of Robert and Donington would open doors for us. I did get a lot of support from people I'd known down the years when it came to helping out with products, but getting hard cash was a different ball game. I needed £250,000 to run the team and, while that wasn't a huge amount, it was like trying to get blood from a stone.

The first twenty knock-backs were a real shock. And then, as time went on and Ann's finger hurt from dialling, that twenty became two hundred. It was rejection after rejection, and we wondered if we'd ever get the team off the ground.

Ann worked at it tirelessly. This was her project. She threw herself into it and slogged her guts out in the effort to get people on board. In the end we realized we needed a different approach, so we pulled sponsors in on deals where they paid small amounts in the first year and then more in the second if they were happy with it.

That worked a treat, because the team did get a lot of media coverage and so most of the backers came back for the second year. It was a gamble but we had no choice. Robert gave us as much track time as we wanted and used his contacts, while I started devoting my time to riders.

The first was James Haydon. He was a fresh-faced, good-looking kid with a great personality, and I liked his spirit and his will to win. Nothing fazed him, and that appealed to me. His problem was his will was too powerful. He would push over the limit in his desire to go faster and was happy to take the crashes. I thought I could drum that out of him and preferred working with someone who was like that than the other way around. You can hold someone back with a bit of careful mentoring, but you can't give someone bottle if they don't have it.

I quickly learned to study young riders and was fascinated by what made them tick. Some are so young that they simply don't know what they're doing – they're winning not because they're good but because they're getting away with it. Others talk a really good race, but the first sign of pain and that's it, they're finished. And then there are those who always blame something else – the tyres, the engines, the team. It's never going to happen for them, either. James, though, had an inner aggression that was great. What I didn't count on was never being able to rein him in.

Like the other riders we had, he lived at our farmhouse. James had a heart of gold, and if there was any farm work that needed to be done, then he'd be out there. He'd train in the morning and at night for a couple of hours. My attitude was, as long as he was putting the hard graft in, then I didn't mind what he did during the day. Much of the time he would play around the yard on pushbikes or go out motocrossing. When Nick Hopkins came to stay with us, too, the pair of them would indulge their competitiveness and drive each other to the point of collapse in the gym. I'd join in, because I hadn't long finished my GP career and so I was still pretty fit, but those two were masochists. After any given session, James would be sitting in one corner, all giddy and light-headed, while Nick would be sick in the other. They nearly killed themselves.

James inflicted a lot of damage on himself when he was riding, too, but I wasn't too worried by that to start with. The way I'd been brought up under Mal Carter meant I regarded the bike as simply the mechanical part of the job. Whether it blew up or got written off, that never bothered me. The only concern I ever had was the rider. You can fix a bike, but if a rider is sidelined for half the season, then it's a disaster that you can't come back from, however great your engine might be.

James crashed a lot in that first year and would always come back to the garage saying sorry to me with his expression.

'James, it doesn't matter. As long as you're OK.'

Money was tight, but I didn't want him thinking that if he crashed, then it was going to cost a fortune. If that thought circulates around your head, then you can't ride to your potential. 'Forget the bike,' I said. 'Just come back safe.'

I was always trying to hold on to James, but he kept coming back from his spills faster and faster. He was absolutely bloody fearless. Nick was the reverse, and you had to give him assurances and egg him into it. They were chalk and cheese. They both could set good times, but the difference was that James would do it in a lap whereas it would take Nick the whole session.

I think James left me too early. He was eighth in the British 250cc Championship in 1992 as a teenager and was second the following year. That was the year he was a wild-card entry to the British 500cc Grand Prix at Donington and came eleventh, the second-youngest Briton after the great John Surtees to gain a world championship point. He moved on because he was ambitious, which is fair enough, but he hadn't got as much experience as he needed and it was hard for him to find his way. I'd just about got hold of him, but then he started crashing a lot because he was trying so hard to impress again. He was in there with the GP elite at the age of twenty, but he needed someone to grab him and tell him to calm down. There was nobody there on the back seat with him, and he fell off an awful lot.

I believe that if I'd kept James and got enough sponsorship, then he would have gone very, very far. He had the natural talent and all the belief you needed. He could fall off and jump back on and put the worst crashes out of his mind. He had it all, but it needed controlling. I never had that chat with him, and that's a big regret. James went his own way, and by the time he was back racing in England he'd been around lots of teams. There was no point in trying to talk him out of it because everyone deserves their chance and he was so positive that it was going to be a huge success that he wouldn't have listened anyway. Nevertheless, I do sometimes wonder what might have been.

There were other good riders who came on board with us. Karl Harris was another James Haydon. Leon put me on to him and said this guy is an unbelievable motocrosser. He'd not done any road racing, but I went along to a motocross race and went up to him as he was ready to go out. He had turned up late and not bothered with practice, because if you got there too early, then sometimes you had to marshal at those meets. Leon nudged me and said: 'That's him.' I walked up to him on the line and he looked at me blankly, not knowing who I was.

'Do you fancy trying road racing?' I asked.

He shrugged and said: 'Yeah, OK.' Then he went out. That was it. I put him on a Superteen bike and he won a few races through pure aggression. The bike

wasn't as good as lots of the others, but he was so determined that he made up for it. Later, he would become
a British champion, and it felt good that I'd given him
his start.

I liked helping riders out. John Reynolds, later a very
popular British champion, was another I tried to advise.
But for all the successes there were a few who didn't
make it. They could always get to what I'd call the level,
but then there was something missing that prevented
them from making that last step. And that's the hardest
step of all. Whether it be lack of confidence or a fear of
pain, something stopped them. But when it worked I
got so much satisfaction from seeing these young up-
and-coming riders make progress.

It came as a shock when Team Great Britain finished,
even though I'd known we were on a three-year deal. I
was enjoying it so much that I'd almost forgotten about
the time. It had been a team effort between me, Ann
and Robert, but we needed the governing bodies to get
behind it and back it. I hope we helped the careers of
some very talented riders but would like to have done
more with it. Maybe if we had there would have been
more British riders in MotoGP in recent times. It left a
void again.

By that point we had another member of the family.
Zoe was born in May 1996 when I was pushing forty.
The year before, I'd been doing some instructing at a
race school for Yamaha when I got one of those

horrible calls. I dropped everything and rushed to the hospital, where Ann had miscarried. It was a terrible time for all of us, but especially for her, and we were delighted when she fell pregnant soon afterwards with Zoe. I always wanted four children, but we stopped at three. I try not to think about the one we lost.

Emma was really into horses by that time, and we went down to Robert Smith's place to buy one. I was pretty inexperienced on horses so I went with Janet, who knew a lot. She was in awe of Robert, who was a champion showjumper and the son of Harvey Smith, and she refused when he asked if she'd like to try his grade-A top-notch horse. I wasn't so shy and said I'd give it a go and started with a little jump.

'Do you want to go higher?' Robert asked.

'Yeah, go on, then.'

So the bar was raised, and I jumped that, too. It carried on like this for a while until the jump was taller than Robert's head.

'Hey, Dad,' he said to Harvey. 'He thinks he can jump this.'

Harvey, the gruffest of Yorkshiremen with an acid tongue, came over to watch and I set off. In truth it was easy, because the horse was so good, and he cleared that, too. After that, Harvey wanted me to try a novice horse around the field. I didn't like to tell him I couldn't trot. Jumping was fine, because it was like spotting a braking point on a bike, but trotting was different. On the novice horse I was in trouble and almost ploughed into the fence. Somehow the horse cleared the jump, to Harvey and Robert's immense amusement. 'Got you out of bloody trouble then, didn't it?' Harvey said.

Horses were Emma's great passion and it was nice to be able to do something with her, because when she moved on to dancing I was out of my element. However, they proved just as dangerous as bikes, as was shown when we later went to buy another horse from a bloke in Halifax. Emma was doing really well by that point and was full of confidence, so we let her go on the horse. What we didn't know was that this animal was wild. It ran straight at a fence and Emma went flying over it. She crashed down flat on her back. The horse came somersaulting afterwards and missed her by inches. It was like Snetterton again but far worse. That did me totally. I felt so guilty about letting her go on that horse without testing it first myself and I was badly shaken up. Emma was bedridden for a week. The image of that horse missing her by such a fine margin remained in my head.

Horses were never going to be enough for me. They were fun and I enjoyed them, but I needed something else. Robert Fearnell was again the man who had the idea for a solution. He knew Honda were talking about doing a race school, because they had one at Cadwell which they weren't happy with. Robert spoke to them and they decided that Donington would be a better prospect. I thought they were talking about me being the chief instructor, but then Robert dropped his bombshell. 'Er, no, that's not it,' he said. 'They want you to run it.' Even Robert thought that might be a bit much for me. My business acumen was hardly proven, and we knew it was going to be a long, hard struggle. Robert came up with the idea of going in with Jim Russell, who ran a car race school. That way I could earn some decent money and use their tried-and-tested structure. Bob McMillan, the Honda boss, came back and said: 'No way. It's Ron or nothing.'

We owed a lot of money, couldn't afford it, and Ann was panicking like mad, saying, 'How do we put a phone line in the office?' We agonized over it for a while but decided we had to go for it. So we remortgaged the house and used the kindness of a number of close friends. Two of them were Bryan and Irene. Bryan was a fan who followed me everywhere, but he was also a shrewd businessman and high up at Hotpoint. Ann leaned on him a lot, but she still died a thousand deaths as she got on with doing all the administration and planning side. I focused on the customers and what would work for them on the track. I'd seen what Yamaha had done at their school, and there were things I thought were wrong. One of those was the fact that they all got changed in the garage by picking up a set of leathers from a pile dumped on the floor. More importantly, I felt the punters were so restricted in what they could do on the track that I failed to see what enjoyment they could get out of it. I opened it up more and, although it caused a few more crashes, it gave ninety per cent of people a hell of a lot more fun.

I ploughed into it with my heart and soul. There was no feeling that these people would be gone in a couple of hours. I talked to them all, gave them tips, set the bikes up. It was nice to pass on some knowledge, and people loved talking about the GP days. We were a bit soft to be in business to be frank, and the first year was a nightmare. We didn't have a clue. People said we had to do a business plan, but we were living from day to day. How the hell could we predict anything? My attitude was if we're going to go down, then let's go down big time, owing a hell of a lot of money. So the bills stacked up. We forgot to budget £4,000 for fuel to run the bikes in, and so that plunged us further into debt. It wasn't a huge sum, but we were treading such a fine line that it all mattered.

The stress was huge, although Ann felt it more than me. She wanted to be liked by everyone, and some of the instructors took advantage of us. Ann got to the stage where she felt physically sick going to the school in the morning, because they would ring in with excuses for being late and ride roughshod all over her. She was too nice a person for that. My attitude to the instructors was, 'If you don't like doing it, then why bother?'

After the first year we sat down and thought it might just work. We didn't make a profit, but we paid lots of people off. There was no money coming in, but we were paying bills at last. Robert said we should look at it as a three-year venture, and every year we thought it would fail because people would get bored, but they kept on coming. They still are. One of them was Johnny Rea, a young kid whose father used to sponsor Joey Dunlop. I gave Johnny his first go on a bike, and it was obvious he was a talent. Little did I know that within a few years he would be riding against Leon in the British Superbike Championship.

My work with Team Great Britain and the race school proved to me how much I like passing on knowledge. I've had several offers to run a team, but the toughest thing is being able to give a long-term commitment. Instead, I help people out in the paddock on any given day. But I didn't really need to run a team again, because I'd already started on a new adventure, the one that is still ongoing and has been the next-best thing to racing in GPs. It's been a roller-coaster ride and it's a work in progress, but I've relished it as much as riding with Freddie Spencer and the rest. This is the story of the Pocket Rocket . . .

15

THE POCKET ROCKET

THE SCARIEST THING ABOUT MOTORCYCLE RACING IS
watching your son do it. You stand there on the pit wall,
watch him go past and start counting the seconds. You
know the dangers, you've tasted them and you dread
them. Being a Haslam, Leon has crossed the line on
numerous occasions, resulting in broken bones, lifelong
scars and late-night escapes from hospitals. I've been
called a terrible parent, and he's been mocked for
having it easy, but you won't change us. We're racers.

He first rode a bike when he was four. It was just a
little thing that he took around the paddock. But it
was really when Team Great Britain was taking off
and there were people like James Haydon and Nick
Hopkins living at the farmhouse, training in the morning
and riding bikes for fun in the afternoon, that he showed
a real interest. One day, when he was eight, he came

up to me and said: 'Dad, why can't I ride bikes?'

I looked at him and smiled. 'You can.'

It started from there. I was as excited as he was at first. I bought him a 60cc motocross bike, and I jumped in with two feet. I got the right tyres and made sure the engine was running well and then we made a practice course on the field at the house. That lasted for precisely two weeks. We went to a couple of meetings and that seemed to be that. He parked up the bike and I thought he'd made his fuss and now we could move on. A couple of weeks passed and then he came up to me again.

'Dad, why aren't we going racing?'

I grinned at him. 'Because you haven't asked.'

'OK, then, can I go?'

After that, he asked every week. Then every week I'd have a problem, because I'd be off to race meetings and he wanted to do more and more. The excitement at seeing him riding soon merged into outright fear at what might go wrong. Leon was fearless and loved the jumping side of motocrossing. The higher the better, as far as he was concerned.

The first bad crash came on the field at the back of the farmhouse. I'd been watching him and his mates messing about and relishing the table tops, the doubles, the trebles. I went back into the house and half an hour later one of his mates came running up. 'Quick! It's Leon – he's had a crash.'

Those words struck like a dagger. I ran out and saw him lying at the bottom of the ramp. He was in a lot of pain, but it didn't look that bad at first. Then I noticed the puncture mark at the top of his leg and realized the bone had come out, pierced the skin and somehow gone back inside again. That was when I knew we had a major problem.

'Don't move, Leon,' I said. 'It'll be OK. I'll call an ambulance.'

I seemed to wait for ever with him at the bottom of that ramp. I wanted him to have some gas and air so that the pain would ebb away, but we stayed there for an eternity. I knew it was bad but had no idea how bad and how long it was going to take to recover until we were in the familiar surroundings of the Queen's Medical Centre. I'd been there countless times in my career, and now I was going back just months after the Snetterton crash, the injuries filtering down from father to son.

Ann had gone in the ambulance with him. She'd done that so many times before with me that it must have been gut-wrenching for her. It was the start of a new cycle, and she could see that. I was coming to the end of the road and Leon was jumping on the bike and taking over. She could see years of anxiety and nerves and pain stretching ahead of that ambulance as it made its way to Nottingham. There was also the feeling of guilt to contend with, although that wasn't too bad locally because we'd got to know all the orthopaedic surgeons over the years.

It was doubly painful for Leon, because he only had to turn up to the next round and he would have won the National Youth Championship, but he was going nowhere for a considerable length of time. He had broken his left femur and had to have plates put in. The doctors removed one of the three main muscles from around the bone. He was left surrounded by external fittings with a scaffolding of bars and bolts. It was an almighty mess. It took the whole winter to heal and I wondered if all this was worth it. He was just a ten-year-old kid and, Christ, I'd seen enough accidents and trauma to last me several lifetimes.

But he was there the next season. We'd got the bits out of his leg and it had healed nicely. He caught up in the championship, and we went to Northern Ireland with a chance of putting the record straight. A year after his accident he was in the same position, and all he needed to do was finish in the final race of the year to claim his first British title.

He was going well enough in practice in the Chambers Memorial when he landed badly after a double table-top jump and broke his right tibia and fibula. This made the previous year's accident look like small beer. There was internal bleeding and muscle pressure building around the break. Ann and I sat outside the operating theatre and were thinking the same things. If it took this to win a title, then forget it. He was only young and had his whole life in front of him. Why put him and us through this? The medical staff felt the same, and, in truth, the way some of them treated us made us feel like scum.

'How can you let this happen to a child?' they asked. 'Why are you letting him ride bikes? Do you want him to kill himself?'

They dug into us hard, and it hurt. Nobody could care for their son more than we did, and the comments cut deep. It was traumatic seeing him like that, but the doctors were distinctly unsympathetic and made no secret of the fact that they blamed us. This time the bone hadn't come out of the skin, but it was a big mess and needed to be lined up. They put him in plaster, and I sat and thought. The only distractions were the squeals of pain from Leon. Every time he moved, it hurt. I winced. I'm no doctor, but common sense told me that once he was in plaster then it shouldn't be hurting. Unfortunately, our efforts to explain this to the medical staff were flawed. Someone even spoke about getting social services involved. We were hanged, drawn and quartered.

For my part, I believed they had made a mess of getting Leon's leg sorted out. It was not personal, simply a matter of wanting the best for my son. We were supposed to be leaving the following day, but Leon was in increasing agony. He was crying from the pain, and we were left there with the fingers pointed at us. By that stage in my life I had got to know Professor Colton from Queen's very well. He was the man who had mended my leg after my 170mph crash at Snetterton. He had also come to the race school one day and made the fatal mistake of giving Ann his card. She dug it out and rang him. The message from him was to get Leon home, so we set about putting a rescue plan into practice. Ann rang another friend who ran a private ambulance service from Donington. It cost £2,500 and we weren't insured, but we got him out of the hospital and bundled him into an ambulance. Then we dashed to an airfield and flew home. Our friend's private ambulance was waiting for us when we arrived, and Leon was taken straight into Queen's, where Professor Colton was waiting for him.

It didn't take him long to determine the extent of the damage. 'It's a good job you did what you did,' he said. 'If you'd waited until the morning then he'd have lost his leg.'

That brought it home. Here was the top man in the country, surrounded by a group of fawning students, sitting down with me and telling me straight that my boy could have had his leg amputated. It turned out that Leon had been suffering from compartment syndrome. The blood vessels were swollen and cutting off the blood supply to his foot. That was where the pain was coming from. It's like trapping a finger in the door.

Eventually, the pain becomes excruciating because there's no blood and the finger drops off.

When they opened up Leon's leg late that night the muscle literally jumped out because of the pressure. He'd been put in plaster before the problem had been sorted out. It was the same injury that Mick Doohan, the multiple world champion, suffered when he crashed at Assen in 1992. He was going to lose the bottom part of his leg, but Dr Costa cut his good leg open and let the blood flow from that into the bad one. 'Another half a day and this would have been off,' Professor Colton said in his deadpan way.

Ann and I took it in turns to sit with Leon during the long and lonely nights. We knew he was now in good hands. I felt angry about what had happened to him in Ireland, but my main concern was the future. I felt so guilty. I looked at him, lying in his bed, having lost the championship for the second year running, and I thought, I've got to get him to stop. I've got to get him out of this world. I was panicking because I felt that he was only doing it because it was what I had always done. I thought he was enjoying it, but it occurred to me that he was forcing himself so hard, to the edge and beyond, because that's what he had seen me do when he was growing up.

I made up my mind. I walked over to him and sat down. 'Leon,' I said. 'I've got something to tell you.' I had his attention straight away. It was as if he knew something important was about to be laid before him. And I gave him the story. 'Now that I've nearly packed up racing I just can't afford this. All the expense – the bikes, the crashes, the doctors – we're going to have to call it a day. I'm sorry, son, but you need to think of doing something else with your life.'

We had words, it escalated into a row and then it went quiet. In fact, he didn't utter another word all night. The following morning Ann arrived for the changeover. I said goodbye and went home. She came back to the house at teatime and what she told me made me fill up to the point of tears. I knew Ann didn't want him racing, either. She had never wanted me to do it. For her it just caused anxiety, but she had never tried to stop me, just as Mam never did. 'I've been speaking to Leon,' she said. 'He daren't ask you himself, but he wants one more chance. He said could I ask you if you'd let him carry on. He says if you give him that chance he won't crash as much and he can cut down on the number of practices to keep the expense down.'

That was the turning point. I thought, Bloody hell, here I am, trying my best to stop him from carrying on, and he wants it so much. I felt terrible, shamed by this young boy's desire. Ann had tried hard to make him see my side. 'Look, Leon,' she told him. 'You're really good at football. Why don't you go for that?'

'It's one in a million, Mum, and, anyway, I love bikes. If it costs too much, I'll get a job.'

She told me all this and I felt so small. All the doubt that I had in my head disappeared. I had just given him the biggest escape route he could have wanted, if he was doing this as some misguided way to please his dad, but he had proved that theory to be rubbish. Ann and I sat in the kitchen and I've never felt so guilty, not about the crash, but about the fact that I'd doubted him.

I went back to the hospital and told him straight. 'Leon, there's no problem. We can do anything you want. My biggest problem was knowing if you really wanted it. You can't give half measures in this game.' I realized then that, while we are two of a kind, we are different people. We react in different ways, and some things can't bridge a generation gap. It was all part of learning to be a father, something you never really know. It's why I asked Leon to give me his own side of the story to see how his recollections varied from mine. This is his version of those early years as the son of Rocket Ron:

I knew my dad was famous. I heard all the family stories about the old days and where he'd come from and how Phil was this incredible talent who was going to go all the way. I knew what had happened to my uncles, but it didn't put me off. I watched the videos of my dad's old races and was proud of what he'd achieved.

I grew up in the paddock. It was all I knew for a long

time. I was six weeks old when I went to my first Grand Prix and I was four when I won my first race, a kids' off-road competition at the Argentinian Grand Prix in 1987. As a toddler I walked into the Honda Britain garage and would merrily bash away at a brand-new £800 exhaust with a hammer. It was normal for me.

It was only when I got to school that having Ron Haslam as my dad caused any problems. There was a bit of jealousy, and I was fighting most weeks. The first year at school was a proving ground, a learning curve. People knew who Rocket Ron was and so they would say to me: 'Who do you think *you* are?' I was lucky that my mum and dad supported me all the way, even when I got suspended from school for fighting over a girl. The other lad had said something to one of my girlfriends at the time. I was just sticking up for her. That was an attitude I'd inherited from my dad. He always said you should stand up for what you believe in. With him, family always came first. After that fight, Mum went into school to try to sort it out, because she was the diplomatic one, while Dad smiled at me and asked me if I'd won. When I told him I had, he was happy enough and that was the end of it.

My relationship with my dad has always been one of brotherly competition. Whatever we do, we always egg each other on, whether it be on bikes or the farm or in the gym. There is that deep instinct that makes us want to beat each other. I've never really rebelled against my parents, because there wasn't anything to rebel against. They were two people who were doing everything to help me do what I wanted. You'd have to be an idiot to rebel in those circumstances.

When Team Great Britain was up and running I loved the atmosphere at the house. It was crowded, and there was always something going on, but I looked up to the guys who lived with us, like James Haydon and Nick Hopkins. They were the only ones who had their own rooms in the house. Mum and Dad were together, I shared with Emma, and Shep, the mechanic, slept on a camp bed in the hall outside.

I suppose it was inevitable that I'd get into bikes. I was immersed in that world from the start. I'd been on bikes around the paddock, but my first full season was when I was eight years old on a 60cc bike. I loved motocrossing. It was hard and it hurt, but my dad made a track on the land at the back of the house and I spent hours out there trying to get better.

I was ten and it was August 1993 when I had the first crash. I was leading the championship with one round to go and I was confident. I was practising back at the farm when I fell. It was a big break, and the femur came through the skin. It hurt like mad, but I was more concerned about the fact that I knew this meant I wasn't going to be able to race. 'My championship,' I said through the tears. 'My championship.'

I had weeks in hospital, but it was the end of the

season, so once the race had passed there was no rush to get back. I was having lots of skin grafts, and there were all these external fixings attached to me. Mum and Dad sat there, and I could tell they were thinking, What have we done? For me it was just part of racing and it never fazed me. My only thought was when we could get a new bike so I could start testing the following January.

When I did it again the following year in Ireland, I couldn't believe it. I remember thinking, Shit, this is a lot more painful than last time. My dad said it wasn't and reminded me about the agony I'd endured twelve months beforehand. 'You were in loads more pain then,' he said, as if that would be some sort of comfort.

It was a week before the last round of the National Youth Motocross Championship. I had to finish in the top four to guarantee the title, and I'd never been out of the top three all year. I felt it was a done deal, but then I didn't even make it to the line. They took me to hospital, where they plastered me with a cast all the way to my hip. I was sitting there with nine other motocross kids, all with broken legs. The track was a bit tough for schoolboys, to be honest, as that line-up of battered bodies proved.

It seemed to me that the doctors couldn't be bothered with us. They asked why any parent would put their kid through this. Even if that was their attitude, they could have looked after me better, but they put me in the cast and left it at that. I had horrific pain in my feet, and my whole leg was numb. The doctors failed to follow that up when I was so clearly in agony. All they did was give me an injection in my backside every three hours to ease the pain. Mum had enough and rang Professor Colton, and he said they should get me back to Queen's. I was drugged up to the eyeballs when they flew me back. I remember getting on the helicopter and vaguely remember opening my eyes as I was wheeled into Queen's, but that was it. I was out of it.

I'd had two major accidents – breaking my femur, tibia and fibula and nearly losing my leg – but I was young and just thought that was normal. I was totally nonplussed, because I knew I was young and could get better. Thirty minutes after I got to Queen's, my muscle jumped out of my leg on to the table. I reckon that if the doctors in Ireland had spent less time having a go at us they might have picked up the syndrome I was suffering from. You get that even now. I sometimes go to a hospital for an X-ray on a wrist and they say: 'You've crashed at 130mph?' There's a total lack of sympathy and they think we're wasting their time.

'Look,' I say, 'I just want an X-ray. Are you going to give me one or not?'

Back then the injuries didn't bother me. Now, if I did my femur, it would be crucial for my entire career, because I need to prove myself and win a championship. I'm at an age where I know how long it takes to come back from a wrist, a leg or a collarbone. I appreciate the risks more than I did when I was lying in Queen's with Professor Colton telling me how close I was to losing my leg. It was the same when my dad had his big crash on the Norton in 1992. It's never nice to see your dad in pain, but I watched that crash and didn't really acknowledge the severity of it. He'd been lucky up until then and hadn't had a really serious break. I didn't think much about it, but it was a defining crash for him. It didn't finish him, but he could see that one more crash could be the difference between normality and never walking again.

When you're a kid you don't see the bigger picture. That was why I was angry when my dad gave me his line about stopping because of the money.

'What are you telling me this for now?' I said. 'I've just lost my championship for the second year running and you're saying you won't take me racing next year. Thanks a bunch.'

We fell out over that. When Mum came in the next day, I told her what my dad had said. She was always the middle ground and the mediator, but she wanted the same outcome as my dad.

'Tell him I'll go racing on my own,' I said.

'Leon.'

'I'll get a job.'

'Leon, you're eleven years old.'

'I'll go with my friends.'

Now I can understand why my dad wanted to put me off. It was a point in our lives where my dad felt really down. He was feeling guilty about what had happened to me. He knew all the work I'd been through only to see the title snatched away from me twice by broken bones. My dad later told me that what I went through would have destroyed most people, but I was desperate to carry on, even to the point where I wanted to do it to spite him.

BOY RACER

•

LEON FLIRTED WITH DISASTER AND LOVED EVERY second, while I stood on the side of a muddy field and could see history repeating itself. He wouldn't settle for second place or gaining half a year's experience. He was in a rush, and that meant he would crash and beat himself up. Motocross has a way of doing that more than any form of motorcycle racing. I'd think, Christ, Leon, you've just come back and you've knocked yourself out and broken your wrist. He crashed so much that it became the norm, but it was anything but normal. His love of the dangerous bits like the high jumps risked more broken bones. He was an accident waiting to happen.

If he wanted to race bikes, then I felt he should be allowed to do it. It had been the same question that my family had wrestled with after Phil's accident at Oliver's

Mount. None of us ever went back to the track in Scarborough, but the desire to keep racing stayed the same even if the venues changed. It was the same question that I pondered after Babe's crash in Holland. If I packed it in because my brothers got killed, then why was I living? All I needed was the knowledge that this was Leon's choice. It hadn't been a test, but I needed to know.

Leon has the same morals as me. The core of my attitude to life is that family is the number-one priority and nothing breaks that. Whatever happens, the family is always right. Leon took that a step further and was like that with his mates, too. Not long after the second accident, one of Leon's friends, Gary May, came to the house. He had a catapult. They were messing about and managed to hit a car. The police were called and it became a big issue. Statements were taken. It was Gary who had fired the catapult, but Leon took the blame and refused to pass the buck. I remember the policeman saying that the shot had hit a car door and then ricocheted through a window and broken something inside a house. I thought that was a hell of a trick shot.

As he got older he would get in trouble with his mates a lot. More often than not it was his refusal to back down that was his undoing. So, if his mate ever got in a fight, he would stand next to him and take the beating even if there were fifteen on the other side. It was an admirable quality, but I told him that you had to be careful with friends, because while you stood up for them the likelihood was that they wouldn't do the same in return. I think I instilled that mutual respect into him, though, and was pleased he grew up sharing the same values. It meant that, when I'd hear stories of kids stealing things from their own houses, I'd be dumbfounded, because that would just never happen here. It's why he's still here, living in one of the old barns. I don't think he'll ever leave.

Finally, in 1995, when he was twelve, Leon did win the National Youth Motocross Championship. He had two plates in his leg and would sometimes complain that he could feel his skin being stretched over the metal, but it didn't seem to bother him too much and he retained his title the following year. The injuries piled up, though, and although I never doubted his motivation any more I did question his ability to withstand the battering.

'What about trying road racing?' I asked him one day. 'I think you'll enjoy it more.'

He wasn't interested. He loved the rush you get from motocross even if it hurt, but I thought that if he made the switch then he wouldn't get injured as much. You get the fatal stuff in road racing, as we all knew too well, but it wasn't as hard. 'It makes sense,' I continued. 'I can throw a scooter in the back and we can go to the same meetings, but I can't go motocrossing with you because I'm with Team Great Britain.'

He thought about it for a minute and then said: 'Go on, then. If it shuts you up, I'll give it a go.'

The first time was a one-make meeting for kids down to the age of thirteen. Leon was totally lacking in enthusiasm for it, but I got him a set of leathers from a company we used and we set off. The race was open to everyone, because scooter racing was new and they had no idea what sponsors they were going to get. They made it as broad as they could, which meant that Leon was in there against some professional 125cc lads. He looked pretty apathetic until he started racing, and then he was transformed. Suddenly, he knew the excitement of winning on tarmac, and he enjoyed that every bit as much as doing his jumps.

There were other things to consider, too. Leon was lazy and he certainly hated cleaning his motocross bike, which I made him do, just as Babe had made me do in another era. After a hard meeting, with mud and worse splattered all over the bike, he would be in the yard cleaning it for three hours. I told him that I would mend the bikes and do the maintenance, but his job was to clean them. He hated that, and the beauty was you didn't need to do that with scooters. The penny dropped. And so he changed his mind and became a road racer.

The first season was great. Leon won the 1997 Gilera Scooter Championship at Cadwell with three races to spare and then told the man from *Motorcycle News* that he wanted to step up on to bigger bikes. After twelve wins from sixteen races, you couldn't blame him, but that title was a minor accolade compared with the media feeding frenzy that had already taken place that summer at the British Grand Prix.

It all started when Leon got the offer to ride a Honda CB500 in a support race called the Newcomers' Cup. The media got wind of it, and the phone didn't stop ringing. Lots of them had got the wrong end of the stick and thought that Leon was riding in the British Grand Prix rather than at it. I was happy to let them go along with the bizarre notion that a fourteen-year-old kid, who weighed six stone something wet through, would be taking on Mick Doohan, the Thunder from Down Under, and Co.

We had to apply for a special licence from the Auto Cycle Union, because sixteen was the minimum age for racing anything more than a scooter. Jim Parker, chairman of the road race committee, said he put Leon's name forward because of 'his outstanding prowess and skill'. Still, the phones kept ringing. All the national papers wanted to write about this boy who was now being called the Pocket Rocket. One journalist asked me: 'Don't you think he's a bit young to be racing in a GP?' I let it go and, a bit mischievously, said he would be all right. Word spread. Even some of the big GP teams thought that Leon was going to be in the 500cc race. It became a bit of an in-joke.

The Newcomers' Cup was still a big deal, though, and Leon was nervous. To be racing in front of that many people at his age was incredible when you consider I had not even had my first race by then. Serge Rosset, my old boss from the Elf project, was there with his new team. They all came out on to the pit wall to watch. Some of the top riders were there too. It gave him such a boost, because they were only there for him. He qualified in pole position against a field of seniors, including James Toseland, and was third off the line. It was a thrill to see him go. He cleared off and won the race. He didn't talk about motocross any more after that.

Toseland, who would go on to become a two-time World Superbike Champion, was two years older and one step ahead. Leon had done well on the CB500, but with his size there wasn't much more he was going to do on it, so I tried to move him into the British 125cc Championship. My aim now was to do what Mal Carter had done for me and give him as much experience as I possibly could in a short space of time. And that meant donning leathers and riding with him.

I've never liked little bikes. I started on Babe's brute, and my first bike was the Panther. But I thought that if I got two 125s and rode around with Leon, then it would be the easiest way for me to see where he was going wrong. I used my contacts at Honda and got a couple of RS125s. That invited a lot of carping from some people. They said Honda Britain gave Leon a bike only because I was his dad. It was water off a duck's back to Leon. He couldn't have cared less. I was glad – you have to be that way in racing, because there's a lot of backstabbing and bitching. If you start listening to them all, then it will screw you up and completely do your head in. That's what happens to Ann, who hears everything, gets increasingly riled and ends up with her hair standing on end.

The truth is that it helps having contacts, but Honda wouldn't have been daft enough to waste bikes if they didn't think Leon was up to it. We started the 1998 season on year-old machines. That's how I remember years now – I relate them to the bike I had at the time. In the first half of that year I could beat Leon fairly easily. For me it wasn't a competition, because he was my son and I was just trying to help him through, but he wanted to beat me terribly. My view was that I would happily beat him or push him if it taught him a lesson.

I started going in the races to pull him along. There was no way I was going to win those races, because I hate little bikes. I know some people looked at me and wondered what I was doing, but I was forty-two and this was a development project just like the Elf and the Norton. The only difference was I was now developing my own son into a GP racer.

It got to the point that year where I decided I didn't

want to do the races. Not because of any shame or embarrassment to be down at that level, but because I didn't want to take sixth place off some young lad on the way up. The place meant nothing to me, so I stopped entering the races, but I would help Leon in the practice and warm-up by pulling him along. That didn't go down well elsewhere, and some of the other riders griped to the officials.

'How can you allow Ron Haslam to go out on the circuit helping Leon when he's not even in the races?'

The officials heeded the complaints, and one of them pulled me after a session. 'Ron, you're going to have to race,' he said.

'Why? That's pointless. I'm not interested in 125 racing. I'm only interested in Leon.'

'I don't care. If you don't race, then you're not allowed to do the meeting.'

'You're being stupid. Tell you what – I'll start the race and then pull in after two laps.'

That annoyed him. 'Do that in two races and we'll take your licence off you.'

I was taken aback. 'Come on, you're being really childish now.'

He wouldn't budge, though, so I had to compete in the races. My best finish was fifth. I felt bad about stealing a place off someone else, but the officials were the ones to blame, not me. I took Leon to Croft and we spent two days' practice sorting out the brakes. It went really well, and I found it so much easier to show him something rather than tell him. I'd tried to explain that to the organizers, of course. I said that two years earlier I was running Team Great Britain in the 250cc class and I used to do all the practices but not the race. They allowed me to pull James Haydon along. What was the difference? Just because it was my lad, they stopped us.

The flip side to trying to accelerate Leon's learning was that he suffered more pain in a short space of time than most people should ever feel. We went to Croft and he did well in the first race and was up to third in the second when the inevitable happened. He was trying so hard to get to the front that he had an enormous highside three laps from the end. I panicked, because it was right in front of me on the penultimate corner. It was what I'd call his first proper road racing crash, and it frightened the life out of me.

Up until then there'd been no barriers. He'd been doing well, so the only thing to do was to go faster until he crashed. It was worse for Ann, because she was on the start–finish straight and so didn't actually see him come off. She just saw the ambulance. She was a wreck, whereas I'd seen him hobble into the back and knew he was going to be OK. That was a case of reality hitting below the belt.

He was all right. Nothing broken. Just a bit banged about. I told him why it had happened. 'Too much angle and too much power, not realizing where the limit was.' He was trying to rush on the inside of someone on the previous corner. He was close to the edge and he needed to know.

I was learning that watching is a very taxing business for a parent. Everyone says the same. Everyone knows the fear. But it was more frightening for me, because I knew from doing the practices about all the things that could go wrong. I also knew him too well. It's the same now. At Cadwell Park in the 2007 British Superbike Championship, I knew he was on the edge in too many places. When it's like that you know something will happen. He might save it and not crash, but something, somewhere is going to go wrong, whether it be him running wide or coming off. Nobody can take it that close without that being the case. The Irish would term it doing more than the bike can do. I know that if Leon is on his limit and needs two more tenths to win, then he'll take them. He might get away with it and he might not. That's the bit that's hard to deal with.

Nobody is immune, though, and I got a rude awakening myself when we turned up at Knockhill. We went out as usual with me in front. It was wet, which never bothered me because I was still good in those conditions. I was dragging him along but soon found I was pulling away very easily. So I went behind him and watched what he was doing and saw the bike flicking him up in the air every so often. Come on, get it sorted, I thought to myself as we sludged around in the rain.

'What's up?' I asked when we came in.

'It's got no grip compared with yours,' he said.

''Course it has,' I replied.

He insisted that I had an advantage, so we swapped Hondas. Sure enough, he was proved right. I followed him and he pulled away from me with alarming ease. Pride hurt, the bike spun from under me as soon as I tried to close. It was only then that I realized we had a hard compound tyre on the back. I don't know how it got there, but I whipped it off and put the soft on. The result was that we were super-fast in the last qualifying session. In fact, we were on a lap that was probably two seconds faster than anyone else. We were building up the speed and were getting quicker and quicker. We were reigning in the rain. And then I fell on my arse. I let go of the handlebars and began sliding in the damp with the bike. I sat on the floor and then, just as I hit the grass over the white line, the bike flipped back up straight. It was the sort of thing that had happened only once before, in that race when I'd left old Percy Tait scratching his head, and I couldn't have done it again if I'd tried. I'd crashed and yet something dragged me back upright. It was incredible, and it completely cocked Leon up. He lost a lot of time wondering what his old man was up to. It didn't make much difference, though. He still won the race and set the fastest lap.

He was seventh in the championship that year, which was a good effort in his first season. He was there as a wild card in the British 125cc Grand Prix at Donington, which had been won the previous year by a rising star named Valentino Rossi. Leon was young and fiery, just like his dad and his Uncle Phil had been, but his lap times were good. We were a fledgling team, but I was the dominant voice then, and what I said went. It caused some friction back then, so it was interesting for me to hear Leon's take on his rise through the ranks and what he really thought about his old man's methods:

In 1997 I had just turned fourteen when I had the chance to race in that one-off CB500 race at the British Grand Prix. That was the turning point. My dad was running the race school at Donington by now, and the CB500 was the bike I would mess around on. It would only get up to about 115mph, but it was more like a real bike than the scooters which had automatic transmission. It was a big deal and I got lots of publicity out of it. Beating Toseland didn't do me any harm either.

It was after qualifying that I realized I could win it and I just shot off. I remember getting a huge bottle of champagne afterwards, even though I was too young to drink or have a road licence, so I gave it to Serge Rosset. It was that race that made me think that I could make a career out of this.

I got a deal to ride the Honda RS125 in the British

Championship in 1998 and felt top of the world. I was a fourteen-year-old kid who was just getting into girls and going out and here I was riding against people more than twice my age. That did present a few problems, though. There was one rider, Alan Green, who was always commenting on me in his local paper. He would be griping about the bike I had and saying, 'If he can't win on that, then he might as well pack up.' He seemed to have some issue against me, but the funny thing was he was the most out-of-control, wildest rider you'd ever seen. It just made it so much more fun when I did beat him.

There were other people who weren't best pleased when I'd wipe them out, but that's just what happens in racing, and most of the other riders were great. It was actually the best fun I've ever had, and I'd hang around with riders like Steve Patrickson, Chris Palmer and Pete Jennings after the races. They were all older, so they'd be drinking beer and they'd give a can to me. I'd been used to that because Dad's mechanics had always tried to get me drunk. So we'd party in the clubhouse until it closed the night before a race. It was the most sociable time I'd had, and the racing was good. The guys who were closest to me in age were five years older, but they were starting out and didn't have the advantage of my dad. It meant that my competition came from the guys who had been doing it for twenty years, and I loved it when I beat someone who was thirty-five.

They might have thought, Who is this little shit? but I was oblivious.

It was a different league from scooter racing. There I'd been winning and it was easy. I'd have half a lap on everyone, so my dad would make me start from the back of the grid. It was stress-free fun and I was a typical teen, juggling racing with my weekly date at Rollerworld and trying to sneak beer into the under-eighteen nightclub in Heanor. I was also playing football three times a week and working on my chat-up lines. But once I got a taste of real competition, I knew things were getting more serious. I was riding for Honda then and had commitments to them and sponsors. People were investing in me, and I didn't want to let them down.

I won at Knockhill and proved I could take on the best in the British 125cc scene. And, of course, the more success you get, the more moans you get. People started saying I was getting an unfair advantage because my dad was helping me, but the truth is he's the sort of person who will sit down and help anyone. Robin Appleyard was a main contender for the title in 1998, and he was one who would spend hours talking to my dad about things. So there were riders who resented me for having expert help but they used my dad in exactly the same way.

Things reached a head at Oulton Park. I crashed on the warm-up lap, so my dad gave me his bike to race.

There's no rule saying you can't do that, but it caused a lot of animosity. Things were said, although most of it was behind my back, because that's what it's like in racing. In the cold light of day we all had the same bikes and the same tyres – the only thing that was different was I had my dad, so they went for that.

It was a good year. I also rode in the British Grand Prix proper, in the 125cc world championship race, and came seventeenth. On the scooter I'd become the youngest winner of a national road-racing crown, and now I was the youngest winner of a British Champion-ship race, as well as the youngest-ever Briton to ride in a GP. It was going in the right direction and I had the best guide, even if sometimes I didn't think that way.

One example of how much my dad gave me came at Oulton Park. There was a blind section on the track where he took about ten seconds out of me. We walked the track, he explained it and then he pulled me round. For someone of my age to learn the braking points and lines would normally take a couple of years, but my dad gave it to me in one thirty-minute session. We still go out on the track now and he stands on corners and tells me what he can see.

Things were moving on up, and the following year, 1999, we decided to go to Spain and compete in their national 125cc championship as well as at home. That was fiercely competitive and a good test for me to see how good I really was. It was also a hectic schedule, which is what my dad had been used to from the Mal Carter days. I was on a super-fast learning curve.

We went out to Spain in a car with my mate Stan and a mechanic called Trick. Stan and I would do our homework in the back of the van or on the ferry and we'd drive all night to get back for the British rounds. Now Stan, whom I've known since we were eleven, is my mechanic. I loved it in Spain – the lifestyle, the weather, the culture – and it was a good test against future MotoGP stars like Toni Elias, whom I beat most weeks. I had to adapt my style, because everyone else's mid-corner speed was greater, and I realized I was going in too hard on the brakes. I took that on board and started ruffling a few feathers. When you compare where I was with my dad at the same age, I already had so much experience. I was racing in two countries and was still only fifteen at the start of the year. At that age my dad hadn't even had a race.

It wasn't all plain sailing, though, and in truth my confidence had been dented in the first round of the 1999 British Championship at Brands Hatch. I was full of motivation after the previous year, and I was two seconds quicker than anybody else before the bike threw me off at Paddock Hill. That crash got inside my head. I didn't openly feel that I was scared or that my confidence had ebbed away; I just felt the bike wasn't working. I couldn't ride around it, so I lied to myself. I struggled to finish in the top three for half the season, and by the time I got back to form on the back of some good displays in Spain I was too far adrift. I finished fifth in the British Championship and was the British under-23 champion, but I knew the reality. I had sampled The Knock and it was scary. And the bad news was there was a hell of a lot worse to come.

17

THE KNOCK REVISITED

LEON DOESN'T BELIEVE IT, BUT I KNOW THAT HAVING ME as a dad can be a hindrance. I know people are always comparing him with me. I know the old timers say he's not as good as his dad. The outsiders look in and say he's only doing it because I've handed it to him on a plate. They don't know how much he wants it or the pain barriers he's been through. If I wasn't here, then Leon would still be as good as he is, but it would have taken longer. All I've done is given him time.

I look back and see how his progression mirrored my own. Where I'd been a young, innocent kid travelling the world to places like Daytona and Macau, it was nearer to home, in Spain, that helped Leon find his feet. It exposed him to a different group of people. In Britain you start a new season, but you're up against the same old names. We wanted to see if he liked that kind of living on the Continent, and he did. He liked it better. It took the pressure off too because, whereas in the UK he would be desperate to win, in Spain he accepted it was a learning experience. Fourth in the Spanish championship was good enough.

In February 2000, at the age of sixteen, he signed his first GP deal with the new Italjet 125cc team. He was eleven years ahead of me. Sometimes I do get a pang of guilt for pushing him so quickly, but it was for his own good as a rider. It wasn't easy with all the crashes and the usual teenage issues. I'm a bit of a perfectionist and so would put my all into everything I did, but Leon could be bone idle. He would go to his mum and say he was shattered and he had homework, which was a red rag to a bullish dad. 'He can't have it all,' I told Ann. 'He can't be out with his mates.' But Leon was a teenager and I'd been through it myself. I remembered the night that Babe beat me for being out with Margaret and the time he banned me from watching Phil race because I wouldn't clean his bike. Now I was on the other side of the fence and could understand. 'If you want to play at this, then fine,' I told Leon. 'But I'm not putting everything into it for three years so that you can go and sit in the pub for the next four.'

There were lots of rows. Teenage angst and paternal concern meant we locked horns. We never came to actual blows, and it was generally left to Ann to smooth things over, but for a time it was hard. He was sixteen, and that's the age when most sons fall out with their dad. It wasn't rebellion so much as us just having different views, but I never ever tried to cajole him into racing. It was done or it wasn't. Simple. Eventually, the pull of the track was too strong for him, just as it had been for me back in the old days in Langley Mill.

The omens for his rookie GP season in 2000 were bleak. The £150,000 sponsorship that was needed was secured late, so Leon had just three days of testing under his belt before his first race in South Africa. Then the tests were marred by an electrical problem that meant he struggled to complete just a few laps. His team-mate was the experienced Czech rider Jaroslav Huleš, and Leon told *Motorcycle News* that it would be a learning year. He wasn't wrong.

For me it was hard, because I was now just a dad, and they aren't welcome in the paddock. A pushy parent or an interfering old man is the last thing a team needs, but I knew that I could be a help to Leon. That made for a difficult relationship with the Italian team. Especially as I felt the Italjet was the most dangerous race bike known to man. The team were nonplussed. They were doing their job, and I could see the disdain in their eyes when they looked at me. It was a disdain that said, 'Oh God, he's brought his dad with him.' I looked at them and thought, I know that bike is going to seize up and throw my son down the road, but I stood back and did nothing, which was one of the toughest things I've ever had to do.

The worst occasion came in the third race of the season at Suzuka when the detonation light on Leon's bike was flashing like crazy on the warm-up lap. Without getting too technical, that light is to warn you that you have a serious problem, and it was obvious that the bike was going to seize. The team's answer staggered me, because all they did was tape it up so Leon couldn't see it. Out of sight, out of mind. I had a dilemma now. I wanted to leap in and tell Leon to come off the grid, but I knew that would be wrong because I was only a parent. I bit my tongue, stood back and waited for the crash.

The team assured Leon they had cured the problem. Four laps later he was up to sixth gear and the bike went end over end at 130mph, leaving him with a broken ankle to go with the badly bruised shoulders, arms and backside that he had suffered earlier that weekend. It was a lose–lose situation for me, and if I'd jumped in and pulled him off the grid the team would have said the bike was fine. I had to take the pragmatic way out, which meant suffering in silence while knowing my son was likely to hurt himself badly.

It was a baptism of fire that year, but there was a silver lining in May when I got the call to come out of retirement at the ripe old age of forty-three and ride in the French 500cc Grand Prix. For me this was something special, as Leon would be riding in the 125cc race on the Italjet, and so we would make a bit of history. The German father-and-son team of Ernst and Reinhard Hiller had competed in a few 500cc GPs together in the early seventies, but it was almost unheard of. I'd still been riding a few races every year since the end of my time with Norton, but it had been largely for fun and for Leon. This was different. Shane Norval, a South African rider, had broken both hands during a crash at the Spanish Grand Prix, so Sabre Sport, an independent British company trying to break into GPs, asked me if I'd be interested in a one-off ride at Le Mans. They knew I could help develop the bike. It was seven years since my last GP at Donington, and a lot of water had flowed under the bridge, but I was up for it.

The hardest bit was telling Ann. She went crazy. 'It was quite violent,' I told a reporter from the *Independent* when he asked how she reacted. She said it was bad enough having to worry about Leon without me as well. As it turned out, she was right to have her doubts. Le Mans is steeped in history, but it's not the most attractive of places, a grim working city with ugly buildings and no pretensions. It was the grim rather than the historical side of the place that I'd sample that weekend. It was going to be my 109th GP – a pretty decent effort, that – but I didn't even make it to the start line after a horrendous highside in the last minute of qualifying. I remember being up in the air for ever and landing squarely on my back. That shook the crap out of me. I couldn't bend my back and was battered to high heaven. Eventually, I managed to move but everything hurt. I went to see my old friend Dr Costa, who diagnosed a torn groin muscle and a broken bone in my back. Meanwhile, Leon's bike seized three times, so he didn't qualify to start, either. The romantic idea of having two generations of Haslams making family history ended with me in agony and him in a sulk.

It was still interesting to see the changes to the GP scene since I'd been away. The other riders were all eating pasta beforehand while I tucked into my fish and chips and mushy peas. On the track they were fast and aggressive, but I don't think they were as good as some of the guys I'd been brought up with – Freddie Spencer, Eddie Lawson, Wayne Gardner and Co. There were hard men out there at Le Mans that weekend, but I was forty-three on a poor bike and I felt I could get up there with them. I'd kept myself in good physical condition and, after all those years, there were still parts of the circuit where I felt as fast as Valentino Rossi, Max Biaggi and their ilk. But I also knew I'd been a fool to myself and done something I shouldn't have. It was not a competitive bike, and I'd tried to ride it as if it were a winner. The excitement was addictive. I couldn't stop myself from trying to get further and further up the field. The adrenalin flowed. Some instinct wouldn't let me just ride round and round, so I went faster until I made a mistake.

It was a big deal for both Leon and myself, but it came to a sorry end, and our racing bond would have to continue in the pits. That was also a rocky ride at times, because of the unwritten law that says teams and dads are a marriage made in hell. That's fair enough, because the dad's solitary interest is in his son and he will tend to stick his nose in to the point that he is a problem. You see it all the time. Later in his career, when Leon signed for Airwaves Ducati, their team manager, Colin Wright, spelled out the situation in the bluntest terms.

'We don't have dads,' he told me.

I could understand his opinion but said: 'Colin, let it run and you let me know if I'm interfering.'

He was still sceptical. 'I'm employing the rider, not his parents,' he went on. 'As parents, I don't want anything to do with you. I don't like you, I don't want to know you. And that gives me a problem, because I respect Ron Haslam very much.'

'Let it run, Colin,' I repeated. 'You won't have a problem.'

And he didn't. No one has. When Leon finishes racing he comes into the garage and talks to me. I want to know what's happening and, if the team are happy, then I might make suggestions. But that first year with Italjet didn't get any better. His confidence was broken and he started to lose belief. He was always trying to solve problems, and he'd see me and Ann only at weekends, because he'd be travelling with the team, who were Italian and barely spoke any English. I brought him back to the UK to race in the British Championship, just to prove to him that he was still fast, and, sure enough, he won three out of four races.

Before that summer was out we had more bad news. We were abroad and soldiering on with Leon and Italjet when Ann came into the motorhome.

'You won't believe what's happened,' she said. I'd got to know that tone over the years and knew something awful was coming. 'It's Joey.' Oh God, no. 'He's been killed.'

I was stunned. Joey Dunlop was a good friend, a rival and a team-mate, and I couldn't believe it. We hadn't kept in close contact over the years, but you didn't need to with someone like Joey. He never said two words anyway, but he had a heart of gold and you knew you were always welcome at his place. Of course, he was also a bloody good rider. Big bikes, small bikes, it didn't matter to him, and, even though he wasn't doing as much racing by the end, he was still competitive.

Like Phil and Babe, he'd died doing what he loved, racing a 125cc bike in a backwater in Estonia, and after the disbelief faded I felt more sorry for his family. Joey was forty-eight but he was one of those people who did everything that he wanted to do in life. Nobody wants to go before their time, but at least Joey could say he left nothing out. I'd actually been thinking about him a lot, because it hadn't been long since he'd proved he was still a class act by winning his fabled treble at the TT. Even if I'd had a reality check at Le Mans, Joey had showed that age was no barrier. He was still fast and still winning, so there was no reason for him to stop. I felt terrible for Linda and the kids, but Joey really *lived* his life and that simple statement says a lot.

It's the bad times that you learn most from. I knew that, and Leon will now say that running around the back on a dodgy Italjet made him a better person. It did his progress little harm, either, as the following year, 2001, he got the chance to join the elite, riding a Honda NSR V-twin for the Shell Advance team in the 500cc world championship. He was there.

The difference between riding a 125 bike and a 500 one is night and day. At one of the first tests Leon was chuffed because he was half a second quicker than Rossi going into a corner, but then got his wake-up call when Rossi got a second on him on the way out. He was only seventeen at the start of that season, but the mileage under his belt was huge, and he started well. Leon was beating the other V-twins, which was the aim, but then Chris Walker, his team-mate, was sacked midway through the season, leaving a vacant seat on the four-cylinder machine. It was too good a chance to turn down, but it didn't help Leon.

He broke his collarbone in his first race on the four cylinder and his confidence went totally. This really was The Knock. It had hit me, it had hit Freddie, and now it was Leon's turn. When you're falling off as much as he was, you finally come to the realization that it bloody well hurts, and that inevitably has the effect of slowing you down. Your confidence in the bike dwindles and then your confidence in yourself follows suit. So there were broken bones and lots of doubt. He was on a four-cylinder Honda, the same type as Rossi, who was winning the championship, but Leon was struggling down among the dead men.

I told him to forget about the results, but he wasn't happy being down in the middle of the pack. The spark went out, and it was a long road to build him back up again. I needed to get him back to that point where a rider thinks he'll never fall off, even though he knows, deep down, that he must. Leon was badly beaten up, and The Knock came at the wrong time for him. I tried all I could. We'd discuss where he was going wrong, and I'd tell him to forget his corner speed and get more out of his brakes, but Leon's aim when he got Walker's bike was to win straight away. That was unrealistic, and he refused to accept where his true result was, the same thing I'd been guilty of at Le Mans. The bike was not working for him, so he pushed until it went pear-shaped. I got more stick at that time from people who said I was rushing him.

I knew that this would make or break Leon, and in the end the crashing calmed him and he became a better rider for it. By the end of the season they put him back on the Honda V-twin and he finished an impressive eleventh in Brazil. But it had been a hell of a time for him, as he explains:

It was a sign that the Italjet experience wasn't going to be a happy one when the chief mechanic punched the team manager. At the time I was nursing bruises from my latest fall. The manager got the sack. That was round three. Dad was beside himself.

I started the 2000 season full of hope and expectation. I was in GPs and was going the Rossi route, learning my trade in the 125cc class before stepping up. Italjet had wanted a British rider, and I was the only up-and-coming one. They'd seen how I'd beaten some of the top guys in Spain and so I had the move I'd dreamed about. It was to be a short-lived dream.

When we'd finalized the deal I flew out to Bologna to meet the team. It was nearly midnight when I arrived and I was knackered. I was usually in bed by ten, but the team manager, Marco Tresoldi, picked up some friends and insisted we all went out for an eight-course meal. I was dropping off at the table while they all chatted away ten to the dozen in Italian, but Tresoldi hadn't finished and so we all went to a nightclub. I was beginning to wonder what I'd let myself in for as I leaned against the bar and shut my eyes. Finally, they'd had enough, and I was dropped off at a flat with my luggage. Each morning I'd get picked up and be taken to the workshop and each afternoon I was deposited back at the flat. I was there for two weeks and couldn't wait to get home.

The first time I actually got on the bike was at a test in Jerez, and that was a shock to my system, because the bike was slower than a bog-standard Honda. As a racer you always try to stay positive, but little bits of doubt were creeping in from day one. When we got to the start of the season we were nowhere. They were always promising to get bits for the bike, but they never showed up. It's fair to say we had issues. It was hard for me in every way. There wasn't much money around, and I was living in the truck with the mechanics in bunk beds with one shower between ten of us. That was OK, and I liked their company, but I was only sixteen and it was odd being away from my mum and dad. They'd fly out at weekends and sometimes they'd sleep in the cab of the truck, but I was on my own.

It was the Suzuka race that brought things to a head. I was on the sighting lap and the detonation light was flashing like crazy. I came in and pointed to it. Tresoldi was the only one who spoke English and he was having none of it.

'Don't worry, don't worry,' he said. 'We changed the light and it's just oversensitive.'

I went back out and highsided at the back of the straight on the fourth lap. I broke a bone in my ankle, and that's when the mechanic floored Tresoldi. He probably had it coming.

There were all sorts of things going on. Luca was the mechanic of my team-mate, Jaroslav Huleš, but he requested to work for me instead. That's unheard of in racing, but I was happy with the arrangement. Luca spoke a few words of English, and he was very talented. He got the bike working better, but there was nothing he or anyone could do about stopping the thing from blowing up. That happened in twelve out of sixteen races. It was an unhappy time. I rode with my hand on the clutch, and my riding went to pot. That was when my dad took the decision to bring me home and get me racing in the British 125cc Championship as well. It was a calculated decision to rebuild my confidence, because he could see that I was drifting backwards with each crash.

It worked, too. In my first race at Oulton Park I cleared off and won. That was such a good feeling after spending so long on my backside. The trouble was I'd feel good about myself after a race at home and then I'd go back and crash in GPs. I did manage to stay on the Italjet in Barcelona, my favourite track, and got tenth place, becoming the youngest British rider to score points in GP racing in the process, and I raced at Knockhill and won by forty seconds. But any thoughts that I might be over the worst were damned when I then had an almighty crash in my next GP.

It was the worst year I've ever had, because my nerves were shredded and my body was a mess. It was only the British rounds that kept me going. There was a young Aussie kid called Casey Stoner in the championship that year and he qualified second to me on the grid at Brands Hatch.

'Watch him,' my dad said. 'He's young and he's fast but he's out of control.'

It was a wet day, which suited me, so I was staggered when Casey tore past and pulled ten seconds on me. I wasn't too concerned, because I thought he was going way too fast and it was just a matter of time before he crashed. But lap after lap went by and he stayed upright. I knew I had to get my finger out, and I rode the wheels off the bike that day. I passed Casey and won, but he'd opened my eyes. He'd been out of control, like my dad had said, but he'd got away with it and I'd been forced over the limit to beat him.

I won three out of four races back in England that year. The only one I didn't win was when my old friend Alan Green T-boned me on the last lap, dropping me to fifth. I came in and was still excited from the race, buzzing after having such a good battle, but Dad was unamused and launched into a bollocking.

'It wasn't my fault. I was T-boned,' I protested.

'You shouldn't have been in the bleeding way!' he

shouted. 'You should have cleared off.' It was a bog-standard bike that wasn't tuned up, but my dad had high standards. 'You should be winning. Your riding should be better.'

The knowledge my dad's got is incredible. That was how we got the chance to ride at the same GP at Le Mans in 2000. My dad had developed a 125cc ignition, and the company he'd done it for sold it to Sabre Sport. I felt proud that weekend, because this was something special, and I knew my dad was still a class rider. I was gutted when we both failed to make it to the start. We were there, and that situation will never ever happen again. People's careers are shorter now and it's impossible to see a father and son riding together.

That ignition was just one of loads of things my dad has developed. He's always in his workshop creating things and fixing stuff. The things he's come up with could have made him a fortune. He develops something, we start using it and then a year later we see that it's being sold in the shops. I remember when a new suspension system came out on a motocross bike with hydraulics and new balancing pressures. It was big news, but the fact is that my dad had done that years beforehand. I keep telling him to copyright stuff and get a patent, but he's not interested. He's never been interested in money.

I had a go on Sabre's 500cc Yamaha at the end of the season and was fast. Word got out and Shell came in with an offer to step up to the elite. They wanted two British riders for the 2001 season and, to be honest, there weren't many of us around at that time. So I signed with Chris Walker as my team-mate. To begin with, there was a good feeling that year. Jeff Hardwick ran the team with a bunch of HRC mechanics, but when I started beating Walker, who was on the V4 to my twin, it went quiet and the atmosphere turned horrible.

My aim was to beat the other V-twins, and it started well. The first race was at Suzuka, where Rossi served notice of his brilliance by winning and giving Max Biaggi, his hated rival, the finger as he went past. I had my own private battle with Haruchika Aoki, a two-times 125cc world champion, on another Honda. We went at it all the way to the line, but I highsided on the last lap and he beat me by a few tenths of a second. It was a dramatic start, and I was happy enough with thirteenth place in my first-ever 500cc race. So was everyone else. I'd become the youngest-ever rider to score points in the elite GP class, and the press were raving.

Chris was having a nightmare on the V4 and crashed a lot. You get selfish as a racer, though, and I was happy with my start. I thought, I'm definitely going to get a factory ride. And, sure enough, Honda were already talking about that. I was gaining a reputation as a rising star and loved rubbing shoulders with the best, even if

I was never going to be in a position to challenge any of them on my bike. Then the cracks started to appear. I crashed at Le Mans and broke my wrist, and that meant I had to miss the next two races, which just so happened to be at my favourite tracks, Barcelona and Mugello. I came back at Assen and did well again, beating a couple of V4s to get thirteenth place, but the bike broke at Donington. It was still looking like a good first year among the top riders on the planet. I didn't feel out of my depth, and then they sacked Chris, I was given the V4 and everything turned to shit.

Chris had a horrific crash at Assen and spent time in hospital, drugged up and with all sorts of tubes attached to him. The team didn't show him much sympathy, because they got rid of him soon afterwards, which meant I got his bike for the German Grand Prix at Sachsenring. It was what I wanted because of the increased power, although the irony was that Sachsenring is such a tight track that I would have been better off on my twin. Immediately, I could understand why Chris had struggled so much, because the power and viciousness of the bigger engine were immense. Chris had other issues too. He was trying to convert it into a superbike like he was used to riding, and that didn't go down well with Honda's top brass. There were a few internal issues that put him in the bad books with management, but the bike was a beast.

I fell in that first race on the V4 in Germany and

broke my collarbone. When I complained about the bike, Honda were unimpressed. They just said that this was the bike that Rossi had been on when he finished second in the championship to Kenny Roberts the previous year. There was no arguing with that, but that was only half the picture. In 1999 Alex Criville was the world champion and so clearly he knew how to ride, but he struggled like hell in 2000 on the bike I was now on. So did Sete Gibernau and Tady Okada. Rossi was the exception rather than the rule, and we all knew that he was a special talent. But Criville and Co. couldn't win on that Honda and, a year on, neither could I. Whatever I did I kept losing the front end. It became torture, and the confidence I'd had earlier in the season disappeared overnight. I'd had problems in 1999 and in 2000, but this was my worst-ever experience of The Knock.

This was when I really needed my dad. I was suffering like mad, with broken wrists and collarbones, but more so in my head. The mental turmoil you go through at those times is terrible. My riding had gone to pieces, and my bold hopes of a factory ride the following year were fading. And then it came to the crunch the night before the Australian Grand Prix at Phillip Island. My dad was never one for beating about the bush. 'Let's pack it in,' he said. 'You're only doing this because I did it.'

I was upset by that. This was all I ever wanted, and I

thought that was understood after what had happened after my crash in Ireland as a kid. Now my dad was telling me it was over.

'It's not my bloody fault!' I yelled. 'It's the bike. It's crap! Nobody could ride that.'

He wasn't budging, though. 'Listen, there's no point in racing if you're not riding to your maximum.'

'I am.'

'No, you're not. You're scared.'

'It's the bike.'

'No, it's you.'

It was tough to take in and I refused to listen. My dad said I should focus on football, and that pushed me over the edge. We started yelling at each other. I wanted to blame the bike or anything but myself, but deep down I knew I couldn't ride around the problems. I couldn't get my confidence back.

'You have to go out there and not be worried about anything,' he told me. 'I lost two of my brothers racing, but it didn't matter to me if I got killed or paralysed. You have to want it that badly, Leon. That bad. If you don't, then the job's not worth doing.'

It was the conversation that saved my career. We stayed up until two in the morning in the house we were renting, and it made me realize that this was all I had. I knew that I had to give it a hundred per cent even when the bike was throwing me all over the track. If something awful happened, then so be it. It was like a light bulb flashed over my head. Before then we'd had lots of arguments. My dad was always hard on me, and that got to me a bit. He thought I was lazy, and I thought he was too strict. It was only after Australia that it clicked why he had been like that. I was no longer a kid who could mix racing with lots of other things. I needed total focus. He never pushed me into bikes, but when I was there he wanted to make sure I wanted it as much as he had. It was only after that last argument that I realized why he had treated me the way he had all those years. It was the night that changed me.

18

NOT JUST A GRUMPY OLD GIT

ANY DOUBTS THAT LEON HAD COME OF AGE WERE quashed once and for all when I picked up the *News of the World* the following year and saw a double-page spread on Leon under the banner headline I FOUND THREE NAKED GIRLS IN MY BED. It talked of the raunchy emails and offers he got from women, not to mention the suitcase of lingerie he evidently carried around. According to that piece, he jumped back on the V-twin for the last race of 2001 in Brazil and headed for the post-race party. Brazil is pretty wild, he said, and the bouncers go out and hand-pick the best-looking girls to fill their nightclubs. Then he talked of how he got back to his hotel room and found the three girls. 'I let my driver sort that one out, but it was a pretty wild time,' he was quoted as saying.

Leon was on the rise and I knew he'd have his fair

share of girls, so I was glad when he settled down. If you have a stable background, it can only help your riding. And the next few years would be a roller coaster for him. He rode the Cybertel Honda in 250s in 2002, but the team was new and it was a struggle. He enjoyed teaming up with Jay Vincent, another British rider, but he'd never even ridden the bike before the first round in Japan. He got in the points in the second round in South Africa, but the bike lacked power and it was another frustrating year. Only a seventh in the wet of Portugal lifted the gloom.

Everything was changing at that time. MotoGP was going four-stroke, and Leon came home to ride the bigger bikes with Renegade Ducati. It was a case of taking one step back to take two steps forward. He signed to ride the Ducati in the British Supersport Championship and, although it wasn't as quick as the Hondas, he was fourth halfway through the season. That's when the team split with Sean Emmett and he was put on the Testastretta in the British Superbike Championship. He finished the season with a lot of mileage under his belt and eleventh place in both series. He was ready to step back on to the international stage with Renegade in the World Superbike Championship. Unfortunately, circumstances conspired against him. Leon takes up the story:

The best-laid plans came a cropper when I slid in for the ball during a Sunday League football match. My foot rolled over the top of the ball and I felt severe pain. I did my cruciate ligament, and that meant I missed out on a hell of a lot of pre-season training. When I did come back, I fell at Oulton Park and dislocated my knee again. At that time I also had an old-fashioned approach to diet and would eat whatever I wanted. I even used to mark all the McDonald's on maps before we travelled anywhere. I could get away with that when I was training, but spending so long off my feet took its toll and I put on a lot of weight. I should have been around ten and a half stone but I ballooned to twelve. I took a lot of stick. Jeremy McWilliams, the old man of the grid, said I looked like Nori Haga, my pudgy-faced team-mate.

I wasn't training anywhere like I should have been and that was reflected in my riding. It was my first full year in World Superbikes, and I didn't give it my best shot. It wasn't a case of getting tired on the bike so much as the mental strength you get from being fit. I know how more flexible I am when I crash and how I bounce back quicker, sometimes literally, from mishaps when I'm in peak condition. I was still getting rostrums in the championship and had a few front-row starts, but for me it was a shocking year. In the first race of the season I followed James Toseland, who would become the champion, but my tyre went off towards the end. I kept pace with him, though, and was beating him and Chris Vermeulen, another rider who would progress to

MotoGP, until we got to America and Laguna Seca. I pushed too hard when the tyres had gone and I high-sided. That left me with a broken wrist and made the rest of the season hard work. I had injections before every race and, although I got rookie of the year and scored a great win at Brands in the British Superbike Championship, I was struggling.

It was time for another reality check. I'd been in GPs and had to come back to England and now I'd been in World Superbikes and I was making the same move. There were options to stay but none of them was right. One option came from Foggy Petronas. I've always got on well with Carl Fogarty, the legendary four-times world champion, and he rings me every year to see what I'm doing, but everybody who went on that bike was suffering like mad. They offered me ten times more money, but I wanted a factory bike, so I came home and signed for Airwaves Ducati. World Superbikes was not the best championship at that point, and it had all gone to Pirelli tyres, so I didn't see it as a massive step backwards. I figured that if I could win in Britain I could win anywhere.

I also realized I couldn't afford to be out of shape. I got in touch with Kirk Gibbons, who had been the personal trainer of Jamie Dobb, the motocross world champion, and we agreed to start working together. I took a vow to stop drinking during the season. When I was fourteen I'd get drunk on one beer, but as I got older it would take me a week to recover from the end-of-season parties. Now I knew I was running out of chances, so I started working like never before. Kirk is a madman and trains twice a day every day, including Christmas Day, and even though he's in his forties is probably one of the fittest people in the country.

I worked harder than I'd ever done and have kept it up since. In 2005 I was paired with James Haydon at Ducati, which was great as we went back such a long way and he'd once lived down the hallway in our house. Unfortunately, James was crocked for the season opener, and so Gregorio Lavilla, the experienced Spanish rider, took over. I was pleased with my efforts for the GSE team. I was on pole for the first races at Brands and got the 999's first win at Oulton Park, but Gregorio ended up winning the title while I was fourth.

The training had been a sacrifice in the first year, but I felt the benefits in 2006 and I was second in the championship. That felt good, but it was disappointing not to clinch it, especially as I felt I could have done on the last day at Brands. Me, Gregorio Lavilla and Ryuichi Kiyonari all had a chance to win. I was pumped up. The wet was a bonus. In the first race I was going well and lying second when the race was stopped because Shane Byrne had crashed in the rain. I stormed away to win the second, but it wasn't enough, and I ended up just eight points adrift of Kiyonari. If the weather hadn't got in the way and the race hadn't been stopped, I think I'd have been the champion. The following year, 2007, the bike wasn't capable of winning the title and, while I was in the hunt and finished third, it was an uphill struggle.

Now I look around and think I'm ready. It's been a hell of an apprenticeship, but I remind myself that my dad didn't even get into GPs until he was twenty-six. James Toseland is the top Brit, but his career was pretty stagnant until he got into the Fila team in World Superbikes. He's worked really hard at his training and has progressed, but as a rider he's not doing anything different from anyone else. Everybody has stepped up their training now. I don't go out and get drunk with my mates any more, and what has surprised me is I don't want to. That might sound boring, but there are still some old-school values being practised in the paddock. I look at Rossi and Colin Edwards, and they're up until two in the morning, having a few beers and playing music, but they do it discreetly. You can't be seen to be like that these days. I don't do it, because I have some distance to go. I need to get to where those guys are. James is the top Brit at the moment and I'm second, but from where I am to where he is is only a couple of years' journey, and he's two years older.

I'm no longer the young kid partying in the club-house until midnight on the eve of a race. I'm friendly with people and socialize, but there's also a sort of hatred there. I want to beat people so badly now that some of the fun has gone. Times change, and now I'm racing against people who are my age or even younger – people like Leon Camier and Cal Crutchlow, who's my team-mate now. I have to make every year count. I will make the sacrifices, whether it means training twenty-four/seven or not going out, because I have to be number one in Britain if I want to be number one in the world. It's why I work with Kirk, why I stopped playing football – it's just too dangerous – and, most important, why I listen to my dad.

I was never pushed down this route, and at times it seemed that my dad was trying to push me down any other one. I now realize I got into GPs at the top end when I wasn't ready. I didn't have the knowledge or understanding. It's only been in the last three years that I've finally felt ready to take on any challenge. Rossi is special, an unbelievable rider, and even on the same bike you'd struggle to match him, but he's not doing anything out of this world. When I was in 500s I beat him in most wet practices, and I know I've beaten top MotoGP riders like Stoner, Elias and Vermeulen. Anybody can do it if they put it all together.

I owe a lot to my dad for this new-found belief, and if I have kids I'll have the same attitude. This is such a hard career to make a living from. You have to question whether the money you can make from a brief period is worth the broken bones you're going to get. Like my dad has done, I'd paint that picture and let my kids decide.

Growing up, I used to wonder just why he said those things to me, why he was always picking holes in my riding. Now I know that anything he says that is horrible is only for my own benefit. Seeing people like Toseland ask him for advice brings that home. He's been there and done it, after all. He's trying to make me better, and I finally realize that he's Rocket Ron, a good teacher, a great racer and a brilliant dad, not just a grumpy old git.

I can say now that Leon could go to MotoGP and he would hold his own. I have no doubts about that whatsoever. One of his greatest assets is the strength of his self-belief. Whether that's right or wrong, the fact is that you need it, and Leon believes he can beat Rossi. Nobody will alter his mindset on that. He's been through so much and has been racing for a decade already. The normal tendency when something is hurting so bad is to take the excuse and not push so hard. Leon will do the opposite. He'll go even harder to prove the injury isn't holding him back. He'll moan about tyres and engines, but he'll never moan about broken ribs and arms. Once, in his motocross days, he had a spiral crack down his arm. It must have been hurting like hell, but he still finished second. I like him for that.

I don't give him compliments. I look for the things he could have done better, regardless of where he might have finished. It's not a case of not appreciating how good he is, but I want him to be even better. Until he gets to Rossi's status, there'll always be people in front of him. There'll always be more to do. We used to argue about it, but he knows I'm only doing it for his benefit.

At first, though, he felt that I was on to him all the time and didn't give him any space. 'Yeah, you won a race but you were slipping a bit at the chicane,' I'd say. If he came sixth, I'd tell him why he wasn't fifth. Maybe then, at the end of the day, I'd say, 'You did well today', and a small comment like that would be a major thing for him.

The biggest thing I can give him now is standing out on the track and watching the other riders. Sometimes, as a rider, you can have a problem but not know how to change it. I can watch someone else and say: 'He's doing it like this and it's working for him.'

The conversations we have are between two riders, not a father and son. I'm ten times harder on him than I was with the lads in Team Great Britain. I'd tell James Haydon something once and if he didn't listen then that was fine. His loss. With Leon I have to make him accept it, and that means we can have disagreements that fester for hours on end. Lots of times I was right and lots of times I wasn't right for him. I won't say I was wrong and I never will. That's the Haslam stubbornness!

Now I feel sure that he'll do it. He's done well in the past, but there's always been more for him to do before he's ready for the top. Even in the 2006 season, when he finished second in the British Superbike Championship, I knew there were a couple of things missing that you need to be a world champion, but the following year he began to put it all together. On equal machinery and tyres he would give Rossi or Casey Stoner, the 2007 MotoGP champion, a run for their money. There's only Rossi who really stands out now. He's unusual, because, like Eddie Lawson in my era, he's lasted a long time. Freddie Spencer was unbeliev-able and achieved a double world championship, but it was a short reign. Lawson and Kenny Roberts were the same as each other – if the bike was competitive, then so were they. The rest could be fantastic and un-beatable on their day, but you knew it could end at any time. I never believed that with Lawson and Roberts, and I don't believe it with Rossi. He's even more out-standing, though, because he's done it through lots of classes and lasted such a long time.

The very young lads tend to crash and burn out quicker, like Freddie did. It will be interesting to see how long Stoner lasts. Leon has an advantage in that he's been around for years but is still young. Now, once he gets into a world championship, I think he's stable enough to win and then carry on winning. He won't just be a flash in the pan, winning at his favourite circuit on the back of six crap races. He has the strength to go the distance.

It's there for him now. You can never say for certain in this sport, because of the politics and the machinery, but I hope you'll soon begin to see the benefit of taking him to GPs as a kid, being out of his depth in every way, surviving the catalogue of crashes on the Italjet's ejector seat, tasting 250s and 500s, and even enduring that nightmare flight back from Northern Ireland with his leg in pieces.

I knew he'd cracked it when I saw him win both races at Donington in 2007. People assume he knows the track like the back of his hand, because I have a race school there, but the fact is that he's never had the best results at his local track. To win both races there showed me that there'd been some sort of change inside him. It wasn't just lap times. If it needs to be pushed over the limit, then he'll do that. He'll put in that extra two per cent. Back in 2006 he had to win both races at Brands Hatch to win the British title, and I knew there was no way any other rider was going to stop him, but then they waved a bloody red flag to stop the race early. That day I knew he would take it as far as it needed. It was the professional approach. Yes or no? Who knows? It might end in disaster, but it was a calculated gamble rather than a hot-headed kid trying too hard.

I look back now over my career and I'm proud of what I achieved. I came from an overcrowded house in Langley Mill and took on the best riders in the world. I rode in more 500cc Grands Prix than any British rider before or since, and my third places in Spain and Germany in 1987 remain the last time a British man scored back-to-back podiums. I developed bikes, made lots of friends, and I've helped lots of young riders get a start. The race school has been another source of satisfaction and, while it can be frustrating and hard work, it's something else I'm proud of. Most of all, though, I'm proud of my family. I've got everything I could have ever dreamed about here with Ann, Leon, Emma and Zoe. The fact that Leon still lives here in the annexe says it all.

Babe, Phil, me and Leon. It's a motorcycling dynasty, I suppose. Who was the best? Babe gave it his best, and I did it through pig-headedness, making a shit-load of mistakes and managing to survive. Phil had the natural talent. He was the first man to get the 100mph lap at the Manx; he was the one rivalling Barry Sheene, when Sheene was the golden boy, with a bike bought over the counter.

And now there's Leon. It took me much longer to gather the sort of experience you need to go for a title. As I write this, he is twenty-four, the same age that Phil was when he died, when he was looking like a world champion in waiting. Leon's ahead of us both.

I hope that people remember me as a talented rider who developed bikes and treated people well. Someone who gave it absolutely everything. Nowadays you'll find me in the pits or in my garage at home, sleeves up, covered in oil, stripping engines. This life consumes you. It gets under your dirty black fingernails, under your shredded skin, in your blood. I feel blessed to have been part of this extraordinary family.

PICTURE ACKNOWLEDGEMENTS

Unless otherwise stated pictures are courtesy of the author. Every effort has been made to obtain the necessary permissions with reference to the copyright material. We apologize for any omissions in this respect and will be pleased to make the appropriate acknowledgements in any future edition.

Section Two
Cadwell Park International: © Ian Buckden; On the Rothmans Honda: © Hero Drent; Accident waiting to happen with no chain at Ballaugh Bridge: © Niels Skillicorn; The mad, bad world of Elf: both © Hero Drent; Troubled times with Suzuki and on the Caviga: both © Hero Drent

INDEX